WHAT DO DRACULAS DO?

essays on contemporary
writers of fiction for
children and young adults

by
DAVID REES

The Scarecrow Press, Inc.
Metuchen, N.J., & London
1990

The author gratefully acknowledges permission to reprint excerpts from the following works:

Aiken, Joan. *Night Birds on Nantucket*. Jonathan Cape, 1966; Doubleday, 1966. Reprinted by permission of A M Heath & Company, Ltd., Authors' Agents.

Gardam, Jane. *The Summer After the Funeral*. Hamish Hamilton, 1973; Macmillan, New York, 1973. Copyright © 1973 by Jane Gardam.

Hautzig, Deborah. *Hey, Dollface*. Hamish Hamilton, 1979; Greenwillow, 1978. Copyright © 1978 by Deborah Hautzig.

Mahy, Margaret. *The Changeover*. J. M. Dent, 1984; Macmillan, New York, 1984.

Southall, Ivan. *Bread and Honey*. Angus & Robertson, 1970. Reprinted by permission of the publisher.

Southall, Ivan. *King of the Sticks*. Methuen Children's Books, 1979; Greenwillow, 1979.

Wrightson, Patricia. *An Older Kind of Magic*. Century Hutchinson, 1972; Harcourt Brace, 1972.

British Library Cataloguing-in-Publication data available

Library of Congress Cataloging-in-Publication Data

Rees, David, 1936–
    What do Draculas do? : essays on contemporary writers of fiction for children and young adults / by David Rees.
        p.   cm.
    Includes bibliographical references and index.
    ISBN 0-8108-2320-9
    1. Children's stories, American—History and criticism.   2. Children's stories, English—History and criticism.   3. Young adult fiction—History and criticism.   I. Title.
PS374.C454R44   1990
813'.54099282—dc20   90-8669

Magic has still a real and important place in our stories—most real when the magic is dark, mysterious, and a little frightening, as it always was.
—Patricia Wrightson, *An Older Kind of Magic*

That was where witches belonged: in bedside stories that scared you stiff when you were six. When you were thirteen, witches were wet.
—Ivan Southall, *Bread and Honey*

For Geoff Fox, Brian Merrick, and Freddie Smith

CONTENTS

ACKNOWLEDGMENTS

Ten of these essays have been printed in other publications. Those on Joan Aiken, William Mayne, and Roald Dahl were published in *Children's Literature in Education,* in the spring, summer and autumn issues of 1988 respectively. "The Wound of Philoctetes" was published in the autumn issue of *Children's Literature in Education* in 1983 under the title, "On Katherine Paterson, Alexander Pope, Myself, and Some Others." The essay on Maurice Sendak appeared in the fall 1988 number of *San Jose Studies.* The other five were published in *The School Librarian:* Esther and Deborah Hautzig in December 1980; Susan Cooper in September 1984; Leon Garfield in May 1988; Mary Norton in August 1988; and Jane Gardam in February 1989.

My thanks are due, for their help and advice, to Mark Cohen, Geoff Fox, Deborah Hautzig, Julia Macrae, Joan Murphy, Jenny Rees, Caroline Roberts, Marian Robinson, Freddie Smith, and—in particular—Lee Kingman Natti for her time, patience, and encouragement.

INTRODUCTION

My younger son, Adam, when he was very small, asked me one evening: "What do Draculas do, Daddy?" At the age he was then he could not pronounce the letters *r* and *s* properly, so the word "Dwaculath" made the question seem all the more childlike. Not thinking or reacting quickly enough, I said, "They drink blood." His little face puckered in alarm, and I knew, too late, that I'd not given the right reply. I should have said something, I suppose, about how they existed in books and in our imaginations, along with the witches, dragons, elves, unicorns and folk-spirits, both good and evil, that he already knew of from the stories he either read for himself or that were read to him. In some way or another, I should have explained that Dracula, like other mythical beings he had encountered, was a spirit who tried to invade us, and that while we might welcome an invasion by a good spirit, in Dracula's case we would resist most strongly.

All authors, it seems to me, are like spirits who intrude on us, or whom we invite in—a witch, it is said, cannot enter a house unless she is asked to do so—and if they are bad authors who write bad books, the result may be like Dracula's effect on the lives of his victims: a corruption. This is, I guess, another way of putting Ted Hughes's famous remark in *Myth and Education:* "Great works of literature . . . are hospitals where we heal . . . when they are evil works they are battlefields where we get injured." This applies as much to children's fiction as it does to adult fiction. Philippa Pearce's *Tom's Midnight Garden* makes me feel enriched, a better person for having read it; Roald Dahl's *Charlie and the Chocolate Factory* makes me feel deprived—it is as if Dracula had done something destructive to my imaginative life, had taken at least a tiny bite.

Not many of the authors I'm writing about in this book, I'm

glad to say, are likely to produce the Dracula effect, even when, as is Margaret Mahy, they are directly concerned with the Dracula theme: Carmody Braque in *The Changeover* is ultimately made to seem very small, almost pathetic, as is the Count of Transylvania himself in Bram Stoker's novel—though en route he appears to be powerful and frightening. He can, our authors are telling us, be defeated—invariably. Which is just as well.

This book of essays on contemporary children's fiction is intended to be a companion volume to my two previous collections of essays on writers for the young, *The Marble in the Water* and *Painted Desert, Green Shade.* My choice of authors this time has largely, though not entirely, been governed by a wish to discuss the work of major figures I did not include in the other two books. They are, with the exception of Mary Norton, men and women whose careers began in the nineteen fifties and nineteen sixties, and whose best work was done during that period and in the nineteen seventies; they are, therefore, some of the creators of what has often been called the second golden age of children's literature. It has been said that there is no such thing as the second golden age of children's literature, but I think there is—or was. If I had to suggest a year in which it started, I would say 1952— the year that saw the publication of E. B. White's *Charlotte's Web* and Mary Norton's *The Borrowers.* But E. B. White is dead now; Mary Norton's career has almost certainly drawn to a close, and the authors I am writing about, with the exception of Margaret Mahy, have not produced many books of great significance in the nineteen eighties. At some date or another as the seventies finished and the eighties began, the second golden age also drew to a close.

The Carnegie Medals awarded by The Library Association in Britain in recent years could perhaps be regarded as evidence to support this assertion. Peter Dickinson, in 1980, was the first author to win the Carnegie for a second time, and since then this feat has been performed by three others: Robert Westall, Jan Mark, and Margaret Mahy—all of them writers whose reputations became firmly established in the seventies. Is this because the number of important authors emerging in the 1980s is few indeed?

Who is the key figure of this second golden age? "Leon Garfield is the best of us," Penelope Lively once said to me. "Leon is the king." I don't agree with this statement, simply because there were too many good exponents of children's literature in the sixties and seventies to single out any one particular person for such an accolade. But it does seem to me, the more I read of the children's fiction of this period, that Leon Garfield may well be the king-*pin*. Many authors, including people as diverse as Joan Aiken, Helen Cresswell, Jane Gardam, and Ivan Southall, come near to him at times in style or theme or the territory their books occupy.

But territory and theme are common property, when all is said and done. Which brings us back to Dracula: the Count of Transylvania lurks in many and various disguises in children's books. The real answer to the question of what do Draculas do is that, like all great mythical and legendary beings, they stimulate our minds and imaginations. By casting a spell—imprisoning us if you like—they paradoxically set us free. As do most of the authors in this collection of essays.

REFERENCES

ROALD DAHL
> *Charlie and the Chocolate Factory,* Knopf, 1964; Allen and Unwin, 1967

TED HUGHES
> "Myth and Education" in *Children's Literature in Education,* March 1970

MARGARET MAHY
> *The Changeover,* Dent, 1984; Macmillan, New York, 1984

MARY NORTON
> *The Borrowers,* Dent, 1952; Harcourt, 1953

PHILIPPA PEARCE
> *Tom's Midnight Garden,* Oxford, 1958; Lippincott, 1959

DAVID REES
> *The Marble in the Water,* Horn Book, 1980
> *Painted Desert, Green Shade,* Horn Book, 1984

BRAM STOKER
Dracula, first published 1897

E. B. WHITE
Charlotte's Web, Harper, 1952; Hamish Hamilton, 1952

FREEDOM AND IMPRISONMENT

Mary Norton

Arrietty drew back from it with a little gasp of dismay.
Was the rest of Peagreen's house somewhere under the
floor? If so, it would be beyond bearing. She thought of
those early years at Firbank, the dusty passages, the dimly lit rooms, the long monotonous days, the sense of
imprisonment, intermingled with fear. She had grown
used to it, that she realised now, but only because she
had known no other life. But now she had tasted freedom, the joy of running, the fun of climbing; the sight of
birds, butterflies, flowers—of sunshine, rain and
dew . . . Not, not that again, not under the floor!

Thus Mary Norton, in *The Borrowers Avenged,* articulates
Arrietty's most deeply rooted feelings. It is in sharp contrast
to what motivates Pod and Homily in all the Borrowers
books, and is therefore not only the basis of the plots of the
stories, but the source of tension in the relationships between the three main characters. Indeed one might go so far
as to say that the twin themes of freedom and imprisonment
are a major theme, perhaps *the* major theme, of all Mary
Norton's work.

She is not a prolific author. In a writing career that spans
more than forty years she has produced only eight books for
children, and one of these, *Poor Stainless,* is brief and slight; a
sort of Borrowers footnote. *Bedknob and Broomstick* and
Are All the Giants Dead? are her only novels other than the
Borrowers series, and they, too, are concerned with freedom
and imprisonment. *Bedknob and Broomstick* was originally
two separate stories, *The Magic Bedknob* (her first book) and
Bonfires and Broomsticks. The children Carey, Charles and
Paul, and their friend, Miss Price, appear in both books, and it
was sensible of Mary Norton to combine the two as one

continuous novel; *The Magic Bedknob* on its own seemed short and somewhat inconclusive. The final result, *Bedknob and Broomstick,* is a very satisfying work. Miss Price, in particular, is a powerful creation:

> You all know somebody rather like Miss Price. She wore grey coats and skirts and had a long thin neck with a scarf round it made of Liberty silk with a Paisley pattern. Her nose was sharply pointed and she had very clean, pink hands. She rode on a high bicycle with a basket in front, and she visited the sick and taught the piano. She lived in a neat little house . . . and the children knew her by sight and always said 'Good morning.' In all the village there was none so ladylike as Miss Price.

Such characters may have almost disappeared from the English rural scene (*The Magic Bedknob* was published in England in 1945); Mary Norton convinces us, however, that we *do* all know somebody rather like Miss Price. But, just as the outside observer of English village characters may only see what is in fact the tip of an iceberg, so Miss Price is not at all what she appears to be. She is 'far from ladylike' Mary Norton tells us later. She can fly on a broomstick and cast spells; she rescues herself and the children from being eaten by cannibals on a South Sea island; she saves a seventeenth-century necromancer from being burned at the stake; she even threatens (a rather unpleasant moment,this) to shut the children up by casting a rattling good spell on them. But Miss Price doesn't revel in her art; she disapproves of it. She sees the practice of witchcraft as somewhat disreputable, like excessive smoking and drinking. She tries to give it up—she destroys her books and gets rid of her jars of newts' eyes and dried mice, but it's no good: she has a weakness for it, and the children, Carey in particular, can usually persuade her to indulge. The conflict in Miss Price is one of the book's strengths. Uncertainty and conflict in adults appear in nearly all Mary Norton's work, and are invariably well done—Homily occasionally finding, despite her fears, that the great outdoors can be pleasant, Miss Menzies reluctantly seeking the help of the police to find the Borrowers, Mrs May telling Kate, against her better judgement, the Borrowers' history;

and so on. Adults, in fact, are very important in Mary Norton's novels. She doesn't make the mistake of thinking that children's fiction should only be about children. The Borrowers stories are always at their best when human adults are involved in the plot; when they are not so evident, as in *The Borrowers Afield* and *The Borrowers Afloat,* the action loses some of its power to hold us, its "spell."

Another pleasure to be found in Mary Norton's books is her sense of humor, and it is present in *Bedknob and Broomstick* as much as it is in her later work. Sometimes it is dry and understated—Charles, for instance, suggesting that Mr Jones, the necromancer who has been transported to the twentieth century, might care to read *Little Arthur's History of England:* 'I mean, it would all be news to Mr Jones from chapter seven onwards'—and this comment on Mr Jones is also subtle and neat:

> 'There are few lives,' he began, rather gloomily but as if he might be going to warm up later, 'sadder than mine . . . '

At other times the humor presents us with a delightful sense of the ludicrous. Miss Price's reaction when she is told that the children have brought Mr Jones from Charles the Second's London to modern Bedfordshire is an example—

> 'No, Carey, I do think this is thoughtless of you. I had made up my mind this was the last trip the bed was going to make and there you go picking up strange necromancers who you know perfectly well have to be taken home again, which means another journey.' She pushed her feet into her bedroom slippers. 'Where did you say he was?'
> 'He's in your bedroom,' said Carey. 'On the bed.'

The tone is that of a cross parent refusing a child's request to take in a stray cat, which is quite unexpected, given the situation: the humor is in the incongruity.

Bedknob and Broomstick is a fine book, immensely readable and amusing. In its more chilling moments it presents us with real fear and excitement—an example of the latter is the excellent description of the witch-burning—and in Miss

Price we have a convincing, rounded character: the conventional spinster who wants to conform to what is expected of her (an exact parallel to Arrietty's feelings that life under the floorboards is like being in prison) and the creative artist who can whizz off to exotic places on a magic bed (Arrietty's "other life" of freedom, the joys of the natural existence out of doors). Freedom also means trouble and danger, but it is preferable, Mary Norton says, to limited, circumscribed safety; a certain kind of reality is dull compared to the experiences of the imagination. In her next book, *The Borrowers,* she returned to the same theme.

The Borrowers stories are central to a tradition in children's fiction that has a long history—what is it like to be a very small person indeed, say only five or six inches high? There are many precedents for this—the dwarfs of the world's fairy tales, for example; the story of Tom Thumb; what happens to Alice in *Alice in Wonderland* when she eats the cake and shrinks; and the Lilliputians in *Gulliver's Travels.* (Vice versa, Gulliver's adventures in Brobdingnag.) *Gulliver's Travels,* of course, was never intended to be a children's book, but generations of children have "borrowed" it from adult literature and found pleasure in it. The interest of the young in minute human beings has something to do with a child's own size: to someone of a very young age an adult is a giant and the eye-view of the world is similar to that of a dwarf, a Lilliputian, a Borrower. Onto this universal theme Mary Norton adds, in all the Borrowers stories, three main characters of universal interest—Pod, Homily, and Arrietty. They are not so much stereotypes as archetypes, a "typical" artisan's family "making do," "getting by," the sex roles sharply defined, and decency, keeping up appearances, being aware of one's place (not too grand, not too humble) being constantly emphasized.

Much of the tension in the books comes from Arrietty's challenges to these assumptions of her parents. Pod—the very name suggests it—is a plodder, limited in his outlook, unimaginative (except when it comes to do-it-yourself ingenuity with gadgets), the protector, the provider, in a sense the family's wage earner: all traditional male roles. Homily cooks and cleans, is obsessively house-proud, jealous of her relatives, snobbish, easily frightened, and has narrow horizons and values; she is a "typical" working-class housewife. Much of the humor of the stories comes from Homily's snobbery and fearfulness:

> They came to a place where some beetles were eating a long-dead mole. 'Don't look,' said Homily, quickening her step and averting her eyes, as though it were a street accident. (*The Borrowers Afield*)

When the family has to live, for a while, in an old discarded boot, Homily has reservations—'I wonder whoever wore it,' she says, and 'I'm not going in no further: there might be something in the toe.' But she is much relieved when Pod tells her it was once a gentleman's boot; 'Thank goodness for that!' she says.

> 'Why, Mother,' asked Arrietty, irritated, 'what's wrong with a working man's boot? Papa's a working man, isn't he?'
> Homily smiled and shook her head in a pitying way. 'It's a question,' she said, 'of quality.' (*The Borrowers Afield*)

Arrietty rejects many of her parents' values: her lack of fear, her predilection for talking to human beings, her love of nature and liberty, run contrary to everything that inspires Pod and Homily—and cause a great deal of trouble. The contrast between her and her mother is best exemplified by their attitudes to the countryside. For Homily it's 'draughts, moths, worms, snakes, and what not'; 'we won't none of us see another spring,' she says. It's 'dogs barking and foxes in the badgers' set and creeping in the night and stealing and rain coming up and nothing to cook on.' For Arrietty it's just the opposite, a world of beauty, mystery, and delight:

> The river seemed full of voices, endless, mysterious murmurs like half-heard conversations. But conversations without pauses—breathless, steady recountings. 'She said to me, I said to her. And then . . . and then . . . and then. . . . ' After a while Arrietty ceased to listen as, so often, she ceased to listen to her mother

when Homily, in the vein, went on and on and on. (*The Borrowers Afloat*)

This idea is echoed in a direct comment by the author herself at the end of *The Borrowers Aloft:*

> Stories never really end. They can go on and on and on—and on: it is just that at some point or another (as Mrs May once said to Kate) the teller ceases to tell them.

So the flow of the river symbolizes the story—and real, rewarding life: both are real life.

The five Borrowers novels vary a little in quality. The best, I think, are the first and the last two, *The Borrowers, The Borrowers Aloft,* and *The Borrowers Avenged.* In these three, humans play strong roles in the plot, and, as I said, the stories seem to generate more excitement when humans are present, particularly when those humans are nasty and selfish. In Mrs Driver and Sidney and Mabel Platter, Mary Norton creates three people who are entirely credible, and very nasty and very selfish indeed. Also, despite the reader's continuing pleasure in Pod, Homily and Arrietty—they always entertain and interest us, and we feel for them, think with them—they don't really develop as characters. They are wholly "there" in the first book. Perhaps it would be too much to expect Pod and Homily, so set in their ways, to alter whatever may happen to them: they never allow experience to change their views or behavior; instead they judge experience by previous experience. But Arrietty doesn't mature as much as one might expect. Other characters in the stories, however, do develop. One of the minor delights of *The Borrowers Avenged* is the change that has taken place in Aunt Lupy since we first met her in *The Borrowers Afield.* Living now in a harmonium in a church vestry, she has "got" religion and become meek and mild—

> 'Welcome,' she said, with a gentle un-Lupyish smile, 'welcome to the house of the Lord . . . '

Homily is amazed by Lupy's new-found generosity:

> She could hardly believe her ears. Lupy *offering* things!

And, seemingly, with real sincerity. Although she did
notice a little quiver about the lips, and a slightly ner-
vous flutter of the eyelids.

But certain old characteristics remain—

'Ours is a long story,' said Homily. 'You tell me yours
first.' Lupy did not need asking twice.

The first of the series, *The Borrowers*, is an achievement of
a very high order. It is Mary Norton's finest book, and, to my
mind, one of the great masterpieces of post-war British children's fiction. Where it scores above all its successors is in its
plot, which has a logic about it like that of a classical tragedy,
so exact and right that it seems effortless—as if the author
didn't have to work at it, just simply tell it. (Which is the kind
of effect almost all novelists aim for, and rarely attain.) Given
the characters—Pod, Homily, Arrietty, the boy, Aunt Sophy,
Mrs Driver and Crampfurl—and the one fatal mistake (Arrietty talking to the boy), all that follows is as inevitable as the
chaos King Lear produces (given the other characters) when
he divides his kingdom; and there are few pieces of narrative,
in any country's literature, as exciting and well-written as the
lead-up to Mrs Driver's discovery of the Borrowers. As in
classical tragedy too, it is hubris that leads to downfall. If
Homily had been content with a few simple gifts from the
boy, everything would have been fine, but she over-reaches
herself, for once gives in to delusions of grandeur: she has to
have more and more things for her house, and of better quality. Materialism and greed are her undoing. So the disap-
pearance of valuable trinkets (quite useless to Homily, but a
wonderful status symbol if the Overmantels or the Harpsi-
chords should drop in for afternoon tea) arouses Mrs Driver's
suspicions. Pod knows the dangers, when Homily, flying too
high, talks about having a 'musical conversazione' and starts
changing into a satin dress for dinner. 'It hung like a sack, but
Homily called it "Grecian."'

Homily, he felt, should call a halt; surely, now, their
home was grand enough; these jewelled snuff-boxes and
diamond-encrusted miniatures, these filigree vanity-
cases and Dresden figurines . . . were not really neces-

sary: what was the good of a shepherdess nearly as tall as
Arrietty or an outsize candlesnuffer?

But Pod has his weaknesses too—he can't bring himself to
deny his wife the pleasures she has never had before.

Mrs Driver's character is revealed to us in comments like
this one—

> Standing there, on that fateful day, in the spring sun-
> shine, feather duster in hand, her little black eyes had
> become slits of anger and cunning. She felt tricked. It
> was, she calculated, as though someone, suspecting her
> dishonesty, were trying to catch her out.

For she is also a "borrower," mainly of Aunt Sophy's vast
stock of madeira, which she and Crampfurl drink in the kitch-
en late at night; and one of the plot's neat come-uppances is
that Mrs Driver's actions result in Aunt Sophy removing the
madeira to her bedroom, where the servants can't touch it.
Mrs Driver's punishment is small, however, considering the
evil way she treats the boy, tormenting him and locking him
up in the bedroom; and evil, too, is her attitude to the Borrowers when she at last discovers them. She can't believe the
evidence of her own eyes: she is that kind of person who,
when confronted with the irrational or the unexpected, vig-
orously acts to expunge it in order to restore the equilibrium
of her world order, regardless of the morality of such behavior.

> 'They'll be moved all right,' she said. 'Don't worry. The
> rat-catcher will know how. Crampfurl's old cat will
> know how. So will the sanitary inspector. And the fire
> brigade, if need be. The police'll know how, I shouldn't
> wonder. No need to worry about moving them. Once
> you've found the nest,' she went on, dropping her voice
> to a vicious whisper as they passed Aunt Sophy's door,
> 'the rest is easy!'

So Pod, Homily and Arrietty are smoked out; their home is
destroyed, and they flee for their lives, escaping just in the
nick of time.

This kind of edge doesn't appear again until the fourth

book of the series, *The Borrowers Aloft*, though this novel does not have the same perfection of structure—too much time, perhaps, is devoted to gadgetry (how to make the balloon work, for instance), and much of the story, being concerned with the imprisonment of Pod, Homily and Arrietty in the Platters' loft, is static. Even the escape itself seems to hold few dangers. But Sidney and Mabel Platter are every bit as unpleasant as Mrs Driver. Their reaction to the irrational and the unexpected is not Mrs Driver's—the desire to kill it—but to exploit it for financial gain. Mr Platter is an undertaker and builder of "gimcrack villas" that spoil the countryside:

> He had a tight kind of face and a pair of rimless glasses which caught the light so that you could not see his eyes. He had, however, a very polite and gentle manner; so you took the eyes on trust. Dear Mr Platter, the mourners said, was always 'so very kind,' and they seldom questioned his bill.

His hobby, gardening, is a warning to us of what he will do when the Borrowers are at his mercy, and that his attitude to them will not be emotional as was Mrs Driver's but cold and cunning:

> All Mr Platter's flowers were kept like captives—firmly tied to stakes: the slightest sway or wriggle was swiftly punished—a lop here or a cut there. Very soon the plants gave in—uncomplaining as guardsmen they would stand to attention in rows . . . A glimpse of Mr Platter with his weeding tools was enough to make the slyest dandelion seed smartly change course in mid-air.

At some point or another, Mary Norton said at the end of *The Borrowers Aloft*, the teller ceases to recount the tale, but this farewell to her creations, in 1961, was premature. Something about the Platters—as well as the Borrowers—continued to preoccupy her, and twenty-two years afterwards she added another novel to the series, *The Borrowers Avenged*. This book deals with two things that are left unsatisfactorily resolved at the end of *The Borrowers Aloft*—the proper punishment for the Platters' misdeeds, and a more suitable home for Pod, Homily and Arrietty than a house that is open to danger in Mr

Pott's model village. Though Mary Norton was nearly eighty when *The Borrowers Avenged* was published, there is no falling off in her abilities; the magic is still there—narrative, humor, characterization are as fine as ever. (There is an interesting parallel with Lucy Boston, who, also in old age, added another novel, *The Stones of Green Knowe,* to her Green Knowe series: but, in this case, the magic had gone.) It is remarkable, too, that after such a long gap in time Mary Norton was able to write a story that sounds as if it was begun the moment *The Borrowers Aloft* had ended; the illusion that time has stood still is perfectly realized.

There are some pleasing additions to Borrowers lore not mentioned in the previous books; their attitude to ghosts, for instance. They aren't at all frightened of ghosts, who are useful because they keep humans away. 'Ghosts is air,' Homily says to Arrietty. 'Ghosts can't hurt you.' She continues:

> 'My mother lived in a house once where there was a headless maiden. Real good times they had with her, as children, running through her and out the other side— kind of fizzy it felt, she said, and a bit cold. It's human beans that can't abide them, for some reason. Never occurs to them that ghosts is too self-centred to take a blind bit of notice of human beans . . . '

Arrietty, however, is rather upset when Pod and Peagreen, carrying a roll of canvas, walk straight through the ghost of the Poor Young Man who had shot himself. Arrietty feels this shows 'a lack of respect'; and despite her acceptance of Peagreen's definition of a ghost as merely 'a photograph on air, on Time,' she always walks round them rather than through them.

The Borrowers Avenged also attempts to answer the charge sometimes made against Mary Norton that as "borrowing" is in fact stealing, she appears to condone theft. In Arrietty's words, we are told that—

> Human beans were made for borrowers, as bread for butter, cows for milking, hens for eggs: you might say (thinking of cows) that borrowers *grazed* on human beans.

—which is an ingenious justification. But Mary Norton had already given us another answer in the first book of the series. When the Borrowers take only what they need—scraps of food nobody would want, old postage stamps for use as pictures on the living-room walls—the "theft" is so trivial it isn't even missed, nor would it be considered by anyone as reprehensible; but when, through vanity or greed, they take items of value, they run the risk of being discovered. This, of course, is what happens in *The Borrowers*—persecution, terror, and flight are the consequences of such actions. So Mary Norton's morality is in fact the reverse of condoning theft. Real stealing, she says, deserves—and is—punished.

The world of the Borrowers books is not modern, post-war England, but the past of seventy or eighty years ago, of Mary Norton's own childhood: an England where big country houses still employed cooks, maids and gardeners; trains ran on branch railway lines; a car was a rare sight; "ladies" spent their spare time arranging altar flowers in churches; a village was a self-contained unit; and people like Mr Platter had only just begun to ruin our countryside by building "gimcrack villas." This Victorian or Edwardian past is re-created frequently in the work of Britain's contemporary writers for children—Philippa Pearce, for instance, or Penelope Farmer, Penelope Lively, Nina Bawden, and usually in books of fantasy rather than realistic fiction. Lucy Boston's Mrs Oldknowe, too, is an Edwardian, not a modern, person. It is, I think, what we do best. It isn't a longing for an idealized golden age, a turning of our backs on present-day problems—the class structure in Philippa Pearce's *The Children of the House,* for example, is overtly condemned, and in *The Borrowers* a system that forces the rural worker to lead a cramped, unimaginative life is implicitly criticized. This evocation of the past is an opening up to the young reader of the world of the historical imagination; imagination, Mary Norton in particular seems to be saying, sets you free. 'Nothing,' she says in *The Borrowers Afield,* 'turns out in fact as you have pictured it,' and speaking in the same novel through Mrs May she gives us this sound advice:

'And what if it were only a story . . . so long as it was a good story? Keep your sense of wonder, child, and don't be so literal. And anything we haven't experienced for ourselves sounds like a story. All we can ever do about such things is'—she hesitated, smiling at Kate's expression—'keep an open mind and try to sift the evidence.'

Mary Norton's only other book, *Are All the Giants Dead?*, is slight in comparison to the achievements of the Borrowers series, but it is nonetheless well worth reading. It is set in a mythical country inhabited by many of the heroes, heroines and villains of popular fairy tales; the Sleeping Princess, Beauty and the Beast, Cinderella and so on live here, but they are not as they were in the stories. They have grown old: Jack the Giant-Killer, and the other Jack (he of the beanstalk) are two old men who have retired from killing ogres and who now run a country pub. It's an amusing book with an exciting plot—the hunting down of the last wicked giant—which shows Mary Norton is, as ever, on the side of the little people. But things are not what they used to be, the two Jacks grumble—

> This land's got so full of kingdoms, and kings, and what-not, you just can't keep pace with them nowadays. And what's more, they all seem to have this one beautiful daughter, with the natural result—you might say—that there aren't enough princes to go round: they all end up marrying swineherds, or woodcutters, or the seventh son of some poor blacksmith.

There is also a continuation of the fun Mary Norton takes in observing petit bourgeois snobbery—

> 'You see, it would be very embarrassing for my father and mother to have a daughter living down a well and married to a toad. They wouldn't know what to say to people.'

An important theme of the story is stated by the news reporter, Mildred—

> 'It is very pleasant to come and visit these people—and they like it—but one must never get too involved in their lives: it always leads to trouble.'

This echoes the Borrowers books—it may be nice, in some few cases, for Borrowers to talk to humans, but involvement brings disaster; or, in other words, the realms of reality and imagination are best kept apart. As Mary Norton has already said, 'Keep your sense of wonder, child.' James, the central character, does keep his sense of wonder, and learns that courage rather than a talisman is needed to face danger, and that—once again—freedom has to be fought for. The giant is eventually killed, and Dulcibel agrees to marry the toad, who, of course, turns into a handsome prince. *Are All the Giants Dead?* is probably just the right book for the child who has almost—but not quite—grown out of the world of the fairy tale; it emphasizes not the literalness of such stories but their importance as metaphors, as blueprints for dealing with situations we haven't yet reached in real life.

Mary Norton's greatness as a writer is that she makes the reader completely believe in the extraordinary worlds she creates. Kate says to Mrs May in *The Borrowers*—

> Factories go on making safety-pins and every day people go on buying safety-pins, and yet, somehow there never is a safety-pin just when you want one. Where are they all? Now, at this minute? Where do they go to?

One of the results of *my* reading Mary Norton over the past thirty years is that she has the power to return me to the child I once was: I, too, look suspiciously at the floorboards when I can't find a safety-pin, 'hoping,' as Thomas Hardy says in *The Oxen,* 'it might be so.'

REFERENCES

MARY NORTON
  The Magic Bedknob, Dent, 1945; Hyperion Press 1943
  Bonfires and Broomsticks, Dent, 1947
  The Borrowers, Dent, 1952; Harcourt, 1953
  The Borrowers Afield, Dent, 1955; Harcourt, 1955
  Bedknob and Broomstick, Dent, 1957; Harcourt, 1957
  The Borrowers Afloat, Dent, 1957; Harcourt, 1957
  The Borrowers Aloft, Dent, 1961; Harcourt, 1961
  Poor Stainless, Dent, 1971; Harcourt, 1971

Are All the Giants Dead?, Dent, 1975, Harcourt, 1975
The Borrowers Avenged, Kestrel, 1982; Harcourt, 1982

L. M. BOSTON
The Stones of Green Knowe, Bodley Head, 1976; Atheneum, 1976

LEWIS CARROLL
Alice in Wonderland, first published 1865

BRIAN FAIRFAX-LUCY and PHILIPPA PEARCE
The Children of the House, Longman 1968; Lippincott, 1968

THOMAS HARDY
The Oxen in *Moments of Vision,* first published 1918

JONATHAN SWIFT
Gulliver's Travels, first published 1726

ENIGMA VARIATIONS

William Mayne

"William Mayne has some claim to be the most important modern English children's writer," said Peter Hunt in *Twentieth Century Children's Writers.* "Certainly no other author has had a comparably sustained output of such individuality and distinction." Naomi Lewis, reviewing *The Jersey Shore,* said "Mayne is a phenomenon. With almost every new book one feels, with a sense of revelation, this must be the best Mayne yet. And what a remarkable best it can be, in idea, and depth, and technique." Margery Fisher, in *Growing Point,* proclaimed the publication of *Earthfasts* to be "a landmark in the progress of children's literature," that it made her feel "language and thought have been new-born."

The voices of the British literary establishment; though it is only fair to add that Peter Hunt qualifies his statement by saying that Mayne is in many ways unsatisfactory as a major figure. There are other voices. In "A Discussion with William Mayne" in *Children's Literature in Education*—a question and answer session between the author and an audience that consisted mostly of teachers—the tone is less adulatory. "It has been said that a writer of top quality ought not to be so productive," the first speaker remarked; to which Mayne replied, "I should have died at thirty-six, like Mozart, then it wouldn't have mattered," which is a bit uppity, to say the least. A third opinion comes from the readers, the children. It is almost a truism that he is much more liked by critics than by children, and a recent check I made through the shelves of two libraries showed that one had no books of his, and the other only *No More School.* Is he, then, that dreaded figure of the children's book world—the writer who is admired only by adults; and, if so, does it matter?

The first speaker at that discussion made an interesting point, for Mayne's output is prodigious; truly "a phenomenon." Since *Follow the Footprints* in 1953, nearly every year has seen the publication of at least one new book by William Mayne; some years two or three or four, and in 1963 there were five. These books come in all shapes and sizes, for Mayne is as much at ease writing for very young children as he is for teenagers, and almost no genre has escaped his attention—realistic fiction, fantasy, folk tale, space stories, school stories, allegory and so on. No essay of this length could possibly discuss his entire work, or even list it; the critic's best approach here is probably to compare and contrast a varied selection from his output.

The few dissenting voices among the commentators suggest that Mayne is not a popular writer with children because he has no conventional narrative skill; his language is too sophisticated and his humor irritatingly childish; he avoids emotion, drama and crisis; and his emphasis on the ordinary and the humdrum leads to ordinary, humdrum books. There is undoubtedly some truth in this, but there are, nevertheless, several novels that amply demonstrate the opposite: *The Incline* certainly has narrative skill; *No More School* is not linguistically rarefied and its humor neither irritating nor childish; *Ravensgill* is certainly dramatic and *Earthfasts* confronts emotion head on; and in *A Grass Rope* the ordinary and the humdrum make a very satisfying novel. It is almost as if Mayne deliberately says: You think I can't do it? I'll show you that I can. Then, afterwards, he writes something else with all the faults again. He loves to tease: this is clear in the books, and in "A Discussion with William Mayne" he admits that his answers were designed to tease the audience. Which, of course, only adds to the irritation.

One thing Mayne does superbly well is place. Place in his novels—usually his native rural Yorkshire—is supremely important: it is charged with power and feeling and is often more striking than any individual character. Almost equally good is his sensitivity to the weather—we are aware the whole time of snow or sunlight, rain or wind. This is particularly good in *Sand,* for example, though it can degenerate to a mannerism: too many sentences in *The Member for the*

Marsh read like a daily weather bulletin. The background of *Sand* is a lonely, derelict seaside resort (*A Game of Dark* has a similar setting, equally well done):

> The sea was an endless grey, with distant white high-lights scattered on it, where waves broke haphazardly. The sound of it came along the road in the quietness of late Sunday afternoon. It was like an empty sponge being squeezed. There was the noise of sand, too, rustling dry in the gutters, taking up little positions behind stones, and then skirmishing out in cross-draughts, rising up in ghostly clouds, then dropping dead on the hard pavement with a faint sigh. It would regroup in the next movement of wind, and be off again, filling the town slowly with sand.

This is Mayne's prose style at its best—low key, forlorn, depressive (which is maybe why children don't take to it), but powerful and brooding.

A town being slowly destroyed by sand blown in from the beaches is, as an idea, original, romantic, and compelling. But, despite a richly satisfying ending that defuses all the tensions that have built up, *Sand* is not a good novel. Mayne avoids all the various narrative possibilities that derive from his chosen theme, and instead tells us a story about a group of boys who dig up the skeleton of a whale and put it in the yard of a nearby school in order to win favor with the girls. The two themes never marry properly, and eventually the sand idea is lost. The book is also marred by poor characterization (the teachers, for instance, are incredible ogres) and by too much dialogue. All the characters talk excessively, in a very "literary" way, and sound exactly alike; their conversation is often mere padding, doing very little to advance the plot. The dialogue annoys, in fact; it is Mayne at his whimsical worst, "clever" in a pejorative sense, full of feeble jokes:

> "We should have brought the shovels," said Harold. "If anyone wants to get them."
>
> "You're the one that's doing nothing," said Peter. "I mean, you're the one that isn't doing anything."
>
> "You said that once," said Harold. "What do you mean?"

"He means he's only pretending to work," said Guy.
"And you're not even pretending to."
Harold considered what Guy had said. "I believe
you're right," he said. "You must have meant something
else, though."

The whimsy coats everything, so that real feeling (affection,
pain, frustration—whatever) is masked, or destroyed, or
evaded. Mayne has a fatal weakness for puns, and *Sand*
abounds with them. They are rarely amusing:

"All it proves is that no one can tell lies when standing
on the Greenwich meridian. That's why they have such
a mean time at Greenwich."

In *Earthfasts*, landscape is as important as it is in *Sand*, and it
begins, similarly, with an arresting idea that is also unfortunately thrown aside or submerged, a third of the way through,
by material that is not of the same level of interest. This book is
Mayne's first excursion into fantasy: in the Yorkshire town of
Garebridge, there is an ancient legend that says King Arthur's
treasure is buried under the castle; in 1742 a drummer boy,
looking for it in a subterranean passage, disappeared and was
never seen again. *Earthfasts* begins with his sudden reap-
pearance in modern times; he's holding a candle that won't
blow out, and he thinks he's been underground for a mere
hour or so:

Keith looked at David, and David was less easy to see as
well, so the drummer boy was not unnaturally fading as
he had unnaturally come. But where had he come from?
What was he? In the first moments that he appeared,
solidifying before them, he might have been a ghost; but
what ghost was so full of talk and noise and wanting to
be at an inn, or at the castle gate in Garebridge?

The amusing and tragic consequences of a teenager from
1742 finding himself unexpectedly and unwillingly in the
twentieth century are very well handled, but the idea is
dropped after sixty pages. Mayne decides at this point to
concentrate on the candle: it belongs to King Arthur, asleep
under the earth, and the King wants it back—an echo of one

of the themes, the attempt of another world to retrieve an object taken into this world, of Alan Garner's *Elidor.* The book now becomes something less than it might have been; it turns into a catalog of extraordinary, supernatural events— standing stones come to life as giants; lightning removes people without trace; a wild boar rampages through the town, and so on—and though these set pieces are done very well, the reader is disappointed by Mayne abandoning what started as a psychological novel. However, the characterization is much better than in *Sand,* and for once emotions—fear, Keith's feelings about David's presumed death—are not avoided. The autumnal atmosphere and the setting are excellent—

> After the high hill trees, those upland willows and thorns, the low-lying beech died on the twig, and still hung there, and the fruit trees, leaving the fruit ripening, began to fall. And after perhaps two weeks the heat began to fall with the leaves: the mornings were no longer muggy, but the air was lying on its sharp side, coming edgeways through bedroom windows and spiky at street corners. There was a day when whiteness touched the roofs, and when the sun came the last of the leaves that would fall were loose, and there was a rustling all day, louder than the rustle of the coming of spring, and more spectacular.

Having discovered fantasy, Mayne was to return to it often. He said, in "A Discussion with William Mayne" that it was "just a tool of the trade," and that is indeed how he uses it. It is not for him a way of exploring the deep and hidden recesses of the personality (except in *A Game of Dark*), or, as in the novels of Penelope Lively or Alan Garner, something that puts us in touch with the historical and mythical past that has molded us. It's merely a bag of tricks, as in Susan Cooper's novels, which makes one feel that a major talent is not working properly. However, some of the later books are, even on this level, impressive; *It* in particular. *It,* once again, has a setting that is magnificently rendered, an English cathedral city—York, though it isn't named as such. The theme is serious: diabolic possession. Alice, an eleven-year-old girl in the twentieth century, is bewitched by a bad-tempered though not very evil spirit from Saxon times. Mayne doesn't handle his idea very seriously, however, though if he did the result would probably not be a children's book. But this novel does show that he can use conventional narrative techniques very well when he wants to; *It* is a good yarn that keeps the reader turning the pages to see what happens next, even if the reactions of some of the characters are somewhat implausible. Mum, for instance, regards her daughter's condition as if it were nothing more frightening than a touch of flu. En passant, there are some splendid perceptions; Mayne's development as a novelist shows an increasingly sure touch in his ability to encapsulate, in little asides, some telling comments about human behavior. Alice's view of her grandfather sums up a problem many children have at some time or another:

> She had been looking round the room at all Grandpa's things and realizing how hopeless it was to expect to achieve anything for herself because he had already done it all, and there on his walls and shelves were the signs of it: the relics of foreign lands, the row of books he had written, and the signed picture of him holding hands with the queen; the things of a complete person who had completed everything.

Probably Mayne's best novels are the three he wrote in the early seventies, *Ravensgill, A Game of Dark,* and *The Incline. Ravensgill* and *The Incline* are realistic stories of considerable narrative power and excitement that share similar plot elements; tales of thwarted love, anger and jealousy, with faint echoes of both *Romeo and Juliet* and Alan Garner's *The Owl Service.* Both also share a similar Yorkshire setting of remote, rugged hills and dales, a landscape that is in part industrialized, but an industrialization that is nineteenth century and in decay. The combination of landscape and industrial decline is a favorite backcloth in Mayne's books—the derelict mineshaft in *A Grass Rope,* the abandoned gravel pit and the disused railway line in *Sand,* and almost every novel of his has ancient trains in it, Victorian rolling-stock and steam engines operating on obscure branch lines. In

Ravensgill, it is an old reservoir with underground passages and waterways which provides the scene for much of the action, and in *The Incline* a slate quarry with its own funicular railway (the incline of the title) that takes the slate down into the valley. In both novels these man-made additions to the rural scene cause a death—in *Ravensgill* Clifford White dies in one of the tunnels, and in *The Incline* the villain, Marrick Lantho, is killed by a wagon of slate as it descends into the valley.

The Incline is the more successful of the two. It has some strong characterization, particularly its dour teenage hero, Mason Ross, and though *Ravensgill* also has people we care about and feel for, and a couple of delightful and convincing eccentrics in the two grandmothers, it is marred by a typical Mayne fault: the withholding of information from one of the chief characters solely for the purpose of keeping the reader in suspense. Bob's discovery of the truth about his grandparents' marriage is simply delayed so the denouement of the story can come in the right place; the unlikely device is that people refuse to tell him the truth because "it's best not to talk of it"—even though everyone else, including his own brother, knows the answers. This is plot manipulation, not the illusion of reality. *The Incline* has no such fault, and, again, has some remarkably effective observations. The first time Mason says "I love you" to Moira is a fine moment:

> "You look hot," said Moira. But it was not hotness that had come to redden Mason's face. It was the shame of having said something so personal to Moira and not being understood, the pity of spoiling a day by saying what he had and understanding what he meant; by understanding and naming his feelings he had destroyed the nervous quality of them. They were labelled now, and displayed to him as something smaller and less worth having than he had expected; as if he had pulled out the middle of a flower in a search for nectar and found the nectar soured by the juice of the flower itself.

Ravensgill's felicitous moments are of a different nature, but equally well conveyed. Bob's feelings about a French grammar book are—

> In its brown paper wrapper it looked more alive than it
> did when it was open, promising interest. But opened
> again it was a dry garden of verse that was not verse.

—and Judith's denunciation of male competitiveness is good;
she calls it "pride and prejudice and sense and sensibility and
your war and peace." She says:

> "I don't see why you have to be better all the time, and
> have to push past everyone . . . All you boys do the
> same, you can't join together and find out who's best at
> something and then help them to do it best."

A Game of Dark, written between *Ravensgill* and *The Incline*, is a quite different sort of achievement. It is Mayne's
finest novel, though it's too odd and too bleak to be popular.
The central character, Donald Jackson, is a very introverted
and lonely teenager. He has "eaten out all the circle of life
round himself"; he "watched himself lighting the fire." His
relationship with his mother is formal and cold; she is a teacher at his school and he finds these two roles of hers a source
of confusion: "She called him Jackson in school, and he called
her Mrs Jackson, and of course the same thing very often at
home." But Donald's chief problems are with his father, a
Methodist preacher who is dying of an incurable illness. His
feelings for his father, who is authoritarian and unloving, indeed unlovable, range from indifference to open dislike. Intensely distressed by his incapacity to love his parents or to
make them love him, Donald retreats into a fantasy world—
he imagines he is a young squire in early Saxon times serving
a lord in a small town which is being attacked by a monstrous, disgusting worm sixty feet long. The worm is slimy,
with an appalling stench, and it eats living things including
people. As his father nears death, Donald knows that he has to
kill the worm, and the moment he does so his father dies.
   A Game of Dark pushes children's literature in a direction
it had never previously taken. Mayne seems to be saying
there isn't anything necessarily wrong, in certain circumstances, for a child to hate his father, indeed, metaphorically,
to kill him; which, even if some of us might well concur, is a
fairly revolutionary statement for a children's book. The

worm also has obviously phallic connotations, and at a deeper, more allusive level, the book is dealing in a very odd way with adolescent sexual terrors—it suggests that Donald loathes and fears his father's maleness and his own developing sexual identity (the imitation of father). The worm is more than a mere symbol of Dad; it embodies everything Donald perceives as rotten and disgusting inside his father *and* himself—"observation, assessment and regulation," he says—and in killing it he appears to be performing a metaphorical castration of both himself and his father. He is also killing "observation, assessment and regulation." Whatever we may think of this, we don't have to agree that Donald is right; we don't have to identify with him. Our reactions are more those of pity and fear, and a certain relief at the book's calm ending—"Donald lay and listened to the quiet, and went to sleep, consolate." He admits that what he has done is "not an honourable deed," and that he now knows how to love his father, which is perhaps a step on the right road. We are left, surprisingly, with the feeling that he will grow up into a sane, whole adult.

The fantasy elements of *A Game of Dark* are excellent; rarely has this "tool of the trade" been put to better use by anyone. Mayne in this novel switches very abruptly from realistic passages to fantasy. No talisman, such as C. S. Lewis's wardrobe, or Philippa Pearce's grandfather clock, is needed as a bridge between one world and another: it is clearly established that the world of the worm is the darker kind of imagining of a rather dark boy; it is wholly in his mind. When the book was published (1971) this use of fantasy was quite novel in a children's story, but it has had its imitators since. "A prodigiously accomplished work of art," Brian Alderson said of it in *The Times,* and so it is: brief, spare, poetic, and absolutely original. Not many children, of course, will appreciate it, which brings us back to the question of does it matter if it is admired only by adults. My answer is that it doesn't matter: *A Game of Dark* exists; it is there for the right child when he or she wants it.

In a quite different vein are the earlier, realistic novels; two of the best of which are *A Grass Rope,* which deservedly won the Carnegie Medal in 1957, and *No More School.* One of the weakest is *The Member for the Marsh* with its unlikely "clever" dialogue, thin characterization, and inability to get a coherent plot together until the last quarter of the book. Even this latter stage of the story is suspect: a group of children discover the remains of a neolithic village in a Somerset marsh, and set out to explore it before the local farmer, who wants to turn the area into a lake, floods it; but Mayne devotes more time to the picnic the children eat than the relics they find, and agrees with the attitude of the children and the farmer—that the marsh is a nuisance, and the neolithic village worthless and uninteresting, best drowned. A dubious piece of morality indeed! There is something very old-fashioned about this book. It's juvenile literature of another age, when children had "adventures" and inter-reacted only with each other; when adults were shadowy figures on the fringe of things (usually issuing instructions about safety) and never spoke adult-to-adult, only adult-to-child; when sexism was a non-existent word—the boys' references to Anne as a dog, and their treatment of her as such, now seem to be jarringly unpleasant. It could be argued that the problem is one of period; *The Member for the Marsh* was published in 1956, a time when supposedly realistic children's fiction was sometimes little more than escapist fantasy, and adult perception of children's literature was often an undervaluing of the genre. But this period had its masterpieces, *The Borrowers* for instance, *Tom's Midnight Garden* and *Charlotte's Web*, and it was only a year after *The Member for the Marsh* that William Mayne wrote the first-rate *A Grass Rope*. The answer lies in that teacher's statement, "a writer of top quality ought not to be so productive." *The Member for the Marsh* is hasty in conception and superficial in execution.

A Grass Rope looks forward to *Earthfasts* in its promise of the supernatural—an ancient legend about a pack of hounds swallowed up by a hill, a unicorn, and buried treasure—but everything is given a natural and reasonable explanation, and imaginative little Mary, who tried to get into the hill and find a unicorn to keep as a pet, is comforted at the end with the present of an orphan fox cub. The setting is a farm in the Yorkshire hills, and the scenery, as ever, is omnipresent and beautifully rendered. The characters are convincing and well contrasted, with adults as much at the center of the story as children, and the girls are not relegated to an inferior role. The dialogue helps rather than hinders the story-line, and the narrative is skillful and exciting. Every fault in *The Member for the Marsh* is here turned into a virtue, and only a year separates the two books! No wonder William Mayne seems like an enigma. Some of the best writing in *A Grass Rope* is concerned with the foxes and the ambivalence about killing them felt by the characters and by the author:

> He watched the fox as if she were on stage. She walked over the grass like a dancer: each leg had its attendant pointing shadow; the gill still made rippling music. The fox made her own ballet, pointing each silent foot, and reached the shadow of the wall.
>
> Under the tractor shed the moonlight moved: a straight gleam pointed to the fox; the night burst round the moving moonlight: twice there was thunder in the air; the fells sent the double report back from bank to bank and scar to scar. Every creature that heard crouched low and fearful; but one crouched animal heard nothing: shot moves faster than sound, and the fox was dead before she fell.
>
> Adam saw his gun standing beside him, and knew he had not fired. "Good," he said.

One is reminded of Betsy Byars' *The Midnight Fox.* The farmer, Mr Owland, sums up the dilemma neatly—"A fox is a better animal than a hen," he says. "But no one can do anything about that. Hens lay eggs: foxes don't."

No More School takes place in a tiny Yorkshire village that has a school with one teacher and only fourteen children. When Miss Oldroyd becomes ill, the children are supposed to go to school in the next village, but they don't want to: they pretend to go there, but in fact they sneak into their own school and teach themselves. It's a bit improbable, but the story is told with such gusto and such good humor that the improbability does not seem to matter. This is a book for the younger age range, and Mayne manages to simplify his language and his concepts without sacrificing anything in the way of narrative skill and poetic imagery. The occasional remark sounds wrong: "You only get schoolitis," said Ruth.

"That's not an illness, it's an opinion," which is a bit too sophisticated in the mouth of a young child, but Bobby's geography lesson sounds exactly right—

> "Geography," he said. "The geography of England. England is an island. That means it has water all round it, except at the top, where it has Scotland instead."

Discipline in this set-up is a problem, but, on the plus side, the children cope with cooking their dinners very well; they do learn a bit, and eventually the astonished teacher comes back to find no harm done. This neat, unpretentious story has an obvious appeal to children. No wonder it is on the library shelves, and *A Game of Dark* is not.

Among Mayne's later books, *The Battlefield, The Jersey Shore* and *All the King's Men* are worthy of comment, *The Battlefield* merely for pointing out that Mayne doesn't learn from his earlier mistakes. Here we have tiresome plotlessness, pages of inconsequential dialogue that are full of weak jokes, rustic stereotypes, and some extremely implausible happenings. The place the title refers to should provide some interest—it is a piece of moorland on which a battle was fought, probably during the Civil War; but no information about it is given. Penelope Lively in *Children and Memory* said—

> To feel the impact of a place like the battlefield at Edge-hill, you must know something of the tormented history of seventeenth-century England, or it is nothing but an attractive piece of Warwickshire landscape.

So, another opportunity is lost.

The Jersey Shore, despite immense critical acclaim ("Perhaps as important a book as he has ever transferred from imagination to print," said Naomi Lewis), seems to me to be a wholly self-indulgent novel that ignores its readers. There is virtually no story-line; the rambling speeches of the grandfather about his past are impenetrably difficult for a child to follow; and, solely for plot purposes, there are omissions of information again (we are not told until the conclusion which of the old man's three wives was Arthur's grandmother). The ending is very controversial. It is not revealed, till the last few pages, that Grandma Florence was black: and though Mayne might well say race and skin color are irrelevant to his story, he has in effect evaded something he possibly didn't want to write about, but should have written about. For race is bound to be an issue, given the circumstances— Florence married a white emigrant from England. Landscape and atmosphere, however, are excellent, and there is some fine characterization, particularly Aunt Deborah, who is a little reminiscent of the aunts in Paula Fox's *How Many Miles to Babylon?* (This might just give the adult expert on children's literature a clue as to skin color, but it won't mean much to the child reader.)

All the King's Men is a delightful book. It consists of three stories that have no connection with each other—the first, set in medieval times, is about dwarfs in a royal palace; the second tells us what happened to a Scottish island boy when he is bewitched by the fairies; and the last has a modern setting and recalls *A Grass Rope,* for it is concerned with an over-imaginative child who wrongly thinks supernatural events are occurring. No connection at all, yet there *seems* to be one: it is the prose style which is the link, luminous, beautiful and poetic, so distinctive that the author's "smudge" of himself is indelibly on all three tales. This is the opening of the first—

> We were on our way to the winter palace. No one watched us go that year. Fonso kept falling off the dog, and there was no one to see it and laugh, neither as we left the merchanty town nor as we passed along the cold roads between town and forest.

And the last begins:

> There were eight cats in the snow. Seven of them came in, but black Boogie stayed where he was, lying under the wall beside the grindstone, in a sheltered place.
> Kirsty knew at once what had happened. He had died. She knew at once. Mum knew as well.

There are only sixteen words in these two passages that consist of more than one syllable. It is exactly the same voice in both, the voice of someone who knows precisely what he is doing, and who is doing it very well.

Mayne's writing seems to me to be instinctive, felt rather than intellectualized; he writes as Evonne Goolagong (Mayne would enjoy the seemingly incongruous comparison) played tennis; "I have no plan, no strategy," she said. Her tennis at its best was compared by commentators to poetry, to dancing—it was full of grace and beauty. She won Wimbledon twice with effortless ease, and lost with equally effortless ease to unknown players far below her in ability and experience. So William Mayne can write one year a near-masterpiece, the next a total dud. His worst failing is dodging issues, avoiding the natural psychological climaxes of his stories, dissipating their impact with weak humor. This refusal to depict emotion, to wear his heart on his sleeve, is all very British, dour Yorkshire and stiff upper lip, but it is very annoying to the would-be admirer. But without him, children's literature would be the poorer: probably no one has ever rendered the power of place so well, and *A Game of Dark* is certainly on my list of the top ten most fascinating of modern children's books.

REFERENCES

WILLIAM MAYNE
  Follow the Footprints, Oxford, 1953
  The Member for the Marsh, Oxford, 1956
  A Grass Rope, Oxford, 1957; Dutton, 1962
  Sand, Hamish Hamilton, 1964; Dutton, 1965
  No More School, Hamish Hamilton, 1965
  Earthfasts, Hamish Hamilton, 1966; Dutton, 1967
  The Battlefield, Hamish Hamilton, 1967; Dutton, 1967
  "A Discussion with William Mayne," *Children's Literature in Education,* July 1970
  Ravensgill, Hamish Hamilton, 1970; Dutton, 1970
  A Game of Dark, Hamish Hamilton, 1971; Dutton, 1971
  The Incline, Hamish Hamilton, 1972; Dutton, 1972
  The Jersey Shore, Hamish Hamilton, 1973; Dutton, 1973
  It, Hamish Hamilton, 1977; Greenwillow, 1978
  All the King's Men, Cape, 1982

BETSY BYARS
  The Midnight Fox, Viking, 1968; Faber, 1970

PAULA FOX
  How Many Miles to Babylon?, David White, 1967; Macmillan, London, 1968

ALAN GARNER
  Elidor, Collins, London, 1965; Walck, 1967
  The Owl Service, Collins, London, 1967; Walck, 1968

D. L. KIRKPATRICK, editor
  Twentieth Century Children's Writers, St. Martin's Press, 1978

PENELOPE LIVELY
  "Children and Memory," *The Horn Book Magazine,* August 1973

MARY NORTON
  The Borrowers, Dent, 1952; Harcourt, 1953

PHILIPPA PEARCE
  Tom's Midnight Garden, Oxford, 1958; Lippincott, 1959

E. B. WHITE
  Charlotte's Web, Harper, 1952; Hamish Hamilton, 1952

THE VIRTUES OF IMPROBABILITY

Joan Aiken

Like William Mayne and Leon Garfield, Joan Aiken is an immensely prolific author. She has written a wealth of books for children—plays, verse, collections of short stories, a dozen full-length stories—as well as many novels for adults. The gusto and enormous energy of her work is only equalled among contemporary children's writers by Leon Garfield, and, like him, she can be called, rather loosely, a historical novelist. Her methods and intentions, however, are very different from his—or, indeed, anyone else's. She is the one author, more than any other, who is able to make a virtue of improbability; the wilder, the more absurd her invention becomes, the better the result. With the exception of *Go Saddle the Sea,* her straightforward, realistic novels are not as successful as the sequence of books that begins with *The Wolves of Willoughby Chase,* which are set in an imaginary, fantastic period of the nineteenth century that bears little resemblance to the real Victorian era; indeed, Queen Victoria in these stories never existed. This sequence of books displays all her gifts at their most beguiling: magnificent plots that are often so lavish in their ingenuity that first-rate ideas can get tossed aside in an almost spendthrift way; a delightful sense of humor; and an increasingly sure ear for language that manifests itself in parody and the dialects, vocabulary and speech rhythms of various periods of history.

This latter ability is not conspicuous in *The Wolves of Willoughby Chase* itself. The dialogue here often sounds wrong, veering uncertainly at times—even in the same sentence—from a pastiche of Victorian English to modern slang; and there are rustic minor characters who are stereotypical and unconvincing. But things show a marked improvement in

Black Hearts in Battersea with the homespun pronounce-
ments of Scottish King James, and in *Night Birds on Nantucket* with the archaic Quaker speech of the Nantucketers.
Then from *The Whispering Mountain* onwards there is a riot
of extraordinary vocabulary and speech rhythms—Welsh
sentence structure, Sussex dialect, Cockney rhyming slang,
nineteenth-century criminal slang, nineteenth-century military slang, anachronistic Elizabethan English, and so on—all
of it handled very deftly by an author who now knows exactly what she is doing.

Like Leon Garfield, Joan Aiken is influenced by Dickens,
but what she takes from him is different from what Garfield
borrows. Description of place and the physical appearance of
people is in Garfield often Dickenslan, as are certain recur-
rent themes—the quest for financial "great expectations";
the exploitation of the innocent child in a crowded, filthy,
urban environment. Only in *Midnight is a Place* does Joan
Aiken explore the latter idea; and, with the exception of the
opening paragraphs, the snow-bound countryside, and the
train journey in *The Wolves of Willoughby Chase,* she spends
remarkably little time—in her first six books—describing
scenery and weather. *The Stolen Lake* is different; here she
pauses quite often to depict the mountains, rivers, vegetation
and wild life of South America, and does it very well. Victorian London in *Black Hearts in Battersea* is not dwelled on
at all, and the industrial northern city of Blastburn, in which
the second half of *The Wolves of Willoughby Chase* is set, is
also ignored: we expect descriptions like Dickens's portrait
of Coketown in *Hard Times* (the two cities seem much
alike), but we have to wait until *Midnight is a Place* for
Blastburn to come into its own.

The Dickensian influence is strongest in the scenes in *The
Wolves of Willoughby Chase* which occur in Mrs Brisket's
school; we are reminded of Wackford Squeers's academy in
Nicholas Nickleby, or Thomas Gradgrind's in *Hard Times.*
But there are few other direct parallels, and by *Night Birds
on Nantucket* Joan Aiken seems to have abandoned Dickens
as a source of ideas and turned to Melville: this book is, in
part, a parody of *Moby Dick*—the gloomy, religious Captain
Casket is a comic version of Captain Ahab, and the flirtatious

pink whale a send-up of the white monster, old Moby himself. (Even in *The Wolves of Willoughby Chase,* the wicked governess, Miss Slighcarp, is more a parody of Charlotte Brontë than Dickens.) The Dickensian influence, however, continues in Joan Aiken's plot methods, the names of her characters— Gripe, Moleskin, Pelmett, Fringe, Fitzpickwick, Firkin, Gusset, Twite, Luggins, Prigman, etcetera—and, most strikingly, in the marvellously atmospheric openings of her books. Linguistically, the first paragraph of *Black Hearts in Battersea* is so close to Dickens it could have been written by him; and just as *Great Expectations* and *Our Mutual Friend* begin with a magnificent hint of something sinister, so does *The Wolves of Willoughby Chase*—

> It was dusk—winter dusk. Snow lay white and shining over the pleated hills, and icicles hung from the forest trees. Snow lay piled on the dark road across Willoughby Wold, but from dawn men had been clearing it with brooms and shovels. There were hundreds of them at work, wrapped in sacking because of the bitter cold, and keeping together in groups for fear of the wolves, grown savage and reckless from hunger.

The opening of *Night Birds on Nantucket* is worth quoting in full: there are few books that present on their first page such a tremendous sense of mystery and excitement, such an invitation to read on and find out what happens next—

> Late in the middle watch of a calm winter's night, many years ago, a square-rigged, three-masted ship, the *Sarah Casket,* was making her way slowly through northern seas, under a blaze of stars. A bitter, teasing cold lurked in the air; long icicles sometimes fell chiming from the spars to the planks beneath. No other sound could be heard in the silent night, save, from far away, the faint barking of seals.
>   On the deck a child lay sleeping in a wooden box filled with straw. Sheepskins covered her warmly. Had it not been for her breath, ascending threadlike into the Arctic air, she would have seemed more like a wax doll than a human being, so still and pale did she lie. Near by squatted a boy, hunched up, his arms round his knees,

gravely watching over her. It was his turn below, and by
rights he should have been in his bunk, but whenever he
had any time to spare he chose to spend it by the sleeping child.

   She had been asleep for more than ten months.

   The main strength of *The Wolves of Willoughby Chase*
sequence is, as I have said, in the breath-taking improbabilities of the plots. The royal family of Britain is the Tudor-
Stuarts; the Hanoverians have been defeated in a civil war
that ended in 1832, and King James III is on the throne. (He is
later succeeded by his son, Richard IV.) The channel tunnel
has been built, and, because of an exceptionally severe
winter, starving wolves from the continent have rushed
through it and now roam the English countryside. Hanoverian villains in *Night Birds on Nantucket* hope to kill King
James by means of a long-range gun that can be fired with
deadly accuracy from one side of the Atlantic to the other; in
The Cuckoo Tree, they plan to destroy Richard IV and the
entire government during the coronation ceremonies by
placing St Paul's cathedral on rollers so that it will run downhill into the Thames; and in *The Stolen Lake*—perhaps the
most ingenious and original book of the series—we are in a
British ex-colony, New Cumbria, which is in South America
and has peasants who speak Latin, an Inca-like capital city
called Bath Regis, man-eating birds, a princess who can ride a
leopard, a queen who is over a thousand years old, and, most
daring of all, a lake that is actually stolen. (The king of the
next-door country removes it when it is frozen; his soldiers
cut the ice into blocks and take them away on teams of
llamas.) With such wonderful extravagances, smaller improbabilities seem to matter not a bit. Sylvia, for instance,
cannot possibly go to the loo on her two-day train journey to
Willoughby Chase (it is stressed that the train has no corridor
to other compartments); the wolves, despite the emphasis on
their slavering jaws, ferocious appetites and tendency to leap
through train windows, can be beaten off with lumps of coal
or croquet mallets; escape from disaster is often ludicrously
easy—in convenient air balloons in *The Stolen Lake* and
Black Hearts in Battersea, or, also in *Black Hearts in Battersea,* by jumping out of a box at the opera into a piece of

embroidery—and in the same novel, the plot is made to cope with fire, flood, wolves, kidnapping, poisoning, explosions and two shipwrecks.

One example of Joan Aiken being prodigal with her ideas is her treatment of the wolves. They are so well done and so important to the first half of *The Wolves of Willoughby Chase* that it is a disappointment that they appear only fleetingly thereafter; they are, of course, replaced by the human wolves of the title, Miss Slighcarp, Mrs Brisket and Mr Grimshaw. Mr Grimshaw is a rare example in Joan Aiken's work of appearances being deceptive; he seems at first to be a kindly old gentleman, coming to the assistance of a frightened little girl. Usually the characters are done with a few brief strokes, and are either wholly good or wholly bad at first sight; Mrs Moleskin in *The Wolves of Willoughby Chase* is an example:

> Bonnie did not last long in the kitchen. The second time that the cook hit her with the frying-pan, Bonnie picked up a sauce-boat full of rancid gravy and dashed it in the cook's face.
>
> There was a fierce struggle, but the cook, one Mrs Moleskin, a large, stout woman with a savage temper, at last thrust Bonnie into the broom cupboard and reported her to Mrs Brisket.

There is little of the ambiguity that one meets in Stevenson's or Garfield's villains—Long John Silver in *Treasure Island,* for instance, or Solomon Trumpet in *Jack Holborn*—though Dido Twite's father is an exception; and people rarely change sides. (Again, there are a few exceptions, such as Professor Breadno in *Night Birds on Nantucket.*) Occasionally a good person may be ambiguous (Grandfather Hughes in *The Whispering Mountain* is selfish and insensitive, yet essentially honest and virtuous), but for the most part the characters are done in black and white. The minor characters, like the villains, are at their most convincing when they are caricatured. The naval lieutenants in *The Stolen Lake* are brought to life through the language they speak, a parody of military slang—

> Lieutenant Windward exclaimed impatiently, "Come, come, my man, what the deuce ails you? This is moon-

shine! Battles—alliances—Ah well, I reckon you are all
tottyheaded yet."

But when Joan Aiken resorts to stereotypes, the results are
not so effective. Lord Malyn in *The Whispering Mountain*
contains too many characteristics of the typical stage baddie
to be interesting, whereas Miss Slighcarp—a superb caricature—always holds our attention. Sometimes brief details
of physical appearance are enough to create an impression of
personality: a Garfield trick. Aunt Tribulation in *Night Birds
on Nantucket* "had black curls and gay black eyes, and her
face was round and rosy and soft, like a pink frosted cake."
She would be quite at home in *The Strange Affair of Adelaide
Harris.* Dr Furneaux in *Black Hearts in Battersea* is described in a similar way:

> As he rose up from behind his desk he reminded Simon
> irresistibly of a prawn. His whiskers waved, his hands
> waved, a pair of snapping black eyes took in every inch
> of Simon from his dusty shoes to the kitten's face poking
> inquisitively out of his jacket.

As far as the heroes and heroines of these books are concerned, the girls are usually more convincing than the boys.
Sylvia, Bonnie and Dido are sharply differentiated, but Simon,
Nate and Owen are too alike. Simon and Owen, in particular,
are too gifted, too cool in a crisis, too mature to seem quite
real. They *always* have an answer. This is perhaps not very
disturbing as everything and everyone in these stories is out-
rageous and fantastic, but in the realistic novels it is a problem. *Midnight is a Place* and *Bridle the Wind* have children
who think, feel, and act as if they were adults, and who overcome difficulties that seem to suggest their real ages are at
least twenty.

    *The Wolves of Willoughby Chase, Black Hearts in Bat-
tersea* and *Night Birds on Nantucket* follow one another in
chronological order. The fourth book of the series, however—*The Whispering Mountain*—is concerned with a different set of characters, and takes place at the same time as
Night Birds on Nantucket. The fifth, *The Cuckoo Tree,* is,
chronologically, the finale of the sequence, using characters

from all its predecessors to bring matters to a satisfying conclusion. *The Stolen Lake,* the last to be written, is about
Dido's adventures between the end of *Night Birds on Nantucket* and the beginning of *The Cuckoo Tree.* Both *The Whispering Mountain* and *The Cuckoo Tree* are concerned with
the idea of rejection, a theme Joan Aiken explores again in
the realistic novels, *Night Fall, Midnight is a Place,* and *Go
Saddle the Sea.* Mr. Hughes, the curator of Pennygaff's museum in *The Whispering Mountain,* cuts his grandson, Owen,
out of his life when he decides—wrongly—that the boy has
stolen the museum's prize exhibit, the harp of Teirtu; and
Dido, who was abandoned by her feckless father in *Black
Hearts in Battersea,* begins to feel alone and unwanted in *The
Cuckoo Tree,* something that did not bother her in *Night
Birds on Nantucket.* But Joan Aiken in *The Cuckoo Tree* is
tying up loose ends, rounding things off; Cris is restored to
her long-lost brother, and Captain Hughes, the father Owen
believed was dead, is returning to his family, alive and
eventually well. Dido is the cuckoo of the title, the bird who
is fostered in other birds' nests (the good ships *Sarah Casket*
and H.M.S. *Thrush*), but the novel ends happily and hopefully;
Dido does not know it, but her old friend Simon, now the
sixth Duke of Battersea, is just about to meet her after an
absence of many years. What would follow would perhaps be
a romantic relationship—which would be quite out of character with the rest of the series. Joan Aiken was wise to finish
it here, just hinting at the possibility.

In *The Whispering Mountain* and *The Cuckoo Tree* the
narrative is tighter and more complex than in the first three
books; the last fifty pages of *The Cuckoo Tree,* which portray
the chaos that precedes the coronation of King Richard IV
and the final come-uppance of the Hanoverian villains, are
unrivalled in the whole sequence for breakneck narrative
gusto, imaginative invention and crazy humor—they are a
sheer delight to read. Both books show an increase in weird
vocabulary, bizarre dialects and all kinds of speech oddities.
Some critics have objected to this, on the grounds that it
creates unnecessary difficulties for the child reader, but the
charge doesn't stand up: meaning is invariably clear through
what has happened previously in the plot—

"Burn my galleyslops, yes! I've no fancy to pass the rest of my days without any fambles or stamps! Ask me, his lordship is own brother to Horny himself—no matter where we huggered he'd search us out in the end. I reckon trying to play him false was a mug's game."

"It was your notion," Bilk said sourly.

"Oh, quit brabbling. All we need to do now is get the tinkleplunk away from little Caliban there, and we're up to our gorges in velvet. Now: you slide round thataway and then let out a shout to startle him, I'll stand yonder to cut him off when he scampers. Agreed?"

"Ay, let's get at him."

"Don't you dare!" Owen bawled, as loud as he could. "You leave him alone! Keep your hands off that harp!"
(*The Whispering Mountain*)

New Cumbria in *The Stolen Lake* is not a country anyone would visit by choice. It is—

excessively dangerous; there are jaguars, giant owls, and bats, spiders seven inches in diameter which can . . . leap thirty feet in one spring; there are alligators, poisonous snakes, hostile savages in the forest armed with poisoned darts, besides huge hairy tusked birds, larger than horses, which can snatch up a grown man in their talons and fly off with him to their eyrie in the mountains.

Joan Aiken spends a lot of time describing these and other horrors, which include the machinations of the wicked Queen Ginevra, who enjoys eating a white paste made from the bones of young girls; but Dido and her companions survive, though our heroine is kidnapped twice, and nearly thrown over a cliff one thousand feet high. Many of the artefacts of this strange place are also described, including a splendidly grotesque train which has a thatched roof, and—

resembled a row of dominoes in process of falling down. The rolling-stock . . . did indeed have a curiously tilted appearance, since most of its journey would be spent going up the side of a slope like a church steeple; consequently while on flat ground the whole thing leaned forward as if engaged in studying its own toenails.

The Stolen Lake has a thoroughly entertaining, complex narrative, and the usual interest in odd words. Joan Aiken is here at the height of her powers: to look back from this point to *The Wolves of Willoughby Chase* is to look from something flawless to a first novel that has, despite its originality and appeal, weaknesses and uncertainties. The plot complexities of *The Stolen Lake* are neatly illustrated by this amusing paragraph:

> It is a considerable shock when somebody you have known (you thought) very well indeed, and have been fond of, proves to be, not only a completely different person from the one you believed to be your friend, but also not to remember you at all. If, on top of that, he turns out to be a king, reborn after thirteen hundred years, the shock is greater still. And if, into the bargain, he is married to one of the wickedest and most horrible people you have ever met, you can hardly help feeling very unhappy about it. Especially if he seems to be showing rather too much interest in a princess who certainly *isn't* his wife.

The linguistic novelties extend to place-names; the thirteen great volcanoes—Ambage and Arrabe, Ertayne and Elamye, Arryke, Damask, Damyake, Pounce, Pampoyle, Garesse, Caley, Calabe and Catelonde—recall the lines in W. J. Turner's poem, *Romance,* that discuss the magic of names, in this case also South American volcanoes:

> Chimborazo, Cotapaxi,
> They had stolen my soul away.

They also suggest another author who delights in invented worlds and has a gift for place names—Ursula Le Guin. The archipelago of Earthsea that Ursula Le Guin created gave birth to three novels (*A Wizard of Earthsea, The Tombs of Atuan,* and *The Farthest Shore*), but the reader is left with the feeling that it could lead to many more: similarly, Joan Aiken's imaginary Britain with its Tudor-Stuart kings and its oldest ally, New Cumbria, suggests the possibility of stories yet to come. Joan Aiken hints at this in her essay, "A Thread of Mystery":

> I try to provide a sense of mystery by references to
> things outside the orbit of the book which the reader
> can pursue or ignore as he pleases. And I take pains to
> know a great deal more about the action and back-
> ground than I put down, so that what is actually written
> is like the tip of an iceberg.

But whatever else she may produce from the eras of James III
and Richard IV, she will find it hard to better *The Stolen Lake.*
  Two of Joan Aiken's realistic novels—*Night Fall* and *The
Shadow Guests*—have a modern setting; the others—*Midnight is a Place, Go Saddle the Sea,* and *Bridle the Wind*—are
set in the nineteenth century. *Night Fall,* written for Macmillan's *Topliner* series, is essentially a minor work, but it has
its virtues. It is both a murder mystery and a romance. The
characterization, however, is not very subtle; the murderer
and the Cornish locals in particular seem little more than
stereotypes. The romantic elements contain some sentimental prose reminiscent of women's magazines—the two men
in Meg's life are both somewhat misty, Barbara Cartland-ish
creations. But the "who-dun-it" narrative is handled well, and
the Cornish background is good, too; this is the real Cornwall
of industrial decline and desolate landscapes, not the picture-
postcard Westcountry of Susan Cooper's *Over Sea, Under
Stone:*

> I drove on faster now, gradually exchanging the rolling
> Devon hillsides for sharper, gnarled, treeless Cornish
> ups-and-downs. The whole countryside had a forlorn,
> windswept, ramshackle air. It was hard to imagine my
> gay, pleasure-loving, company-loving mother volun-
> tarily coming to spend a holiday in this bleak part.

There are also some apt observations on the subject of self-
satisfied men patronizing women, and the occasional striking
image:

> I had come down here to try and dig out memory, like a
> buried splinter; what was the use of turning tail at the
> first twinge of the needle?

As pot-boilers go, many are a lot worse than *Night Fall.*

Cosmo, the central character in *The Shadow Guests,* is another of Joan Aiken's young heroes who has lost a parent, and/or sibling: it is almost an obsessive theme in her work. Meg, Dido, Simon and Sophie, Tobit and Cris, Sylvia, Owen, Penitence are all in the same situation. Often these characters have to suffer rejection by the remaining parent or relative—Owen, Meg, Sim and Dido are examples. Cosmo, in addition, suffers from the knowledge that his family is burdened by a curse that goes back to Roman times: the eldest son always dies young, unmarried, in a fight. As the novel progresses he meets some of the eldest sons from previous ages—a device similar to that used by Lucy Boston in the first three books of the Green Knowe series—and, through learning their history, he comes to terms with the fact that his first-born son may die in the same way. *The Shadow Guests* is one of Joan Aiken's few excursions into the supernatural, and it is not altogether successful. She admitted in "A Thread of Mystery" that—

> it takes a very special kind of talent . . . Tolkien can do
> it, Alan Garner can, William Mayne can, but I'm doubtful
> whether I can.

Cosmo's experiences with the ghosts, however, help him to solve the problems he has with his class-mates at school. The best writing in the book depicts boarding-school life: the boredom of routine, and the petty nastiness that is sometimes displayed when children gang up together. (Joan Aiken uses this theme again in *Go Saddle the Sea,* where it is also well handled.) This is a sad but truthful comment:

> He could already see that to be Bun's friend was to share
> his isolation; it was like touching a leper and catching
> his disease.

There are some good perceptions too—that people, for instance, may offer sympathy only because they need it themselves; it can be a "stupid, spongy craving." But *The Shadow Guests* fails because it doesn't really know which slot it belongs to—it is in part a children's story, in part young adult fiction. Cosmo, like other central characters in Joan Aiken's books, thinks and feels too maturely to be convincing. Also, too much of the dialogue, especially when Eunice is speaking, merely exists to impart information.

Midnight is a Place is a more ambitious work than either *Night Fall* or *The Shadow Guests.* It is set in nineteenth-century Blastburn, the hideous industrial town that was first mentioned in *The Wolves of Willoughby Chase,* but none of the characters from that book appears in this one. It is a wholly realistic piece—which is a pity, as many of the audacious ideas Joan Aiken gets away with in the fantasies do not succeed in a straightforward historical novel. Coincidence, for example, improbability, or making the villains totally villainous and the good people entirely good, spoil *Midnight is a Place.* Anna-Marie is absurdly adult for her age, far too knowing; Lady Murgatroyd living for years in the ice-house, undetected, is just not credible; Sir Randolph Grimsby is a cardboard, two-dimensional villain; and the harsh working and living conditions that are forced on Lucas and Anna-Marie leave them remarkably unscathed. (The plight of children in Victorian industrial society is done much better, in contemporary children's fiction, in William Rayner's *Big Mister.*) Long before the story ends one ceases to care very much about what is going to happen to any of the characters: it's impossible to suspend one's disbelief. The theme and the background details remind one of Leon Garfield, in particular the emphasis on the consequences of chance:

> How queer it seemed that a dozen words, spoken in a temper, could travel so far, like a tidal wave or an earthquake, could alter the lives of people in distant countries, people who were not even born at the time the words were spoken.

Garfield, however, would have done it all with rather more conviction. But there are some good descriptive passages that recall the Dickens of *Hard Times,* even if they lack his savage intensity. These are Blastburn's factories—

> None of these places looked as if they were built by human beings or used by them. Huge, dark, irregular

shapes rose up all around; they were like pinnacles in a
rocky desert, like ruined prehistoric remains or like the
broken toys of some giant's baby. The potteries were
enormous funnels, the gasworks huge flower-pots, the
collieries monstrous pyramids, with skeleton wheels the
size of whole church-fronts which stood above them
against the fiery sky.

One minor theme that is well-conceived is the Luddite men-
tality. Peter Dickinson in his first two books, *The Weathermonger* and *Heartsease,* also used this idea, but it is better
explored in *Midnight is a Place.*

In contrast, *Go Saddle the Sea,* as an attempt at historical
realism, is entirely successful. It is a picaresque novel, told in
the first person, and it recalls Cervantes or Fielding in method, though not in content or style—each incident is a little,
self-contained episode, often introducing characters who do
not reappear elsewhere, the one unifying factor being the
narrator, Felix, who is present all the time. This is the structure of *Don Quixote* or *Joseph Andrews.* The setting is early
nineteenth-century Spain, and the story is an account of Felix's adventures: he is a cheerful, physical, extrovert boy, half-
English and half-Spanish, who runs away from his grandfather's stifling, aristocratic household because he is treated
badly. He rides or walks across most of northern Spain to
Santander, then sails to England in order to find his English
relatives who turn out to be very different—but no more
congenial—than the Spaniards he has deserted. En route he
meets a gallery of typical Joan Aiken rogues and eccentrics
and some pleasant, charitable people who help and befriend
him; also an amiable mule and a very amusing talking parrot.
Felix, for the most part, is credible and attractive—we care
about him, and what may happen to him—even though there
are one or two moments where he behaves, or thinks, in a
way that is too adult for his years. The main reason why this
book succeeds, however, is the deliberately adopted tone of
voice of the narration, a simple well-handled pastiche of nineteenth-century vocabulary and sentence structure that never
falters at any point. It is an excellent instrument for Joan
Aiken's purposes—

Next befell me a very strange adventure, which makes
me shudder, even now, when I recall it, so singular, so
utterly uncanny were the circumstances, and so dreadful might the end have been, if matters had turned out
differently.

There are some pleasing, unfussy descriptions of Spain—a
country Joan Aiken seems to love (as I do) not only for its
scenery, but its people, their customs and way of life—that
are often done with a striking, original image—

The house-roofs, here, were made of huge slates and
came down almost to the ground, as a protection from
the mountain rains. Up above the houses, on the sides of
the mountain, almost like cloths hanging on a line, were
the small fields, with cattle grazing; they seemed so
steep I wondered that the cattle did not fall down the
chimneys. A little church, up above, clung to a crag like
a stone-martin perched on a cliffside.

There are also some excellent comments on the weather
("the snow-flakes appeared black like a cloud of grasshop-
pers"), and people's physical appearance—"big ears that
spread out so wide you could see the light through them, like
those of burros"—and a very nice description of England
from Felix who has not yet arrived there: a splendid amalgam
of prejudice and absurdity—

They eat their meat half-raw; beer and cider are drunk
mostly, for wine is very dear; the bread is abominably
bitter; the hedges are mean and insignificant, being full
of nettles, thistles, and thorns instead of oak and vine;
they burn a black, shining stone everywhere instead of
wood; their candles are made of tallow, very coarse and
stinking, for wax is too dear; their clothes are not gay or
colourful, as in Spain, but mainly grey or brown; there
are no goats in England; they have no aqueducts or
wayside fountains; their streets are wide, for the sun
never shines, and they need no shade; their night-watchmen cry out every half-hour all through the night, telling
the state of the weather—a needless service, for it is
always raining . . .

Go Saddle the Sea is an exciting adventure story with a well-paced narrative, full of incident, humor and enjoyable characters.

The sequel, *Bridle the Wind*, in which Felix does the journey in reverse (he has decided his Spanish grandfather is preferable to his English grandfather) is a disappointment. The adopted tone of voice slips—Felix often sounds more like Joan Aiken than himself—and the picaresque method is unfortunately replaced by a conventional plot structure that lacks probability and relies too much on coincidence. Felix and the other main character, Juan, consistently seem older than they really are, and they far too conveniently overhear the conversations of the villains. (This is a sloppy device to short-circuit narrative longueurs that also mars parts of *The Whispering Mountain* and *The Cuckoo Tree*.) The relationship between Felix and Juan is done quite well, but the disclosure at the end that Juan is really a girl (Juana) seems to lack point—the same idea, in Gene Kemp's *The Turbulent Term of Tyke Tiler*, did serve a useful purpose. The best scenes in the book are the early chapters in the monastery; the monks are credible and human, particularly the mad, sinister abbot who virtually imprisons Felix and Juan because he needs more novices. But the way the second half of the narrative is influenced by supernatural events is a serious fault, as if something from a different genre had strayed into the wrong novel—the "magic" seems like a cheap bag of tricks, another lame device to solve plot problems. There are some good descriptive passages, particularly of the Pyrenees, but the references to local life and culture, which, in *Go Saddle the Sea*, were so naturally introduced and integrated into the story, are here an intrusive digression: the author undoubtedly has a real affection for the Basque people, their music and language, the scenery—but she has much too strong a desire to tell us about it, to teach us history and geography lessons.

Joan Aiken, in "A Thread of Mystery," said she didn't think her books were great literature—they weren't "worth a lot of analysis"—but she wanted to give children the same sort of pleasure she had derived from her own childhood reading. In the fantasies she succeeds admirably in giving us *all* pleasure, children and adults alike; in most of the realistic novels the pleasure is less. Her main achievement is the creation of a world, in *The Wolves of Willoughby Chase* series, that is uniquely odd, hilarious, exuberant, and endlessly imaginative. She is the only writer I can think of whose work is at its best when it is at its most crazily improbable: this is also "a very special kind of talent."

REFERENCES

JOAN AIKEN
The Wolves of Willoughby Chase, Cape, 1962; Doubleday 1963.
Black Hearts in Battersea, Cape, 1965; Doubleday, 1964
Night Birds on Nantucket, Cape, 1966; Doubleday, 1966
The Whispering Mountain, Cape, 1968; Doubleday, 1969
Night Fall, Macmillan, London, 1969; Holt Rinehart, 1971
"A Thread of Mystery," *Children's Literature in Education,* July 1970
The Cuckoo Tree, Cape, 1971; Doubleday, 1971
Midnight is a Place, Cape, 1974; Viking, 1974
Go Saddle the Sea, Cape, 1978; Doubleday, 1977
The Shadow Guests, Cape, 1980; Delacorte, 1980
The Stolen Lake, Cape, 1981; Delacorte, 1981
Bridle the Wind, Cape, 1983; Delacorte, 1983

MIGUEL DE CERVANTES
Don Quixote, first published 1605

SUSAN COOPER
Over Sea, Under Stone, Cape, 1965; Harcourt Brace 1966

CHARLES DICKENS
Nicholas Nickleby, first published 1839
Hard Times, first published 1854
Great Expectations, first published 1861
Our Mutual Friend, first published 1865

PETER DICKINSON
The Weathermonger, Gollancz, 1968; Atlantic/Little, Brown, 1969
Heartsease, Gollancz, 1969; Atlantic/Little, Brown, 1969

HENRY FIELDING
   Joseph Andrews, first published 1742

LEON GARFIELD
   Jack Holborn, Constable, 1964; Pantheon, 1965
   The Strange Affair of Adelaide Harris, Longman, 1971; Pan-
      theon, 1971

GENE KEMP
   The Turbulent Term of Tyke Tiler, Faber, 1977; Merrimack,
      1980

URSULA LE GUIN
   A Wizard of Earthsea, Parnassus, 1968; Gollancz, 1971
   The Tombs of Atuan, Atheneum, 1971; Gollancz, 1972
   The Farthest Shore, Atheneum, 1972; Gollancz, 1973

HERMAN MELVILLE
   Moby Dick, first published in 1851

WILLIAM RAYNER
   Big Mister, Collins, London, 1974

R. L. STEVENSON
   Treasure Island, first published 1883

W. J. TURNER
   Romance, first published 1916

SUNDAY SCHOOL TEACHER

Madeleine L'Engle

When Madeleine L'Engle's third novel for children, *Meet the Austins,* was published in 1960, the reviews were written in superlatives. "An unusually good family story," said *The Bulletin of the Center for Children's Books;* "the family is wonderful . . . no suggestion of sentimentality or precocity." "A nicer family would be hard to find," *The Chicago Tribune* stated; "the book is beautifully written." *The New York Times* decided that it was a story "far better than most . . . There are intimate details of home life that everyone will recognize with pleasure." Most of Madeleine L'Engle's subsequent output has been greeted with favorable reviews, and she has been rewarded with the Newbery Medal for *A Wrinkle in Time,* and she was a runner-up for the most prestigious prize of all, the Hans Christian Andersen Award. She is, therefore, someone who should be taken seriously by the critics. *Twentieth Century Children's Writers* says she is "one of the truly important writers of juvenile fiction in recent decades," but also comments on her faults; the *Oxford Companion to Children's Literature,* however, is less kind—"Her emphasis on family togetherness and the warmth of parental love is perilously near the sugary, and she always writes about 'talented' (if not positively precocious) children in comfortably-off homes." John Rowe Townsend, in *A Sense of Story,* places her work in the category of "good bad books"; she "may confuse or embarrass or irritate," but she is "unlikely to bore the reader."

The truth is that Madeleine L'Engle has a considerable capacity to bore the reader, not least by wearisome repetition of themes, characters, and situations; and unless the reader is white, upper middle-class, tremendously gifted, and a com-

mitted Christian, he or she is unlikely to find much in her
work to identify with. *The New York Times,* in stating that
Meet the Austins contained "intimate details of home life that
everyone will recognize with pleasure," must have assumed
that all its readers were like the Austins, who are, in fact, by
any standards unusual—and, to my mind, somewhat repellent and smug. "Aren't you sorry for people who don't
laugh?" John says to his sister, who answers with "Yes. And
people who don't love music and books." The Austins say
grace at meals and sing a lot (they all have good singing
voices, like most of the characters in Madeleine L'Engle's
novels: almost every male, for instance, is a fine baritone or a
lovely tenor), and they say prayers aloud at bedtime, often
with embarrassing gush—

> "Oh, God, thank you for letting Maggy stay with us and
> making her not break so many of my toys any more
> especially Elephant's Child, and thank you, God, for my
> good dinner, for the meat and mashed potatoes and
> gravy and 'sparagus, oh, no, God, I forgot, I don't like
> 'sparagus, and thank you for the milk and rolls and but-
> ter, Amen."

The Austins are talented people who take to the arts and
sciences with an almost effortless ease; they also talk a great
deal about God—when an old family friend dies in a plane
crash, it is "the hand of God." They have, however, little
awareness of what lies outside their narrow world: ethnic
minorities, non-Christian religions, the working class, social
problems. *Meet the Austins* is an old-fashioned, Victorian
book that thrusts its young characters through a series of
moral hoops; tests and temptations that deal with lying, stealing, disobedience, carelessness, and so on. It is written in
banal, breathless first-person prose—the most frequently
used word is "and":

> We got to Boston in the late afternoon and took baths
> and went for a walk on the Common and fed the swans
> and then went and had a lovely roast beef dinner at our
> hotel and then, when we expected to be sent up to bed,
> Mother and Daddy told us they were going to take us to
> Symphony Hall to hear the orchestra, because we didn't

get many chances at home to hear live music, and no matter how wonderful our records are, they're still canned.

As Nicholas Tucker said, reviewing Judy Blume's *Forever* in the *Times Literary Supplement,* "talking straight from the adolescent's mouth can act as camouflage for slack writing."

Meet the Austins has three sequels, *The Moon by Night, The Young Unicorns* and *A Ring of Endless Light.* In *The Moon by Night* the Austins go on a camping holiday and drive across America from coast to coast. The opportunity to write about landscape is largely missed; "I won't describe it," Vicky says of Santa Fe, "because anybody can look it up in the *National Geographic"*—which suggests the author is saying she cannot rise to the challenge. The Austins' attitude to the places they see can be patronizing: New Mexico, Vicky tells us, is "gorgeous" but also depressing, because "it seemed so *poor.* At home in Thornhill nobody is really poor," and Tennessee is "really a beautiful state, and everybody we talked to at filling stations and markets and places were lovely and drawly and friendly." Like *Meet the Austins, The Moon by Night* is basically plotless. It consists of do's and don'ts about camping, God, quotations from Psalm 23, and sermons on various subjects. One of the boys Vicky meets, Andy, is beautiful, with parents who are university professors, and he quotes Chaucer. The precocity of the Austin children and their friends is a continual irritation. Vicky writes poetry; Suzy has "always been a beauty" and is going to be a doctor; John is "tall and good looking," "terrifically intelligent, but not a bit of a grind," and "good at sports, too," In fact he talks more like an encyclopedia than a human being—

> "The Visigoths and the Vandals were the four hundreds, Theodoric of the Ostrogoths was five hundreds, and, oh, yes, it was Frankish kings of Gaul in the six hundreds, but there wasn't any strong central government. And wasn't it in the six hundreds that Jerusalem was taken over by the Mohammedans?"

Conversation in Madeleine L'Engle's novels often consists of speeches of this nature, or question and answer sessions

more like a classroom assignment than family talk. Andy—
unconsciously—amuses the reader with the statement,
"When I talk I want to find out about things. Or impart useful
information."

The plotless novel built around a lengthy car journey is
much better done by Paula Fox in *Portrait of Ivan,* and the
main theme of *The Young Unicorns*—a man impersonating
his brother for nefarious reasons—is more successfully handled by Leon Garfield in *Jack Holborn.* At least *The Young
Unicorns* has a plot, albeit an improbable one: the Austins
have to prevent a mad actor (who's pretending to be the
Bishop of New York) from using laser beams on people's
minds to make them docile zombies; he wants to do this, we
are told, to avert catastrophic disaster in the city—but what
that disaster is remains vague. There are new characters in
this book, incredibly gifted children again; an ex-gangland kid
who has a beautiful singing voice and is a marvellous cor
anglais soloist (one is reminded of yobbo Pennington in K. M.
Peyton's *Pennington's Seventeenth Summer,* who turns out
to be a brilliant musician), and blind Emily, who is an infant
prodigy pianist and who sings chorale preludes in the bath.
Conversations about the Meaning of Life abound, and the
usual preachiness. Much of the action takes place in a New
York cathedral, and the author attempts, frequently, to evoke
its splendor and atmosphere. She has, however, a limited
supply of adjectives—"the great central altar," "the great
slumbering body of the Cathedral," "the great pile of stone,"
"two great candlesticks on the altar," "the great rose window," "Bishop Potter's great white marble sarcophagus,"
"the great arched vault," etcetera.

A Ring of Endless Light is a return to plotlessness. Vicky
goes for walks with Leo who's nice but not sexy, flies in
aeroplanes with Zachary who's sexy but not nice, and talks to
dolphins with Adam who's both nice *and* sexy. No prizes
given for guessing Adam wins out in the end. There are inter-
minable philosophical discussions about free will, death, the
universe, God, vegetarianism, life-support machines, astrono-
my, marine biology, and so on; and the teenage characters—
intensely moralistic, serious and with no sense of humor—

speak not like adolescents but mature middle-aged men and women:

> "In this psych course I took, it's called *archaic understanding.*"
> "What's that?"
> "It's understanding things in their deepest sense. All children are born with archaic understanding, and then school comes along, and the pragmatic Cartesian world—"
> "Cartesian?"
> "After Descartes."
> "Oh. Yeah." I felt stupid, so I added, "*I think, therefore I am.*"

This is eighteen-year-old Adam instructing Vicky. The book is full of repetitions—holding hands, singing, classical music, looking at the stars, food, grace before meals; there is a daily weather report, and almost every menu is given in detail. This extract is characteristic, and, as elsewhere, adds nothing to the story—

> I set the table and made the salad dressing and cut up celery and scallions and green peppers, washed the lettuce, and then fixed the tomatoes and put them in a small bowl to be added later. I looked in the refrigerator to see if I could figure out what Mother had planned for supper. There were peas, so I shelled them. I saw some hamburger and a basket of mushrooms, so I figured at least I could make Poor Man's Beef Stroganoff, which I set about doing.

The main theme of *A Ring of Endless Light* is coping with death—Commander Rodney dies, at the beginning of the book, of a heart attack. But Madeleine L'Engle is not content with this—she repeats the idea again and again—Binnie dies of leukemia, and Grandfather is dying of the same disease; Zachary's mother has died recently, and he wants to commit suicide; one of the dolphins gives birth to a still-born baby; Jeb, knocked down by a motor cyclist, nearly dies; Zachary feels he caused Commander Rodney's death; and Adam feels he caused Joshua's death—an event from an earlier novel,

The Arm of the Starfish. Less than half-way through therefore, the reader loses interest in the theme, so a remark like "It was a quiet day. We didn't get cosmic about anything" seems unintentionally funny; as does Zachary's comment that John is "repellently secure." And as for smugness, Vicky could scarcely be bettered when declining a glass of champagne— "I felt more grownup being free to refuse than I would have if I'd felt I had to prove something by accepting." It seems extraordinary that *A Ring of Endless Light* was a runner-up for the Newbery Medal.

Adam is the central character in *The Arm of the Starfish,* a stock cloak-and-dagger story about crooks trying to steal the results of hush-hush scientific research, and, like *The Young Unicorns,* it is improbable and unconvincing. Adam works for a famous marine biologist; his parents are university professors, and he falls for a spectacularly beautiful girl, Kali. Although he is a scientist, he speaks four languages, knows a great deal about literature and classical music, has a "wonderful" singing voice, is an expert swimmer, and, when a shark tries to eat Kali, he stabs it to death with one swift blow. He is quite ready to "make a sacrifice" for his country, and of Kali he says: "She *is* very attractive. I mean, any red-blooded American male . . . " His age? Sixteen.

If meeting the Austins is a daunting experience, we have to observe the talented Murrys in four books—*A Wrinkle in Time* and its sequels—and the saintly O'Keefes in no less than six (three of the Murry novels and *A House Like a Lotus, Dragons in the Waters,* and *The Arm of the Starfish*). While it is true that young readers often enjoy sequels and series books, such repetition of character as occurs in Madeleine L'Engle is either a sign of laziness or an inability to broaden her scope. After the Austins, however, one is grateful for the Murrys, even if Mrs Murry is beautiful as well as being a good mother, a brilliant scientist and a Nobel prizewinner, and Dad chats on the phone about security matters with the President of the United States. Also, their twin sons are brilliant athletes, their youngest child exceptionally gifted, and their daughter's boyfriend, Calvin O'Keefe, is the president of his class, a basketball star, and has "aura." But Meg, the daughter and the main character in *A Wrinkle in Time,* is, thankfully, a credible, ordinary teenage girl, though in subsequent books, as Calvin's wife, she is "beautiful" and a bit goody-goody.

A number of publishers rejected *A Wrinkle in Time*, which seems as extraordinary as *A Ring of Endless Light* being considered for the Newbery Medal. Farrar, Straus and Giroux eventually took it, and in so doing gave us Madeleine L'Engle's most well-known and most attractive book. It has an exciting plot that keeps the reader turning the pages; its Christian ethos is implied rather than preached; its villains are suitably villainous, and Meg and some of the minor characters are people we like and feel for. It is generally considered to be a work of science fiction (though fantasy, I think, would be a more apt definition) and because it won the Newbery Medal, it is, as Francis Molson points out in *Twentieth Century Children's Writers*, historically important—

> The first juvenile sf novel not only admitted into the mainstream of children's literature but also honoured in a significant way—thus heralding juvenile sf's coming of age.

Mrs Whatsit, Mrs Which and Mrs Who are delightful inventions, unpredictable and mysterious guardian figures, reminiscent of angels, or kindly versions of the witches in *Macbeth*, Eumenides; but the book's triumph is Meg—at times bad-tempered, confused, awkward, and lacking in confidence, at others considerate and loving. She desperately misses her father, who has been away from home for months: the best scenes in the novel are those that show the depths of her feelings for him, her reunion with him, and the acute distress she experiences when she realizes that he is far from perfect. "The feeling of complete reassurance and safety that his presence always gave her" changes to disappointment, which—

> was as dark and corrosive in her as the Black Thing. The ugly words tumbled from her cold lips even as she herself could not believe that it was to her father, her beloved longed-for father, that she was talking to in this way.

The sci-fi paraphernalia—far-flung planets, the evil brain IT, the Medium, inter-galactic travel—are also convincingly done. There are weaknesses, however. Calvin and Charles Wallace are not credible, and the latter's exceptional powers are mere contrivances to side-step plot difficulties. There is also towards the end too much repetition, particularly of Meg's pleas to her father to return to Camazotz and save Charles Wallace from IT. But these are small blemishes. If Madeleine L'Engle could always write as well as this, she would perhaps be "truly important."

Of the three sequels, *Many Waters* is the best. Meg's twin brothers, Sandy and Dennys, now aged fifteen, are at the center of this story: their journey through time and space takes them to Israel in Biblical times, when Noah is just about to build the ark. Both boys fall in love with the same girl, one of Noah's daughters, and because she is not to be saved from the coming flood, they hope to transport her back with them to twentieth-century America. Twin boys falling for the same girl is the main theme of another young adult novel, Penelope Farmer's *Year King,* but Madeleine L'Engle does not deal with the romantic and sexual implications as fully as Penelope Farmer does; and in the end she evades the issue somewhat— Sandy and Dennys are not allowed to alter the course of history, and they return home without Yalith. (*Bedknob and Broomstick* by Mary Norton has as one of its themes the removal of a person from an earlier century to the present day, but it is given a much more light-hearted treatment.) *Many Waters* has a neatly constructed plot, deft characteriza-tion—the quarrels between the members of Noah's family are particularly well done—and good, too, are the mythical animals, unicorns, griffins, and manticores. There are also some pithy comments on Old Testament sexism. Occasion-ally the twins' American slang jars when put against the heightened, poetic style of most of the writing, but on the whole the prose is an improvement on much of Madeleine L'Engle's earlier work—

> The moon set, its path whiter than the desert sands dwindling into shadow. The stars moved in their joyous dance across the sky. The horizon was dark with that deep darkness which comes just before the dawn.

A vulture flew down, seemingly out of nowhere, stretching its naked neck, settling its dark feathers.

—Vultures are underestimated. Without us, disease would wipe out all life. We clean up garbage, feces, dead bodies of man and beast. We are not appreciated.

No sound was heard and yet the words seemed scratched upon the air.

A Wind in the Door is a failure on several counts. Its plot is slow and lacks real conflict; it has too much dialogue and an excessive amount of scientific jargon. Charles Wallace is now totally impossible; however blessed with unusual gifts a six-year-old might be, such speeches as this are merely tiresome—

> "Well, billions of years ago they probably swam into what eventually became our eukaryotic cells and they've just stayed there. They have their own DNA and RNA, which means they're quite separate from us. They have a symbiotic relationship with us, and the amazing thing is that we're completely dependent on them for our oxygen."

The writing has two other characteristic faults. In Madeleine L'Engle's books the emotional moments between the sexes are often dangerously sentimental, close to women's magazine material—

> She burst into hysterical tears of relief.
> He vaulted over the wall to her, his strong, thin arms tight round her, holding her. "Meg. Meg, what is it?"
> . . . He continued to hold her strongly, comfortingly.

Also, at the big climaxes when the supernatural forces of good or evil are manifesting themselves, the writing becomes vague and inadequate: as does Susan Cooper's when she is describing the powers of the Light or the Dark in *The Dark Is Rising*. Both authors reach for too many fuzzy adjectives— "ineffable," "great," "tremendous," "utter," "complete," etcetera. Here is Meg observing the birth of a star—

> Ahead of her was a tremendous rhythmic swirl of wind
> and flame, but it was wind and flame quite different from
> the cherubim's; this was a dance, a dance ordered and
> graceful, and yet giving an impression of complete and
> utter freedom, of ineffable joy. As the dance progressed,
> the movement accelerated, and the pattern became
> clearer, closer, wind and flame moving together, and
> there was joy, and song, melody soaring, gathering to-
> gether as wind and fire united.

To describe absolute good and absolute evil is, of course, a
virtually impossible task. Milton more or less succeeded, and
Wordsworth too, but the rest of us should maybe not even
try. It is a pity that *A Wind in the Door* is unconvincing,
because its main theme is highly original (Meg, Calvin, and
their teacher, Mr Jenkins, are dwarfed to an almost in-
finitesimal size so that they can enter Charles Wallace's
bloodstream and help his immune system fight a killer disease), and the author's attempt, here and in other books, to
use scientific research and discoveries at the center of a story
is to be applauded—all too often, despite living in such an
immensely technological age as this is, contemporary writers
of children's fiction ignore the sciences.

The plot of *A Swiftly Tilting Planet* is concerned with the
threats of a South American dictator, Mad Dog Branzillo, to
destroy the world in a nuclear holocaust; Charles Wallace
travels back through time (while the rest of his family is
eating Thanksgiving dinner) to meet Branzillo's ancestors
and cause him to be born not as the "mad dog" but as a man
of peace, El Zarco, the Blue-eyed. It is really a set of inter-
linked short stories, and because of this it lacks narrative
momentum. The writing at times sounds tired, the word
"joy" in particular being used indiscriminately and excessively. Charles Wallace, in his journeys, has a number of en-
counters with the cosmic forces of good and evil. The evil
ones, the Echtroi, always lose, and they are about as ineffec-
tual and tedious as the Dark in Susan Cooper—they manufac-
ture some unpleasant bits of weather, some hideous noises,
and a few nasty smells, but that is all; there is no real drama. It
is also very strange that Charles Wallace, despite his magnificent intellectual abilities, acute sensitivities, and extraordi-

nary capacity for seeing into other people's minds, cannot deduce what any reader can deduce early on in the story— the obvious connection between Mrs O'Keefe and Mad Dog Branzillo through the family names, Madoc, Madog, Maddox, Mad Dog.

The other books are not sequences like the Austin and Murry novels, though members of the O'Keefe family figure in two of them, and Sandy Murry appears in *A House Like a Lotus.* (He's now a successful lawyer, and brother Dennys is a brilliant neurosurgeon!) Madeleine L'Engle's first attempt at writing for children was *And Both Were Young,* which was published in 1949. It is an unexceptional boarding-school story, dealing with the hackneyed theme of the new girl's first term, her gradual acceptance into the "gang," and her development from being a misfit into the most popular child in the class. The setting is unusual (Switzerland) but there are some stock characters and situations—jolly Mme. Perceval whom all the girls *adore,* horrid Miss Tulip who dishes out order marks and deportment marks left, right and center, and Philippa, the heroine, who's so inept at skiing that Fraulein Hauser refuses to teach her: but Mme. Perceval gives her private lessons, and of course Philippa is marvellous at it, and would have won the skiing competition had she not stopped to rescue a girl who's injured her ankle. It is a teendream book of the period, but not a badly written example of the genre; Enid Blyton's *First Term at Mallory Towers* and many others are a lot worse. Some characteristic and annoying L'Engle mannerisms are already present—in the cosy Laurens family, Dad's a professor, Mum's a singer, and teenage Paul, as well as being handsome, speaks four languages. Paul is adopted; his real parents disappeared during the war, and he hasn't come to terms with their loss. The theme is interesting, but unfortunately it is only touched on—mentioned, then dropped.

And Both Were Young was followed by *Camilla Dickinson* (1951), which was revised and republished fourteen years later as *Camilla.* The basic idea, reminiscent of Henry James's *What Maisie Knew,* holds our attention—Camilla's parents' marriage is on the rocks; Mum is having an affair with another man and at one point attempts suicide; Mum and Dad

battle for only-child Camilla's loyalty. It is, however, unnecessarily parallelled by the relationship between Camilla's
best friend's parents—Luisa's reports on what goes on between Mona and Bill add little to what we observe in the
Dickinson menage. It's a pity that these four adults are so
unsympathetic and insensitive; Camilla's mother in particular
is too hysterical to be credible. The writing is of poorer
quality than in *And Both Were Young*—

> "And we can talk. Usually a girl you can talk with isn't—
> doesn't have any—but you do. You sit there and you
> talk about God and you look just beautiful."
> When Frank said that it was as though something
> warm and lovely had exploded right in the middle of my
> stomach and, like the sun, sent rays of happiness all
> through my body.

Frank, Luisa's brother and Camilla's first boyfriend, is pompous, solemn, humorless, and unbelievably adult for his years;
an unfortunate precursor of John Austin. He talks in speeches,
many of them about God or the stars, and it's very difficult to
see why Camilla should be attracted to him. God looms pretty big in this novel, as does the evil of drinking alcohol (the
latter a theme the author uses much too often in subsequent
books). Frank's friend Dave is as dreadful as Frank—

> "No man can participate in mass murder and not lose his
> understanding of the value of human life. But it has a
> value, Camilla. Life is the greatest gift that could ever be
> conceived, but before any of us ever were born those
> who had gone before us had already deprived it of half
> its value. A daffodil pushing up through the dark earth to
> the spring, knowing somehow deep in its roots that
> spring and light and sunshine will come, has more cour-
> age and more knowledge of the value of life than any
> human being I've met. Model yourself after the daffodil,
> Camilla."

There is a great deal more of this kind of stuff. *Camilla* could
have been a worthwhile story about first love and a teenager's perceptions of a crumbling marriage, but it ends up by
being a sermon instead of a novel, and it ceases, long before it
ends, either to interest or to entertain.

Prelude, another story with a neurotic mother and a failed upper-crust marriage (Dad's a composer and Mum was a concert pianist), is better than *Camilla;* it has a tighter plot and, although there is some moralizing about alcohol, it is relatively free from preachiness. In the second half of the book Madeleine L'Engle writes again about boarding-school life in Switzerland, but in a more realistic way than she did in *And Both Were Young;* these low-key episodes are some of the most effective in the novel. One interesting theme—skated upon rather than being fully worked out—is lesbianism; Katherine and her friend Sarah are subjected to a third-degree interrogation by the headmistress after they have been caught by one of the teachers in an affectionate, and in fact totally innocent, embrace. This interrogation is, from the point of view of plot development, too long, but at the same time it seems to be cut off before anything of note emerges. One has the feeling that the author, or her editor, removed something from the text here; maybe such matters were thought to be unsuitable in a young adult novel—though a decade later it probably would not have been questioned.

A House Like a Lotus is written in the manner of *A Ring of Endless Light*—essentially plotless with much sermonizing (cigarettes, marijuana, alcohol, marriage, death and nuclear war are some of the topics); a great deal of dialogue that simply imparts information; and the usual absurdly precocious kids—Polly, aged seventeen, speaks six languages, Charles, aged fifteen, "knows more about marine biology than a lot of college graduates," and Xan, aged fourteen, is "a basketball star at school, is handsome, and adored by girls." A considerable amount of time is spent looking at the stars (again); the menu of the day is given full coverage (again); and dreary Zachary spends his money taking the heroine out on various trips (again) and gets very little in return (again). The setting in this book is Greece and Cyprus, but—again— there is not much evocation of place. What is new is the author's attempt to tackle the issue of lesbianism in a much more in-depth way than she did in *Prelude.* Her handling of the subject would probably earn full marks from some liberal heterosexuals—she's sympathetic; and to her assumed audience of straight teenagers she stresses the importance of

tolerance and compassion, of leaving what goes on in the
bedroom to remain in the bedroom: it's not a matter for
discussion at the dinner table or for cruel jokes at school.
This is an unusual stance for a committed Christian, but likely
to annoy lesbians and gay men, for she falls into the cliché
perpetuated by so many writers: you can have a homosexual
character if you show that person as being morally weak
and/or you let him/her die. Max, the lesbian in question, is a
brilliant artist and stinking rich (she owns Waterford chan-
deliers and a Picasso); she's also wonderfully intelligent and
kind: but she drinks and she's dying of an incurable disease. In
one of her drunken states she makes a pass at Polly. (Or does
she? This important moment is left curiously vague.) The
stereotypical lesbian in fiction is unattractive, with cropped
hair; Ursula, Max's lover, we are told, "was stocky and had
grey-brown hair, short and crisply curly." Homosexual readers are left, as happens so often, with the feeling that there is
nothing of relevance to them.

Finally, *Dragons in the Waters* is another cloak-and-dagger
story, this time a successful one, despite conversations about
God and the stars, and children who talk like adults—

> "Simon, this is the end of the twentieth century. Things
> are falling apart. The centre doesn't hold. We don't have
> time for courtliness and the finer niceties of courtesy—
> and I've learned that the hard way!"

Thus speaks Polly O'Keefe (having, presumably, absorbed
Yeats's *The Second Coming*) at fourteen! Her younger brother's ability to have dreams that predict the future is a weak
device that avoids plot complexities (just as Charles Wallace's "powers" in *A Wrinkle in Time* solve problems too
easily). But *Dragons in the Waters* is a rattling good yarn
with convincing villains, dangers that sound credible, and a
nice cast of eccentric minor characters. Much of the action
takes place on board a ship, and there are some good stage
props here—a valuable portrait that mysteriously disappears,
a hearse with a bullet-hole in its windscreen and a lot of
guilty people with pasts to hide. The book ends up in an
imaginary piece of South American landscape (shades of Conrad, and one remembers, too, Joan Aiken's *The Stolen Lake*)

which seems authentic and colorful. There is another Joan Aiken parallel, this time with *The Shadow Guests*—a curse inherited through generations that kills off son after son. The detective bits have echoes of Dorothy L. Sayers and Agatha Christie, but *Dragons in the Waters* is none the worse for that. Not the least of its pleasures is the central character, Simon, a lonely, withdrawn boy who is not particularly gifted in any way—a child who seems real.

Madeleine L'Engle's work is very uneven. She can write an excellent plot, but she mostly doesn't; her daring is admirable, but on the whole it leads to acute embarrassment. Admirable, too, is an author who will put science and scientists at the center of a novel for children—but one questions whether she has done her homework adequately; the behavior of the dolphins in *A Ring of Endless Light,* for instance, seems invented and romantic rather than zoologically accurate. She wants to impart her experience and values to the young reader, but her preaching does not persuade; and she has in mind too narrow an audience—white, conservative, upper middle-class, intellectual. Lastly, and most off-putting, is her Christian commitment. Propaganda never makes good fiction no matter what is being advocated; religion as propaganda in a novel is as boring as Communism sermonized, or gay rights, the class struggle, feminism, anything. The committed Christian need not write like this. Katherine Paterson is a good example of someone who doesn't—the Christianity in *Jacob Have I Loved* is far more persuasive than it is in any book of Madeleine L'Engle's. Madeleine L'Engle all too often sounds like a Sunday school teacher, not a novelist.

REFERENCES

MADELEINE L'ENGLE
>   *And Both Were Young,* Lothrop, 1949
>   *Camilla Dickinson,* Simon & Schuster, 1951; Secker & Warburg, 1952; as *Camilla,* Crowell, 1965
>   *Meet the Austins,* Vanguard, 1960; Collins, London, 1966
>   *A Wrinkle in Time,* Farrar Straus, 1962; Constable, 1964
>   *The Moon by Night,* Farrar Straus, 1963
>   *The Arm of the Starfish,* Farrar Straus, 1965

The Young Unicorns, Farrar Straus, 1968; Gollancz, 1970
Prelude, Vanguard, 1969; Gollancz, 1972
A Wind in the Door, Farrar Straus, 1973; Methuen, 1975
Dragons in the Waters, Farrar Straus, 1976
A Swiftly Tilting Planet, Farrar Straus, 1978; Souvenir Press, 1980
A Ring of Endless Light, Farrar Straus, 1980
A House Like a Lotus, Farrar Straus, 1984
Many Waters, Farrar Straus, 1986

JOAN AIKEN
The Shadow Guests, Cape, 1980; Delacorte, 1980
The Stolen Lake, Cape, 1981; Delacorte, 1981

JUDY BLUME
Forever, Bradbury, 1975; Gollancz, 1976

ENID BLYTON
First Term at Mallory Towers, Methuen, 1946

HUMPHREY CARPENTER and MARI PRICHARD
The Oxford Companion to Children's Literature, Oxford University Press, London, 1984; O.U.P. New York, 1984

SUSAN COOPER
The Dark Is Rising, Chatto, 1973; Atheneum, 1973

PENELOPE FARMER
Year King, Chatto, 1977; Atheneum, 1977

PAULA FOX
Portrait of Ivan, Bradbury, 1969; Macmillan, London, 1970

LEON GARFIELD
Jack Holborn, Constable, 1964; Pantheon, 1965

HENRY JAMES
What Maisie Knew, first published 1897

D. L. KIRKPATRICK, editor
Twentieth Century Children's Writers, St. Martin's Press, 1978

MARY NORTON
Bedknob and Broomstick, Dent, 1957; Harcourt, 1957; originally as *The Magic Bedknob,* Dent, 1945; Hyperion Press, 1943; and *Bonfires and Broomsticks,* Dent, 1947

KATHERINE PATERSON
Jacob Have I Loved, Crowell, 1980; Gollancz, 1981

K. M. PEYTON
Pennington's Seventeenth Summer, Oxford University Press, 1970; as *Pennington's Last Term,* Crowell, 1971

JOHN ROWE TOWNSEND
A Sense of Story, Longman, 1971; Lippincott, 1971; revised edition as *A Sounding of Storytellers,* Kestrel, 1979; Lippincott, 1979

NICHOLAS TUCKER
review in the *Times Literary Supplement* of *Forever* (Judy Blume), 1976

W. B. YEATS
The Second Coming, first published 1921

KING OF WILD THINGS

Maurice Sendak

When *Where the Wild Things Are* was published in 1963, Maurice Sendak had already built for himself a considerable reputation as an illustrator of children's books, and he had also written and illustrated four books of his own. Though many of the themes, verbal and pictorial, that are found in *Where the Wild Things Are* (and the two great picture books that followed it, *In the Night Kitchen* and *Outside Over There*) are present in the earlier stories, there is little in them to prepare the reader for the immense leap forward it shows in imaginative skill and execution.

Kenny, the hero of Sendak's first book, *Kenny's Window,* is a characteristic Sendak child: lonely, frustrated and bored; a small boy who deals with his feelings by inventing games, and who brings some kind of order and sense into his life through dreams and imaginative play. It's a well-written tale that immediately shows Sendak has gifts as a writer; in fact the story is more interesting than the pictures, which, though technically adequate, are pallid and somewhat self-effacing, no more than illustrations of the words. The writing skill is shown throughout; "It smells like winter is melting," Kenny says, and—

> It was snowing and Kenny watched the large flakes melt against his window. They ran down the glass in long sad drips.
> "My window is crying," thought Kenny. He turned his head sideways and looked up at the sky. "I wonder why snow looks dirty up there and clean down here."
> "Why does it?" he asked aloud, but no one answered.

The balance, however, is wrong: there is too much text and not enough art-work, and there are flaws in the narrative structure. The ending is inconclusive, and some basic information is lacking, such as why are Kenny's parents hardly ever mentioned; does he have any brothers or sisters? The concepts involved in the rooster's questions are a little difficult for the young reader—what is an only goat, for example, and do you always want what you think you want? However, the book moves effortlessly—and satisfyingly—from reality to fantasy and vice versa; and some of the pictorial devices that Sendak uses so frequently in his later work are here—the cross-hatching, the lovely old-fashioned bed, the importance given to windows, to the moon.

The pictures in *Very Far Away,* Sendak's second book, are less tentative than those in *Kenny's Window,* but the story, although it tackles some major themes—sibling rivalry and a young child's anger with his mother—is diffuse and disappointing. Sendak deals much more profoundly with the first of these issues in *Outside Over There* and the second in *Where the Wild Things Are.* Martin, unlike Max in *Where the Wild Things Are,* is not allowed to confront his feelings, which results in the narrative lacking drama and fizzling out. He is the first of a number of central characters in Sendak's books whose Christian name begins with the same letter as the author's own: Sendak is perhaps pointing out that the boy is himself, an idea that is reinforced by the pictures of nearly all the heroes from *The Nutshell Library* onwards—they are self-portraits.

The Sign on Rosie's Door is an advance on its predecessors; a well-written, if somewhat episodic, story in which the pictures begin to do something other than just illustrate the words. The aggressive, unfriendly relationship between Pudgy and Sal is not mentioned in the text, but its course is well portrayed in the pictures, as is the crowded, rather stifling urban setting. The drawings of children in motion— falling, dancing, bending over, running, fighting—are done with an assured skill and fluency that hints at the masterpieces to follow, and for the first time considerable emphasis is put on the use of costume in children's games: dressing up in unusual clothes makes it easier to leave the boredom, loneliness and frustration of reality, and either be someone else (as Rosie does), or confront feelings that are normally repressed (Max in *Where the Wild Things Are*), or find new skills (Ida in *Outside Over There*). Mickey's nudity in *In the Night Kitchen* has a similar function—being naked in front of others is a sort of costume too. The story-line of *The Sign on Rosie's Door* is low-key and depressed in mood, an interesting contrast with the pictures, which are warm, lively and affectionate. It's a sad tale—Rosie is a creative artist and needs an audience, but she can only hold the other children's attention fleetingly. The one occasion she sings *On the Sunny Side of the Street,* uninterrupted and all the way through, is when she's alone. Even at the end, after the games are finished and she's in her bedroom, she is still wanting to be someone else, in this case the cat: she goes to sleep on the rug, and the cat sleeps in the bed. The story is almost all dialogue; it is like a play—or the kind of show Rosie wants to perform in. The brevity and realism of this dialogue, and its ability to suggest more than it says, is excellent—

> "Is that you, Rosie?" Dolly asked.
> There was no answer.
> "Please tell us who you are," said Kathy.
> "I'm Alinda the lost girl."
> "Who lost you?" asked Pudgy.
> "I lost myself," answered Alinda.
> "Aren't you really Rosie though?" asked Pudgy.
> "I used to be Rosie," Alinda said, "but not any more."
> They all sat down on the cellar door.
> "Who is going to find you?" asked Sal.
> "Magic Man," said Alinda.
> "Who's he?"
> "My best friend," answered Alinda.
> "And what happens when he finds you?" Kathy asked.
> "He will tell me what to do," explained Alinda.

The Nutshell Library is in four volumes: an alphabet book, *Alligators All Round;* a counting book, *One Was Johnny;* a book of months, *Chicken Soup with Rice;* and a cautionary tale, *Pierre.* The last three are written in verse, which Sendak handles with the same ease he had shown in the dialogue of *The Sign on Rosie's Door.* This quartet was originally published as miniatures—each book measured two and a half inches by four inches—boxed in a simulated wooden crate designed by Sendak himself. The whole thing shows his remarkable ingenuity and successful realization of original ideas. *Alligators All Round,* perhaps because of its subject matter—the letters of the alphabet—is a smaller achievement than the other three, but the pictures are entertaining and thoroughly individual. *Chicken Soup with Rice,* which aims to demonstrate the usefulness of soup in every month of the year, has a delightful sense of humor in both its pictures and its words. Particularly good are the drawings of a whale spouting soup and a Christmas tree decorated with soup bowls, and the crazy and felicitous rhymes for June—

> In June
> I saw a charming group
> of roses all begin
> to droop.
> I pepped them up
> with chicken soup!

—and July—

> In July
> I'll take a peep
> into the cool
> and fishy deep
> where chicken soup
> is selling cheap.

The latter is accompanied by a picture of a very snobby-looking turtle on the sea-bed, wearing a chef's hat and stirring a tureen.

Pierre is the story of a boy who doesn't care but is made to care when a lion eats him. (The lion ill in bed after his meal is one of the best pictures in the book.) The idea obviously owes something to the *Cautionary Tales* of Hilaire Belloc— the penalty for Jim's disobedience was to be eaten by a lion— but Sendak's story, unlike Belloc's, has a happy ending; the lion disgorges the boy, frightened but unharmed, which is reminiscent of Red Riding Hood's grandmother being rescued from the wolf's stomach. Being eaten alive is a recurring theme in Sendak's work. In *Kenny's Window* Bucky, the teddy bear, is threatened with this fate; and in *Where the Wild*

Things Are, Higglety Pigglety Pop! and *In the Night Kitchen*
the idea is richly ambiguous: a destructive act, and an act of
love. ("We'll eat you up—we love you so," the wild things
say to Max.) The anti-social, self-centered hero is another
recurring theme, as is the threatening lion; and, in the pictures, Pierre's bed is almost the same as Kenny's, and Pierre is
Max/Mickey/Hector/Maurice Sendak—and Johnny in *One
Was Johnny,* the most interesting and personal book of the
quartet. Sendak, in Selma G. Lanes's biography, *The Art of
Maurice Sendak,* is portrayed as a solitary, reclusive man,
living alone with his dogs; and *One Was Johnny* is the story of
a boy who lives by himself and likes it like that—it shows the
increasing annoyance he experiences when he is plagued by
a series of uninvited guests, a rat, a cat, a dog, a turtle, a
monkey, a blackbird, a tiger, and a robber. In verse that recalls both *Sing a Song of Sixpence* and *This is the Farmer
Sowing his Corn,* he threatens to eat them if they don't go
away; wisely, they depart, one by one. The cheeky, selfish
blackbird is repeated in later books, and so is the dog, Sendak's own, a sealyham called Jennie, who first appeared as
Baby in *Kenny's Window.*

It is not easy to avoid superlatives in a discussion of *Where
the Wild Things Are.* It is the most popular and the most
controversial picture book ever published, and its sales have
been huge. It is also, quite simply, the best picture book ever
published. Sendak would not again write so good a text: it is
spare, poetic prose of great beauty, and every word of it
sounds exactly right. (*In the Night Kitchen* and *Outside Over
There* have occasional uncertainties in assonance or rhythm,
and a few moments that sound ordinary or flat when something heightened is needed.) Its pictures are a perpetual delight and astonishment. In the scene that shows Max chasing
the dog, Sendak draws his finest picture of Jennie, and Max
leaping after her is a masterly portrait of a body in motion—
energy, savagery and speed personified. The wild things, too,
are something like perfection: the ferocity of their claws and
teeth always rendered impotent by the bizarre shortness of
their legs and arms, by the goofy stupidity displayed on their
faces, and the heavy, galumphing nature of their movements.
The juxtaposition of words and pictures is utterly original

and could not be bettered: as Max retreats into fantasy, the pictures grow in size like an orchestral crescendo and push the text nearer and nearer to the edge or the bottom of the pages, and at the climax—the wild rumpus—words disappear altogether. They are not needed; the pictures say it all: a noisy, frenzied disco, then a pause for breath as everyone quietly swings from the trees, and finally a companionable, family-like atmosphere as the wild things dance a grotesque hokey-cokey. After this, with Max returning to reality, the wildness diminuendoes; the words now force the pictures to shrink, and on the very last page with its reassuring statement about Max's supper ("and it was still hot") there is, for the only time in the book, no picture at all. The whole device produces a very satisfying, rounded shape and structure.

The subject matter of *Where the Wild Things Are* is aggression, the savage lurking beneath the civilized veneer in people. It is the way in which Max unleashes his aggression and the anger he displays when his mother sends him to bed without any supper, that has disturbed critics just as much as—if not more than—the likelihood of the pictures frightening children. Max's wolf suit (which has the same sharp claws as most of the wild things) has an identical function to Rosie's hat, high-heeled shoes and grown-up dress: it gives him the licence to behave in a way that is usually not possible, to experience impulses and emotions that are otherwise repressed. As Rosie becomes Alinda, star of the stage, so Max becomes a "wild thing," strangling his toy dog with string suspended from a washing-line that looks like barbed wire, and hammering nails in the wall till the plaster cracks. No wonder Max, when he threatens to eat his mother, is sent to bed without eating anything. And it is no wonder, too, that Max is angry: his aggressive feelings have been punished; they have not been allowed a proper outlet. His mother depriving him of food is saying, "I don't love you at the moment." The wild things are Max's aggression and anger brought to life: he invents them, then tames them, and finally does not need them. It's his mother's love he wants. (And the supper that symbolizes that.) Quiet now, the aggression properly worked out, he returns to Mother, love, and security—and his supper. The ending is triumphant: it exorcises all the preceding alarms and fears. When Max pushes the hood of his wolf suit to the back of his head, we see for the first time that he is a vulnerable small boy, not a primitive savage: this is a moment of immense relief and pleasure.

There are many familiar Sendak ideas in both the words and the pictures. The cross-hatching, the dream-like night-time scenario, the brilliant moon, the old-fashioned bed, are examples; there is even a lion, or a parody of one, in the wild thing bowing to Max when he is made king of all wild things. There are also new themes that recur in later books—the sailing boat reappears in *Outside Over There*; the happy, smiling boy in a boat in *As I Went Over the Water*. An object that turns into something else is another new idea—Max's room becomes the trees of a forest; his tent becomes a cave which is then his bed. In *In the Night Kitchen* the dough turns into an aeroplane; the trees Ida can see from her window in *Outside Over There* are replaced by a storm-tossed ship on an ocean, and the hooded, faceless friars (the goblins) are in fact babies. Eating in *Where the Wild Things Are* is almost obsessional, as it is in *Higglety Pigglety Pop!* Max wants to eat his mother; the wild things want to eat him; Max sends the wild things to bed without any supper; Max wants to eat his own supper, is deprived of it, then given it. Love and rejection of love are implied in this, as well as the more obvious ideas of destruction and fear of destruction. Eating the sacred host at religious services is an act of love (Roman Catholics believe they are devouring the real body of Christ); swallowing is a way we can make love, sexually. Sendak said the wild things were in part based on his Jewish aunts and uncles who annoyed and embarrassed him as a child with comments like "You're so cute I could eat you up." We tend to think of them, initially, as savage *animals*, but they are drawn with many human features. Some have human heads and hair-styles, one has human feet, and the skin of another is a striped tee-shirt. The third scene of the wild rumpus, the hokey-cokey, is a gathering of elderly relatives enjoying themselves at a party.

One further point of interest is that Max, when he begins to imagine his bedroom is a forest, is on the left-hand side of the page looking to the right, and he remains in this position in almost all the pictures until he returns to reality. Conversely, the wild things invariably enter from the right and mostly look to the left. The one picture in which this situation is completely reversed shows Max as lonely (he's sitting in his tent, like a sulky Achilles, on the extreme right-hand side). At this point he gives up being king of the wild things, which, although he has physically been where the wild things are for some time, suggests he has only just arrived there emotionally. To be the wildest thing of all is to be alone, deprived of love. This small detail helps to demonstrate the extraordinary care Sendak took with this book. The three hundred and thirty-eight words of the text have the same feeling as the pictures of being worked out meticulously, attention paid to every possible nuance.

Hector Protector and *As I Went Over the Water,* slight pieces compared with *Where the Wild Things Are,* nevertheless show Sendak's art developing in new directions. They are picture stories that illustrate a nursery rhyme which is in both cases no more than four lines long; and they were published together as one book. In no other work of Sendak's is there such emphasis on the pictures as opposed to the text; the pictures vastly extend what the words say, so much so that they do all kinds of things not even hinted at verbally. It is as if the rhymes were merely the bare bones, the art-work the living detail: the first two lines of *Hector Protector,* for instance—

> Hector Protector was dressed all in green,
> Hector Protector was sent to the Queen.

—are illustrated by no less than eleven pictures that show Hector fighting with his mother because he hates the idea of being dressed in green; Hector angry that he has to take a present to the Queen (a cake his mother has baked); Hector shouting "I hate the Queen!"; a fierce lion and a nasty snake that he tames and takes with him to the palace; and his dramatic arrival, interrupting Queen Victoria while she is reading a Mother Goose book of nursery rhymes. There is also another of Sendak's cheeky blackbirds who eventually gets to eat the cake, and who looks wonderfully sick afterwards.

These two works make a delightful book, but Sendak is in

danger of repeating himself; they are both too much influenced by *Where the Wild Things Are.* The pictures have the same dark, dream-like coloring and cross-hatching; Jennie makes yet another appearance; and Hector not only looks like Max, but shows no fear when he is in costume, tames wild animals as Max tames the wild things, and his mother sends him to bed without any supper because she's angry with him. *As I Went Over the Water* has a monster somewhat like a wild thing, albeit less frightening in appearance; a boy (costumed) in a ship; two blackbirds; and the boy becomes friends with the monster. It is all a little déjà vu.

In *Higglety Pigglety Pop!* Sendak makes up for almost banishing words by writing his longest story, and producing a book that is the opposite of *Hector Protector*—the one work of his in which pictures are totally subordinate to the text, even more so than in *Kenny's Window.* It is Jennie's final appearance (she died a month after the book was published), but this time she is the central character rather than a bit-part player. *Higglety Pigglety Pop!* tells the story of a dog who leaves home because she is dissatisfied with having every material comfort; she wants experience, so she gets a job as a nursemaid to a baby who won't eat. Her task is to make the baby eat; if she fails she will be eaten herself—by a lion who lives in the cellar. She does fail, but she escapes from the lion; she then talks about life with an unhappy ash tree, and eventually becomes the leading lady in the World Mother Goose Theatre, performing a dramatized version of the nursery rhyme, *Higglety Pigglety Pop!* Most of the people she has met en route, including the lion (now docile), star in the play, which it seems will have a run that will last for ever. She is content; she *really* has "everything." *Higglety Pigglety Pop!* is too enigmatic and private to be particularly satisfying, though certain characteristic Sendak themes appear; for instance, a child (here a baby) being made to acknowledge and overcome its anger and destructive impulses. Jennie was dying while Sendak was writing the book, and earlier in the same year he himself nearly died from a heart attack; death and immortality are ideas hidden away beneath the text—the World Mother Goose Theatre is perhaps a symbol of children's literature itself, and Sendak may well be meditating on the place he and his dog will share in it after they both are dead. Some of the pictures—they are all, unusually for Sendak, black and white drawings—are beautiful, romantic night scenes, but one misses the energy, the humor, and the dramatic confrontations of *Hector Protector, Where the Wild Things Are,* and *The Nutshell Library.*

This low-key, rather static tale was followed by Sendak's most vigorous and joyful work, *In the Night Kitchen.* The pictures are a startling contrast with anything he had done before: here he ceases to ally himself with European influences on painting and illustrating, and explores the comic-strip traditions of his American childhood. The colors are garish primary colors, the objects stark and flat; bold black outlining replaces cross-hatching, and the words, except on the final page, are all drawn inside the pictures. The story is less easy to interpret than *Where the Wild Things Are;* it's allusive and elusive, with many ambiguities. Do the bakers, for instance, know that Mickey is in the dough when they are kneading it, or are they so unintelligent that they really think he *is* the milk? And why isn't there any milk in the bakery? Three nursery rhymes—*I see the moon, Blow, wind, blow* and *Pat-a-cake, pat-a-cake, baker's man*—are influences on the story, as well as the fairy tale of Hansel and Gretel; there are also some familiar ideas in the pictures: Mickey looks like Sendak; moons abound and there is another old-fashioned bed (Max's, but dwarfed—Mickey is younger than Max). The toy aeroplane above the bed becomes a larger aeroplane, made of dough, that flies; and at one point Mickey is costumed in a sleeping-suit of dough.

Mickey, however, spends more time out of his clothes than in them, which caused as much of a furore when the book was published as had the supposedly terrifying monsters in *Where the Wild Things Are.* Sendak on a previous occasion drew a naked child, a girl, in the frontispiece he did for George Macdonald's *The Light Princess,* and it was not received adversely. Maybe this is a comment on a sexist world that relishes pictures of the female nude, but complains when it sees an unclothed male; but it is more likely that the *nature* of Mickey's nudity offended people rather than the mere fact of it. Mickey revels in being naked, flaunts it in front of others.

The picture in which he falls into the bowl of dough and meets the bakers for the first time is joyful, without shame. Other pictures are equally provocative: when Mickey is fashioning the dough into an aeroplane, one of the wings looks like a giant penis, and he is playing with it; the milk bottle throughout is phallic; and the picture of Mickey in the top of the bottle pouring milk into the dough beneath is—well—ejaculatory. (It may also suggest urinating.) Most striking of all is Mickey standing proudly on the bottle, the measuring-cup on his head like an upside down chamber-pot, shouting "Cock-a-doodle Doo!"—a gleeful display of uninhibited sexuality. So, one begins to think about the words—"I'm in the milk and the milk's in me," and "So the bakers they mixed it and beat it" takes on a sexual implication; and "baker" which has a connection in sound with "masturbator." I think Sendak is doing something in *In the Night Kitchen* that is profoundly healthy and wise: saying to the anxious child that nakedness and sexuality are normal, pleasurable, and good. (And possibly that urinating—bed-wetting?—is nothing to be ashamed of.) One can only feel pity for those troubled librarians and teachers who, in their copies of the book, painted diapers over Mickey's genitals.

Sendak has said that one of the story's ideas came from a childhood memory of a bakery, the slogan of which was "Sunshine Bakers—We Bake While You Sleep!" Why he chose, however, to draw the bakers as three identical Oliver Hardy look-alikes is unclear; perhaps he wanted to link the tribute the book is to the pop art of the thirties to the popular cinema of that period. It is also a tribute to his own urban childhood: it's dedicated to his parents, and the sky-line of New York City is present in most of the pictures, a marvellous jumble of densely crowded buildings, all of which are in fact the gadgets, bottles, tins, jars and cartons of the kitchen itself. Even a train, on closer inspection, turns out to be loaves of bread. The sky is done extremely well: a midnight blue that isn't quite natural, the darkness of the night made just a little pale (as it always is in a city) by the electric light shining up into it. The pictures of Mickey flying and falling have a superb freedom and fluidity; the child never plunges—he floats, and, as he sinks gently into the milk bottle, the look on his face is ecstatic. It is the way we fly in our dreams. Another touch linking Mickey with Sendak is when Mickey pops out of the cake (was the author remembering Spats's birthday cake in the film *Some Like It Hot?*) wearing a little hat of dough which looks like a Jewish skull-cap. Finally, the pictures of Mickey, now clothed and still very happy as he slides back into bed, show that bed as gloriously warm and comfortable. It was all a dream: and it serves to demonstrate how important our dream lives are in our attempts to explore and understand our feelings.

In 1976 Sendak produced *Seven Little Monsters* and *Some Swell Pup,* both of which were disliked by the critics. They are in fact very lightweight, though *Some Swell Pup,* a dog-training manual for children, has some splendid pictures. *Seven Little Monsters* is so thin—a brief text, and a few drawings of monsters who are no more than anaemic cousins of the wild things—that the result is merely for the coffee-table; one wonders why he bothered to do it at all. 1981, however, saw the publication of his third great picture book, *Outside Over There*. In *The Art of Maurice Sendak* he is quoted as saying—

> They are all variations on the same theme: how children master various feelings— anger, boredom, fear, frustration, jealousy— and manage to come to grips with the realities of their lives.

Boredom, fear and jealousy are uppermost in *Outside Over There*: Ida is supposed to look after her baby sister, but she is much more interested in practising on her wonder horn; she neglects the baby, who is stolen by goblins. She eventually rescues the child by playing frenzied music which makes the goblins (now naked babies) dance so much that they melt and become a stream. Sendak says he was influenced considerably by the plot and the music of *The Magic Flute*; the pictures with their enchanting, idealized landscapes suggest something of the atmosphere of that opera, and one of them shows Mozart in a summerhouse, composing at the piano. The kidnapped baby is parallelled in the opera by the Queen of the Night's lost daughter; the horn has similar functions to Tamino's flute and Papageno's bells; the three ladies with their shining swords become in Sendak's pictures faceless monks (goblins) with huge spears; and Ida's faith, patience and courage are tested as Sarastro tests Tamino. Sendak, however, does not reproduce the opera's curious plot convolutions—the Queen of the Night, the sympathetic, sorrowing mother improbably transformed into a villain; and the evil Sarastro being shown in reality as good and wise.

The text, though it begins well enough—"When Papa was away at sea, and Mama in the arbour, Ida played her wonder horn to rock the baby still—but never watched"—is not as perfect as *Where the Wild Things Are.* "Now Ida in a hurry snatched her Mama's yellow rain cloak, tucked her horn safe in a pocket, and made a serious mistake" attempts too much in one sentence, and ends by sounding banal; "The ice thing dripped and stared, and Ida mad knew goblins had been there" forces words against their will into an iambic rhythm and an odd half-rhyme. The pictures, however, are magnificent. Gone are the vivid colors, the night scenes, the cross-hatching of earlier books; these paintings are soft and luminous, with gentle pinks and blues, and benign yellows and greens predominating. They have a sort of midsummer magic about them—and, indeed, Shakespeare's *A Midsummer Night's Dream* hinges on a child stolen by the Queen of the Fairies. Several of them are deliberately reminiscent of famous European art: the rain cloak recalls Titian and Tintoretto; Ida and the baby are a madonna and child in the manner of Rafael or Leonardo. Ida, flying, owes something to Michelangelo's Sistine Chapel ceiling; the baby in the egg-shell is a reminder of Botticelli's *Birth of Venus;* the goblins as babies are like the fat cherubims of many religious works of art; and the opening scene hints at Turner or Claude Lorraine, one of their sea-ports at sunset minus the crowds. The landscape throughout suggests a late eighteenth-century view of nature—ordered, park-like, with grottoes, lakes, rustic bridges, ruins. Presenting the goblins at first as hooded, faceless monks or friars is, both in idea and execution, superb; they look very sinister, like evil religious fanatics from the Inquisition—but perhaps the most sinister pictures are of the substitute baby, "the ice thing," particularly when it is melting. Even though it represents Ida's feelings about her sister—the child is a nuisance; it would be better if she didn't exist—the unexpected granting of the wish is horrifying.

Sendak had drawn a picture of goblins stealing a baby in a previous work, the frontispiece to Lore Segal and Randall Jarrell's *The Juniper Tree and Other Tales from Grimm,* and some of the pictures in *Higglety Pigglety Pop!* are of the bad-tempered baby Jennie has to nurse. With the five goblins as babies, Sendak said he was thinking of the Dionne quintuplets, who figured in newspaper stories during his childhood, and the kidnapping was influenced by memories of the stealing of the Lindbergh child. (The villain, like the goblins, used a ladder.) Other echoes and repeated ideas are the inclusion of Sendak's own dog (an alsatian this time) and costume—Ida in the rain cloak can act in a way that is different from her normal behavior, as did Max in the wolf suit and Mickey when naked; the baby's strange hat, which resembles a lampshade, recalls Mickey adorned with the measuring cup; the goblins' dance is a faint echo of the rumpus in *Where the Wild Things Are* and has a similar climactic function. The ice child melts and Ida makes the goblins melt: Max, deprived of his supper, deprived the wild things of theirs. The sunflowers grow as rapidly as Max's forest, and the view out of the window shifts with great rapidity, from trees to a boat to a storm at sea. The total effect of all this is a book that is enormously rich and satisfying. It was published on both a children's and an adult list: a recognition of Sendak's unique achievement as a writer and illustrator, an acknowledgment that his picture books are not just useful toys for very young children, but works of art that can be enjoyed and appreciated by all. His place in the "World Mother Goose Theatre" of children's literature is that he, more than anyone else, has changed our ideas of the picture book out of all recognition.

His own comments, in the speech he made in 1964 accepting the Caldecott Medal, admirably sum up what he has attempted to do in his work—

> We want to protect our children from new and painful experiences that are beyond their emotional comprehension and that intensify anxiety; and to a point we can prevent exposure to such experiences. That is obvious. But what is just as obvious—and what is too often

overlooked—is the fact that from their earliest years children live on familiar terms with disrupting emotions, that fear and anxiety are an intrinsic part of their everyday lives, that they continually cope with frustration as best they can. And it is through fantasy that children achieve catharsis.

REFERENCES

MAURICE SENDAK
> *Kenny's Window,* Harper & Row, 1956
> *Very Far Away,* Harper & Row, 1957; World's Work, 1959
> *The Sign on Rosie's Door,* Harper & Row, 1960; Bodley Head, 1969
> *The Nutshell Library (Alligators All Round; Pierre; One Was Johnny; Chicken Soup with Rice),* Harper & Row, 1962; Collins, London, 1964
> *Where the Wild Things Are,* Harper & Row, 1963; Bodley Head, 1967
> *Hector Protector* and *As I Went Over the Water,* Harper & Row, 1965
> *Higglety Pigglety Pop!,* Harper & Row, 1967; Bodley Head, 1969
> *In the Night Kitchen,* Harper & Row, 1970; Bodley Head, 1971
> *Seven Little Monsters,* Harper & Row, 1976; Bodley Head, 1977
> *Some Swell Pup,* Farrar Straus, 1976; Bodley Head, 1976
> *Outside Over There,* Harper & Row, 1981; Bodley Head, 1981

HILAIRE BELLOC
> *Cautionary Tales,* first published 1918

SELMA G. LANES
> *The Art of Maurice Sendak,* Harry N. Abrams, 1980; Bodley Head, 1981

GEORGE MACDONALD
> *The Light Princess* (illustrated by Maurice Sendak), Farrar Straus, 1969

LORE SEGAL and RANDALL JARRELL
> *The Juniper Tree and Other Tales from Grimm* (illustrated by Maurice Sendak), Farrar Straus, 1973

FROM RUSSIA WITH LOVE?

Esther and Deborah Hautzig

The Endless Steppe by Esther Hautzig was published in America as an adult book, but in Britain it appeared on a children's list, and as such, proved remarkably successful. The decision to publish it as a book for children was both wise and imaginative. *The Endless Steppe* is a first-person narrative, told by a girl who is ten years old at the beginning of the story and fifteen at the end. More important than this, the story is firmly rooted in a pattern and tradition of writing that has belonged to the world of children for centuries. The theme of human beings stripped of the luxuries and trappings of civilization, forced to rely on improvisation and their own resources to survive, has always been popular, as far back as when *Robinson Crusoe* was wrested by the young from adult literature. There is a strong tradition of tales of this kind in the nineteenth century too. *The Swiss Family Robinson, Coral Island, Treasure Island* come immediately to mind. In the twentieth century there are other obvious examples: Ivan Southall's adventure stories, A. Rutgers van der Loeff's *Children on the Oregon Trail,* and William Golding's *Lord of the Flies* give further evidence of children borrowing from the adult novel. The Second World War provided fresh material for the genre—Anne Holm's *I Am David* and Ian Serraillier's *The Silver Sword.* But the outstanding example, a book so gripping and well told that it makes all similar war stories pale in comparison, is *The Endless Steppe.*

This book's authenticity of detail and background, its utterly convincing sense of deprivation and disorientation, make *The Silver Sword,* which is exciting, competently written, and still widely read, seem like any second-rate children's adventure story dressed up for this occasion in Second World War cos-

tume, with some nasty Germans and a not very well individualized mid-European landscape. Some of the good characters are in danger for most of the time—which is why the
reader turns the pages eagerly—but they are usually rescued
before anything too dreadful occurs. There is no sense of
appalling hardship, of hunger, of suffering as in Esther
Hautzig's book; no genuine feeling at any point that all will not
come right in the end; no real dilemmas in which hope and
despair are equally balanced. In *The Endless Steppe* these
things are the very fabric of the novel, and therein lies its
superiority.

The Endless Steppe is thinly-disguised autobiography. It actually happened to Esther Hautzig, and that, in part, is the
reason for the book's strength. No feat of the creative mind
could even now adequately describe the plight of European
Jews in the 1940s: the mass migrations of people, the depor-
tations, the killings, the struggle to survive. It is still too awe-
some and too extraordinary to be assimilated and rendered as
fiction by someone who did not live through it; unlike, say,
the material of *Robinson Crusoe,* which can be brought alive
without first-hand experience, because it is the common
property of the human imagination—though it needs, of
course, the writing genius of Defoe to turn it into a great
novel.

The central character in the book, Esther Rudomin, was
ten in 1939, the only child of well-to-do Jewish parents who
owned a profitable business in Vilna, then in north-east Poland. (It is now part of the USSR.) Vilna was occupied soon
after the outbreak of the war by the Russians, a fact which,
the author frankly recognizes, saved her parents, her grandmother and herself from certain death. Under Soviet rule,
life—middle-class, comfortable and secure—continued much
as it always had. But one hot day in June 1941, suddenly
and without any kind of warning, Esther's world was destroyed. She was lying on her bed at the time, reading a
mystery story and thinking she might go out into the garden
and water the roses. Russian soldiers burst into the house and
informed the Rudomins that they were to be deported as
class enemies. They had ten minutes to pack their belongings.
Memories of this event are recalled by the author with an

almost Chekhovian poignancy. As the family is herded into
the lorry outside, she sees the dining-room curtains flapping
out of the window in the morning sunshine, and acquaintances, quite unaware of what is happening, walking down
the street to do their day's shopping.

Six weeks in a sealed cattle-truck on a train to Siberia, work
in a gypsum mine: it is attention to detail, the minutiae of
existence, which more than anything else makes the emotional impact of the book so forceful. Release follows when
Germany invades Russia. It is impossible, of course, to return
to Vilna; so the family stays on in Siberia for the duration of
the war, living in a hut in a small unfriendly town, fighting
starvation, freezing cold, petty officialdom, disease. Like the
narrator in Byron's *The Prisoner of Chillon*, Esther grows to
accept it, even to love some of it: it has become her world.
Freedom, in 1945, she views with distress; she doesn't want
to go back to Poland, much to her mother's uncomprehending astonishment. They do return, of course, and discover
that all the other members of their family—aunts, uncles,
cousins—have been murdered by the Germans.

I have said that the autobiographical nature of the book is
partly why *The Endless Steppe* is so vivid and memorable. It
isn't—it couldn't be—the sole reason. Other people have
suffered similar experiences, but they haven't written books
of comparable stature. This is where Esther Hautzig the creative artist succeeds better than some others: not only to
endure the distress of reliving that period of her life, but to
select and reject event and detail, to impose shape and pattern, to see, if possible, underlying meaning, and above all to
write the whole thing in memorable English (for her, a for-
eign language). This is what conveys to the reader the authenticity of the almost unimaginable.

A few examples will illustrate her abilities. The evocation
of landscape and weather, for instance, is excellent. Here is
Esther facing a Siberian snowstorm:

> As far as the eye could see, all around, wherever I
> looked, snow was lifting and spiralling from the steppe.
> The swirling mass of wind-driven snow is called the
> *buran*. The *buran* in itself, as it rises from the steppe, is
> dangerous enough; with its whirlpools making one total-

ly blind, it is more dangerous than falling snow. As I stood there for a second, I felt as if the whole huge steppe was revolving under my feet. Then, as it does in Siberia in a great winter storm, the world went black. The wind blew up with a force that knocked me sideways, and now the snow was coming both from the earth and from the sky. The world was a maniacal, gyrating black funnel of noise and I was in the bottom of it. Alone. Completely alone.

When the family is released from the six weeks in the cattle-truck, Esther doesn't know where she is. The shock of her discovery that they are in Siberia is extremely well done:

> The flatness of this land was awesome. There wasn't a hill in sight; it was an enormous unrippled sea of parched and lifeless grass.
>   'Tata, why is the earth so flat here?'
>   'These must be steppes, Esther.'
>   'Steppes? But steppes are in Siberia.'
>   'This is Siberia,' he said quietly.
>   If I had been told I had been transported to the moon, I could not have been more stunned.
>   'Siberia?' My voice trembled. 'But Siberia is full of snow.'
>   'It will be,' my father said.

How did they survive, mentally and emotionally? Their physical survival was, to some extent, pure chance, the fortunes of war; but why didn't they crack up under the strain? Many tiny details point to reasons like inner toughness, dignity, even joie de vivre and optimism in the face of overwhelming odds: Grandmother wearing a chic Garbo hat and carrying a silver-handled umbrella all that time in the cattle-truck; Mrs. Rudomin, unable to bathe or wash properly for six weeks, using a bottle of *L'Heure Bleu* scent. Years later, in Deborah Hautzig's *Hey, Dollface!*, the heroine, Val, finds a handkerchief of Esther's mother's smelling of the same scent: Mrs. Rudomin has just died of cancer in New York. There is also the closeness that perhaps only a Jewish family has, the refusal of any of them to indulge in useless recrimination or loss of temper, and an iron will to live. They have a belief that never wavers that they *will* survive.

Turning to *Hey, Dollface!*, written by Esther Hautzig's daughter, Deborah, is at first sight like observing something from a different planet. Linguistically they have little in common. The English of *The Endless Steppe*, a very British English—

> Popravka ordered us to eat quickly—how long did he think it would take to swallow one piece of bread? my father inquired under his breath—and said that when the whistle blew again we were to return to work. We sat on the floor in our places in the school-house. We cut our bread, which weighed more for being under-done, and our cheeses in half, and ate it; the other half we wrapped in handkerchiefs, scarves paper if anyone had any, whatever was at hand, and put away for supper.

—has been replaced by something much more contemporary and American:

> Mom had left us enough food for a wedding reception, and Chloe spent ages with her head stuck in the refrigerator, deciding what she wanted. We ended up taking everything out and putting it on the table, and settled into the big green kitchen chairs. Kitchens are really the best places to sit and talk in.
>
> 'Dig in,' I said happily, as Chloe swallowed a piece of chicken. 'Hey, you know, Patty's been running around saying she thinks she's pregnant.'
>
> 'Oh, phooey. She's a virgin.'
>
> 'How do you know?'
>
> 'Because,' Chloe said patiently, as though talking to a child, 'the ones who do it don't run around yapping about it.'
>
> 'Oh,' I said lamely. 'Who does it?'
>
> 'Oh, Rollins does, probably, and North.'
>
> 'How do you know?' I persisted.
>
> '*Boy*, you're a pest. I just *know*. I know the kind of guys they run around with.'
>
> 'Wow.' I couldn't imagine either one of them having sex with anyone. 'Isn't that kind of young?'

Judy Blume ought to take a look at this passage: it has an authentic ring to it that the dialogue spoken by her teenagers

lacks, particularly when they're talking about sex. As far as
sex in *Hey, Dollface!* is concerned, the reader is in for a
surprise, maybe a shock. The story is about an intense friendship between two fifteen-year-old girls that has strong lesbian
overtones; in fact it is hinted that after the book has finished,
when the girls are older, it may develop into a deeper, perhaps sexual relationship. Such a theme isn't unique in teenage
literature, but it is so unusual that a novel like *Hey, Dollface!*
was long overdue when it appeared. There is no subject on
which the educated public is more profoundly ignorant or
has more absurd prejudices than homosexuality, and the
needs of young people who are growing up gay, with the
hostility and worries that heterosexual adolescents don't
have to face, have for far too long been ignored. If only for
this reason *Hey, Dollface!* would be worth reading, but Deborah Hautzig's merits as a writer are not to be dismissed, and
when one realizes that Esther of *The Endless Steppe* is Val's
mother in *Hey, Dollface!* the book becomes particularly
interesting.

Here is Esther, the Polish Jew who suffered deportation to
Siberia and every sort of hardship and terror, now an American 'Mom,' preoccupied with husband, children and running
a flat, and growing embarrassed and helpless when her teenage daughter asks questions about how often married people
have sex and whether homosexuality is normal. It's a far cry
from considerations like where is the next meal coming from,
and will everyone be starved to death or shot. Yet it *is* the
same person. There's the same love of life, the same steely
will. And Deborah is clearly her mother's daughter: despite
the obvious differences between the two novels, they have
several features in common. In both books the characterization of the women is very strong, particularly the central
characters. Esther and Val have a similar sparkle, a curiosity
about life, an intellectual restlessness that questions, continues to question in the face of stiff adult opposition, and
usually wins in the end. Both books are almost straight autobiography, childhood and adolescence not so much remembered by an adult as lived through a second time. And the
Jewish upbringing: the ghetto closeness of a persecuted minority in the one becomes an accepted, scarcely-to-be-com-

mented-on, fact of existence in the other, because in New York such things are unremarkable. It is almost a history of the American dream: the down-trodden European minority in *The Endless Steppe* transformed into the democratic free citizens of *Hey, Dollface!,* and living in a society where even an unusual sexual orientation is, if not totally acceptable, not regarded as a major wickedness. Both novels are inspired by a tremendous belief in freedom—from political oppression in the one, from pressures to conform in the other. 'A young girl's heart is indestructible,' Esther says. 'Perpetually hungry and cold, in the land of exile, I fell in love for the first time.' And Val comments:

> 'We're trying to put ourselves into slots, and con-
> demning ourselves for not being able to.'
> 'We don't have to fit into any slots,' Chloe said. 'So
> let's stop trying.'

But the experiences of mother and daughter are so obviously unalike that freedom, when it comes, is not only of a quite different nature for Val, but much easier to accept and cope with than it is for Esther. Esther is scarred in a way that Val could never be. For Val, freedom is a normal step on the road to adulthood, a simple matter of maturity and choice:

> I'd been looking for some kind of judgement or ap-
> proval, but when I asked adults like Miss Udry or Mom
> they didn't know any more than I did. But *I* can decide! I
> thought. I've been so worried about what other people
> would think I never asked myself what *I* thought. It isn't
> wrong, I thought; it isn't bad. Maybe for someone else it
> would be, but it isn't for me.

For Esther it is much more difficult. She can say 'But we're alive. Our exile had saved our lives. Now we felt ourselves to be supremely lucky to have been deported to Siberia. Hunger, cold, and misery were nothing; life had been granted us,' but sense, beneath that, another more complex set of emotions.

The inconclusive nature of the ending of both books is another similarity. In *The Endless Steppe,* Esther and her mother are re-united with 'Tata' at the railway station in

Lodz, but the reader may ask, what happened then? The house in Vilna has become the headquarters of the local NKVD; and Vilna, in any case, is now no longer in Poland. How did the family fare in post-war Poland? How long did they stay there? Why, and when, did they leave? Interesting though the answers to these questions are, they are not relevant to the novel. The last sentence— 'The years out there on the steppe had come to an end; our exile was over'—is entirely appropriate. *Hey, Dollface!* ends with neither of the girls 'coming out' as gay, even to themselves. Whether they are likely to prefer their own sex for good is a question left in mid-air. Some critics have complained that this is a 'cop-out,' an evasion of issues. It isn't. It's much more likely that fifteen-year-olds who are homosexual (even those who are one hundred per cent homosexual—and Val and Chloe are to some extent attracted to boys) would find difficulty in admitting to themselves that they are so inclined. And not just because of social pressures. To find out and accept that one's sexual orientation is different from the norm is not necessarily a blinding flash of insight, a once-and-for-all realization; it can be a slow and gradual process that may take years. If Chloe and Val had been seventeen or eighteen, one might possibly say that the ending of *Hey, Dollface!* is evasive. But at fifteen the inconclusiveness seems right: fifteen is a very inconclusive age.

Beneath the surface of *Hey Dollface!* the tragic circumstances of Esther Hautzig's early life are hinted at. It would be impossible for her daughter to escape the family's extraordinary past, but it is all to Deborah Hautzig's credit that she is not overawed by this terrible legacy. She doesn't limp along in her mother's shadow. She has said that she hopes that one day she, too, will write her version of those appalling years of European history, from the distant viewpoint of the second-generation American immigrant. This should prove very interesting indeed.

Taken separately, these two books are absorbing. Both are firmly in the center of certain traditions of writing for the young: the one, the adventure story in which the child faces overwhelming odds; the other, the realistic teenage novel that shows the adolescent grappling with his or her first adult problems. Taken together, they become something more: a portrait of a certain section of European Jewry facing the darkest hour of its history, and what happened, years afterwards, to some of its survivors and their descendants.

REFERENCES

DEBORAH HAUTZIG
  Hey, Dollface!, Greenwillow, 1978; Hamish Hamilton, 1979

ESTHER HAUTZIG
  The Endless Steppe, Crowell, 1968; Hamish Hamilton, 1969

R. M. BALLANTYNE
  Coral Island, first published 1857

GEORGE BYRON
  The Prisoner of Chillon, first published 1816

DANIEL DEFOE
  Robinson Crusoe, first published 1719

WILLIAM GOLDING
  Lord of the Flies, Faber, 1954; Putnam, 1959

ANNE HOLM
  I Am David, Methuen, 1965; in U.S.A. as *North to Freedom,*
  Harcourt, 1965

IAN SERRAILLIER
  The Silver Sword, Cape, 1956; Phillips, 1959

R. L. STEVENSON
  Treasure Island, first published 1883

A. RUTGERS VAN DER LOEFF
  Children on the Oregon Trail, U.L.P., 1961; in U.S.A. as *Oregon
  at Last,* Morrow, 1962

JOHANN DAVID WYSS
  The Swiss Family Robinson, first published in English, 1814

ABORIGINALS AND HAPPY FOLK

Patricia Wrightson

Thirty years ago our television screens were without Australian soap operas—good, bad, or indifferent—and we had little or no knowledge of Australian films, novels, and children's books. It is difficult to imagine now, so exposed are we to Australian culture of all sorts—we take it for granted. As far as children's literature was concerned, Australia in the nineteen fifties had no writers of international repute, and the books it produced that were read in the world outside mostly inhabited one kind of genre—middle-class kids enjoying themselves on camping holidays, the sex roles very sharply defined: the boys had all the fun; the girls were frightened and tearful; Dad gave lots of practical advice on how to deal with the great outdoors, and Mum cooked bacon and eggs at all the crucial moments. It was the kind of children's literature that abounded in England before the Second World War, of which Arthur Ransome was the finest exponent. The Australian version could be described as sub-Ransomese.

Patricia Wrightson and Ivan Southall are the two Australian authors who have done most to change all this, who have made Australian children's books come of age; but their writing roots are in this genre. Southall is considered primarily as a creator of realistic fiction and Patricia Wrightson as a creator of fantasy—"I have at present two preoccupations," she says in *Twentieth Century Children's Writers,* "richness of fantasy as a means; and the use of Aboriginal folk-spirits (fairies and monsters) to enrich Australia's contemporary fantasy"—but five of her first six books are realistic novels, and they include her most well-known work, *I Own the Racecourse!*

The Crooked Snake, with which she made her debut, and

its successor, *The Bunyip Hole,* contain only a few hints of
the imagination and intellect that would eventually produce
novels of such striking originality as *The Nargun and the
Stars* and *A Little Fear. The Crooked Snake* has a well-worn
theme—children forming a secret society—and is encapsulated in a virtually adultless world where the "good" kids
outwit and defeat the "bad" kids (an older bunch of vandals
and bullies) and are duly rewarded at the end by grateful
grown-ups. It's escapist stuff, fantasy in the pejorative sense of
the word; plot is all-important, and the dialogue consists
mostly of the issuing of instructions about what to do next.
There are, however, many worse examples of this kind of
story; it is readable—one enjoys turning the pages—and the
descriptive passages reveal a writer of some talent:

> It was quite different from the soaring forests of gum
> they had been in, where the trunks rise clear like the
> columns of old churches and the cool light comes
> through high arches of grey-green leaves. This was like
> being under the sea . . . Even the light was green except
> in clearer patches where the sun splashed in.

The Bunyip Hole contains similar ideas—nice, practical
children camping in the hills and the outwitting of a pair of
nasty vandals—and similar faults: too much of the dialogue is
orders and instructions; the slang ("Good man, Binty," or
"Jumping rabbits!") is not always convincing; and some of the
characterization and sex roles are a bit stereotypical. But it is a
better novel than *The Crooked Snake.* One of the characters,
Binty Collins, *is* well-drawn, a rounded portrait of a fearful,
over-imaginative boy; and the excitement and danger the plot
provides are more genuinely felt than in *The Crooked Snake.*
The sense of place is good too; there are some competent
descriptions of hill country, rivers and waterfalls. The respon-
sibility older children assume—or refuse to assume—for their
younger siblings and their more vulnerable friends is a major
theme in much of Patricia Wrightson's work, and it makes its
first appearance here; it is well-handled, with some pleasingly
humorous touches—Ken and Val, afraid their parents will not
give them permission to camp out because their sister is too
young,

looked at Joan in a calculating way, as a victim whose
sacrifice might save the rest of them. Joan knew that
look and grew restless.

"I'm big now," she said firmly. "I can clean my teeth,
too."

The Rocks of Honey begins in pedestrian fashion, but ends
up by being a surprisingly different book from what the reader expects; it moves from a standard plot of kids enjoying the
countryside and having picnics in the bush to a subtle consideration of ownership, and an exploration of the uneasy rela-
tions between Aboriginals and white communities: we are
already a long way from secret societies and jolly camping
trips. The three main characters are convincing creations.
Barney, the all-Australian white male, is brash, bossy and insensitive in his dealings with both Winnie and the Aboriginal
boy, Eustace; he is sexist *and* racist: completely unattractive.
Winnie, a prickly, withdrawn girl is aware of this and suffers,
mostly in silence, but Eustace, much less sure than either of
status, and feeling inferior to both because of the color of his
skin, behaves like an Uncle Tom figure, a white man's "good"
black, and goes along with whatever Barney says. Until the
three of them find an ancient stone axe buried in the rocks on
the summit of a mountain: this brings into the open all the
tensions that lie between them. To Barney, it is finders keep-
ers; "What you want with that?" Eustace's uncle asks him, and
he replies, "Just to have it, that's all." Eustace begins to realize
that this is an outrage—a relic of his ancestors being shown
off to uncomprehending whites as some bauble to gawp at—
a real slur on his race and color. Winnie, for quite different
reasons, agrees with him that the axe should be returned to
where it was found, and this is what happens eventually,
though Barney's acceptance of this decision comes not from
seeing Eustace's point of view, but because he decides the
axe is dangerous—it is the cause of three mysterious acci-
dents, in one of which he is injured. The strength of *The
Rocks of Honey* also lies in its sombre conclusions. Only
Eustace grows a little during the course of the story; Barney
and Winnie do not. Barney is no nearer to having any understanding of, or sensitivity to, the opposite sex or Aboriginal

people than he was at the beginning. But *The Rocks of Honey* is not a masterpiece—more the work of a writer feeling her way out of safe, easy fiction into something more difficult and more serious; interesting though the subject-matter is, Patricia Wrightson is not yet fully in control of her material. The transition, for example, half-way through from the plot of an ordinary children's book into something more profound is curiously abrupt, and both the chapter describing how and why the axe was originally buried in the rocks, and the moralizing on the last pages, show that the writer hasn't made the story itself do everything it needed to do.

In *The Feather Star* Patricia Wrightson comes to maturity as an author; the story does do everything it needed to do— there is not a fault anywhere. It stands apart from the rest of her work in that it is her only venture into the genre of the realistic teenage novel, and her only book in which an adolescent girl is the central character. So good is it on teenage awkwardness, embarrassment and confusion, on how fifteen-year-old girls cope, and don't cope, with the opposite sex, on their preoccupation with appearance, clothes, hair-styles and so on, that one is astonished that Patricia Wrightson had not dealt with such themes before—she sounds as practised as if she had been doing it for years. The conversations between Lindy and Fleece about their ambitions and frustrations are marvellous pieces of authentic teenage dialogue. The plot works very differently from its predecessors; there is no strong story-line overriding every other consideration—it is built like a mosaic from fragments: little incidents, bits of conversation, seemingly inconsequential actions. The pace is leisurely. Setting scene and mood and delineating character, in the first third of the book, are of paramount importance, so much so that one wonders what sort of story will eventually emerge, if any—a technique Patricia Wrightson also employs in *Down to Earth, An Older Kind of Magic,* and *The Nargun and the Stars.*

The story comes out of the characters and its development is in fact all-absorbing. It is concerned with the destruction of innocence, the painful shift from childhood to a more adult view of the world. Lindy, on holiday with her family in a

remote seaside village, makes friends with three of the local
teenagers, and experiences a happy, but ultimately false,
sense of security in their companionship—

> She looked at the black shapes that were Bill and Ian and
> Fleece, who yesterday morning had been strangers to
> her. Fleece, who loved pretty things and kept her love in
> a brown-paper parcel under the old iron roof. Bill, who
> kept poetry hidden in his mind. Ian, who was going to
> conquer the stars if the old man would let him. They
> were sitting on a star now, four good friends, and this
> star was theirs.

But four good friends they are not; they are mere acquaintances, and Lindy's childlike, wrong-headed perceptions are
rudely shattered when Fleece's "love in a brown-paper par-
cel" (a night-dress she has made) is torn up by a cat. Fleece's
hurt becomes more painful when Ian uses the dress to deco-
rate a scarecrow; Lindy, trying to comfort her, receives nothing but abuse for her efforts; and both girls turn furiously on
Ian, who takes refuge in mocking Bill's poetry. The friendships were suddenly made and are just as suddenly broken. It
is symbolized by the feather star, a sea creature Lindy observes in a cave—this, too, is broken, ironically by the same
cat who ripped up the dress. Some sort of wary reconciliation
comes about between the four "friends," but none with Abel,
an embittered, drunken old man who dislikes them all; he had
"eyes like dull brown glass" and a head "like greasy brown
wood with a silly little collar of white fur around it," and his
violent ill-temper causes Lindy to weep—

> for useless misery and bitterness; for age with its eyes on
> the ground refusing life, wasting all the adventure and
> beauty of a whirling planet in space . . . So Lindy sobbed
> while childhood stole away and Bill patted her awk-
> wardly on the shoulder.

The smaller, but no less significant, details of the book are
excellent—the descriptions of the beach and the nearby
countryside; the sexual attraction between Bill and Lindy; the
silent, despised girl, Annie Tippett—"You go on home, Annie
Tippett, or I'll tell your grandmother" is a refrain that recurs

throughout the book; Lindy's easily satisfied younger brother; Lindy's mother's touching concern for her daughter; the quality of the writing—

> Water bubbled into the pool and washed out and the weed moved with it, softly forward, softly back. The wind came creeping round the rock and moved in Lindy's hair, lifting it forward, lifting it back.

If *The Feather Star* was quite unlike its predecessors, *Down to Earth* is different again, and also something Patricia Wrightson did not attempt to repeat—a novel about a being from another planet visiting Earth, and the events, both humorous and nearly catastrophic, that ensue when he tries to explain who he is. The police want to lock him up when he fails to understand the uses of money; psychiatrists and doctors think he's mad; and as he appears to be a young boy, the Child Welfare people want to take him into care. Eventually the United Nations and the Security Council become involved . . . He is saved from too much unpleasantness, and is enabled to return to his spaceship, by an assorted group of kids who believe his story and protect him—again, the theme of children looking after their peers and siblings. As usual, the characters of the children are sharply differentiated, and their relationships with each other are very convincingly handled; particularly good is strong-minded, independent Cathy, who always manages to stop bossy, organizing George from becoming too much of a male chauvinist. But insensitive putdowns of girls are present, as before:

> At this point Elizabeth leaned across from her table to say: "My Uncle Alec has a white M.G. He got it painted specially."
> "White's only for lairs," said David quellingly. "He probably spends more time cleaning it than driving it."
> Elizabeth subsided meekly . . .

Elizabeth in fact is a middle-class version of Annie Tippett, and has an identical function in the story.

As in *The Feather Star,* the plot is initially slow; again the author needs time to establish character and evoke place. The place, urban Sydney, makes its first appearance in Patricia Wrightson's work (all her previous novels had a rural background), and it remains the setting for the two subsequent books, *I Own the Racecourse!* and *An Older Kind of Magic.* In all three, Sydney is written about with love and affection, and in great detail, as if the author knows it inside out. It is invariably observed through a child's eyes: a city of wonder, beauty, and excitement for kids (though in *An Older Kind of Magic* some of the more unpleasant aspects of modern city life—traffic, pollution, concrete, the cheap magic of advertising—are stressed). No child, Patricia Wrightson seems to be saying, could possibly be bored in Sydney; there is so much to do, to see and hear, to divert one's attention—

> There was a Saturday night activity in all the irregular streets climbing up and down from the harbour. Cars sped along them like whining insects with bright staring eyes drawn to the lights of King's Cross or swarming purposefully about the stadium. The street lamps hung from their poles like drops of light. The buildings, all the mixed-up huddle of them, small and shabby, old and gracious, new and self-important, had retreated into the twilight and crouched there blinking owlishly from lighted windows. The lights on the north shore made a phosphorous glow, and the bridge was a green-lit archway from shore to shore.

Down to Earth is a gently satirical story that pokes fun at people seeing only what they think they see, or what they want to see, and at unimaginative adults who panic when confronted with the unfamiliar. There are some nicely eccentric minor characters, the Cat Woman for instance (Patricia Wrightson uses her again, though somewhat differently, in her short novel for younger readers, *Night Outside*); an attractive dog—dogs have important roles in many of the subsequent books—and, throughout, a great deal of humor:

> "Can you think of anything worse for a spaceman than getting mixed up with Child Welfare? They'll probably want to see him through his apprenticeship, and he's got to catch a flying saucer on Sunday night."

I Own the Racecourse! deservedly brought Patricia Wrightson international acclaim. Its principal theme is the same as that of *Down to Earth*—the outsider, the boy who is so odd that he needs the protection of other children to stop him from getting into serious trouble—but Andy is not a spaceman visiting Earth; he is a retarded child, lost in his own fantasies and inventions, who believes that he owns the local racecourse when a tramp "sells" it to him for three dollars. His minders, the neighbourhood kids Terry, Mike, Joe and Matt, quarrel about how they should cope with this, though they are united in their aim that Andy, for his own good, must be made to realize that he does *not* own the racecourse. But how can it be done without causing him too much hurt? They are unable to find a solution. The adults are no help; in fact they make matters worse by regarding it all as a joke, treating Andy as if he did own Beecham Park, and making a sort of mascot of him—then eventually getting cross when he becomes a nuisance at race meetings. There are some fascinating comments about illusion and reality:

> The problem . . . was to make Andy see what was real and what was not. Joe could see that that might be hard for someone like Andy. Easy enough to know that a house was real, or a loaf of bread, for instance; but what about things like atoms, or Mount Everest, or war? A lot of people never saw those things at all, but they were real, just the same. For someone like Andy, it must often be pretty hard to tell which things were real and which weren't. If someone came along and told him that he owned Beecham Park, how was Andy to know that wasn't as real as atoms? All the more reason, thought Joe, for making Andy understand.

But Andy does "possess the racecourse in his mind," and, as Mike points out, its officials behave in such a way that to all intents and purposes he *does* own it; Matt comments, allusively, "When everyone thought Mrs. Whitlock was going to die, nobody told *her* about it."

Sydney, again, is beautifully evoked—the crowds of people, the night lights, the barely suppressed excitement of this most exuberant of cities—and, as usual, the relationships within a group of young boys are handled superbly. There is also a pack of very engaging stray dogs whom Andy befriends. Good, too, are the adults, in particular Bert Hammond, the head groundsman, who treats Andy with great sympathy and understanding, allowing him to do the things he wants to do—weeding flowerbeds, sweeping up litter, and generally improving the look of "his" racecourse. So who in fact, Patricia Wrightson seems to be asking, *does* own the racecourse? "He's got to have things," Mike says of Andy, but is ownership simply a matter of buying and possessing material objects, or is it occupying a space, mentally and emotionally, as people refer to a rock on a beach as "my" rock, to a beloved landscape or town as "mine"? We are back to the questions raised in *The Rocks of Honey;* who owns the axe? Andy can't own the horses, Mike points out, but he can "own" the race—

> "Real?" said Mike. "What's real? The trainers speak to him in the street and let him lead their dogs and call him 'The Owner.' That's real, isn't it?"

These are particularly significant questions for a white Australian to ask. Aboriginals had no concept of ownership as we understand the word; they thought territory could not be owned at all.

Andy is a first-rate creation—loveable, harmless, and very vulnerable. The book's greatest strengths are the way he causes the plot to develop, and the perfect resolution of its ending. One reads *I Own the Racecourse!* as one reads Philippa Pearce's *Tom's Midnight Garden,* with a mounting sense of panic and horror: both authors seem to be writing themselves into situations that must end in appalling tragedy when the story (and the reader) is demanding an opposite movement—then, in the conclusion, the proper answer is found, not by a cheap trick, but it's been there all along, hidden so skillfully that we never saw it until it is made obvious. The real owners buy the racecourse back from Andy—for ten dollars. He is quite content with this—and his profit.

An Older Kind of Magic shows a marked change in direction; it is the first of Patricia Wrightson's books to use as the basis for its plot the spirits and monsters of Aboriginal legend.

"It is time we stopped trying to see elves and dragons and unicorns in Australia," she says in the epilogue to the novel. "They have never belonged here, and no ingenuity can make them real. We need to look for another kind of magic, a kind that must have been shaped by the land itself at the edge of Australian vision." It doesn't quite come off: Like *The Rocks of Honey, An Older Kind of Magic* is an experimental, transitional work; the author has new things to do, but she hasn't yet found the right way of doing them. Maybe this is because she is still too wrapped up in her previous concerns: relationships between children in an urban environment, the inferior role of girls, ownership, and the "magic" of Sydney suggest that this should have been another realistic story; the spirits who manipulate events so that the children, Selina, Rupert and Benny, achieve what they want—the abandonment of Sir Mortimer Wyvern's plans to turn part of the Botanical Gardens into a car park—are both an uneasy intrusion from another genre, and a bit too much of a device or short cut to cause a happy ending. Also, the necessity of an epilogue to explain the magic suggests that she didn't quite feel the novel itself stands up on its own.

The pace is, as usual, leisurely; much of the first third of the book is devoted to establishing character and relationships, and a wonderfully rich and compelling portrait of Sydney. In no other of her novels is the atmosphere of Australia's premier city so strongly present: Sydney itself is virtually the main character. But the author's attitude has changed; it is now ambiguous, not so much a hymn of praise as it was—

> Selina went running back to the pond. As she went she began to hear, from all round the Gardens, the voice of the city shouting its huge city-song. The great Going Home had begun.
>
> The spinning of tyres, the beating of feet, and the deep, loud droning of the bridge; the grumble and whine of motors; and somewhere, softly, the splashing of fountains. The city roared its song, pouring rivers of cars down every street and rivers of people into every station. Pavements throbbed with the underground rushing of trains. Policemen beckoned, traffic lights flashed, and streets were packed solid. High above Cir-

cular Quay little cars ran like strings of beads along the
expressway into the pumpkin-gold dazzle of the sun.
Trains beat at their rails, buses mooed and howled; the
city shouted.

This is a love-hate relationship; and it gives an edge to the
writing throughout, which is of a very high order—luminous,
poetic prose—and to the images chosen to illustrate the dilemmas of a big, modern city: the display dummies from shop
windows being transformed by the spirits into a crowd of
demonstrators who protest about the proposed car park is
one of the most memorable of these images; humorous, striking and original.

The Nargun and the Stars is a much more satisfactory
book, a fine fusion of realism and fantasy. It is the first novel
of Patricia Wrightson's that has adults at the center of the
action, and the only one about people she later calls Inlanders—the rural whites who inhabit the interior of the continent, and whose way of life is vastly different from, and
hostile to, modern urban Australia. Charlie and Edie, elderly
farming brother and sister, are, like Aboriginals, in touch with
the land, the Australia of mountain, forest, and desert, and
aware of the roles its various spirits play. This gentle, old-
fashioned, rustic couple adopt a distant relative, Simon, a
sullen, depressive orphan boy; their loving care tames him
and he begins to love them in return, and finds that there is a
rightful place for him to exist happily and grow. This by itself
would have made an absorbing story, but the plot mainly
revolves round the problems caused by a Nargun, a primeval
stone monster, who has shifted over a period of centuries
from the place, geographically speaking, where it belongs and
is now threatening to destroy Charlie's and Edie's farm. This,
and other Aboriginal myths Patricia Wrightson uses in subsequent books, are all concerned with displacement: spirits and
monsters, it would seem, have certain clearly defined functions in clearly defined areas—when they move out of those
areas, trouble ensues. So, in *The Ice Is Coming,* the Ninyas,
the ice-makers, create havoc when they start to travel (ice
appears in Queensland, for instance, in the summer); in *The
Dark Bright Water* a lost water spirit causes springs to dry
and deserts to bloom; in *Behind the Wind* it is Wulgaru, death

itself, who has left his territory and is claiming victims he is not entitled to.

The fantasy in *The Nargun and the Stars* is more convincing than in *An Older Kind of Magic* because the spirits aren't used to achieve what the humans should have achieved by themselves; the Nyols, the Turongs and the Potkoorok lend a little assistance, but only for their own selfish reasons—Charlie, Edie and Simon have to defeat the Nargun by their own efforts. It is a nice touch, too, that when the Nargun is eventually imprisoned in a cave under the mountain Simon feels sorry for it, and it is reassuring to know that it won't be there till the end of time. The Nargun is not evil, and it has its own right and proper functions. It will win in the end; it can wait "for a mountain to crumble or a river to break through"—centuries, of course, after Simon is old or dead.

This novel has a similar background to Virginia Hamilton's *M. C. Higgins, the Great*—remote hill people threatened by a mountain; in the Hamilton novel the possibility of destruction by slurry, in the Wrightson, destruction by falling rock. In both books, landscape and a sense of place are very important elements in the writing, which, also in both, is poetic prose of considerable beauty. On Wongadilla mountain "the world fell dizzily away into vistas of far blue ridges," and Simon experiences "in the silence of the ridges and spurs all round—a great quiet, like a roomful of giants thinking"; in bed at night he listens to the wind, "the stealthy slither of the mat along his floor and the crying of the pine outside the window." He listens "with every inch of his skin" to "the song of frogs creaking and hiccuping up to the moon," to—

> The cluck and chinkle of the creek down there in the gully; the louder rush and babble of the river; the quiet mutter of water running over the ground and sopping into his shoes, and somewhere the singing of water over high rocks.

The Nargun and the Stars also contains Patricia Wrightson's pithiest comment on ownership—when Simon points out to Charlie that he is the owner of the land, not the man in charge, Charlie retorts: "For sixty years or so maybe, but how long do you think the Potkoorok's owned it?"

It seems inevitable that a writer so interested in Aboriginal folk-lore as Patricia Wrightson should eventually place an Aboriginal character at the center of a novel. Wirrun, in *The Ice Is Coming* and its sequels, *The Dark Bright Water* and *Behind the Wind,* is that character, a young man who does casual work on Inlanders' farms or at one of the Happy Folk's (the urban, coastal white Australians) petrol stations. This trilogy of novels, collectively called *The Book of Wirrun* or *The Song of Wirrun,* is Patricia Wrightson's most ambitious work, and comparisons with other contemporary authors who use myth—Ursula Le Guin, Alan Garner, Susan Cooper, and William Mayne—are in order, for though these books are wholly Australian and their stories Aboriginal, their themes are similar to those of the *Earthsea* trilogy or *The Dark Is Rising* quintet. Patricia Wrightson is closer to Ursula Le Guin in aims and methods than to Garner, Mayne or Susan Cooper; indeed the *Earthsea* trilogy may have served as some sort of model for the Wirrun books. In *The Ice Is Coming* Wirrun is tested in many of the traditionally masculine tasks and pursuits, as is Ged in *A Wizard of Earthsea;* and in *Behind the Wind,* as in *The Farthest Shore,* a proper role and place for death is the quest of the hero. In the central book of both trilogies attention turns to a female character, though the Yunggamurra is not as important a figure in *The Dark Bright Water* as is Tenar in *The Tombs of Atuan.*

Patricia Wrightson's achievement in the Wirrun trilogy is vastly superior to Susan Cooper's *The Dark Is Rising* sequence, but it falls short of Ursula Le Guin's. Though the writing is often excellent (less so, in fact, in *Behind the Wind*), the plots well-turned, the climaxes good (particularly in *The Ice Is Coming,* which daringly uses a magnificent and unexpected *anti*-climax at the critical moment—the supposed monster of monsters, the Eldest Nargun, turns out to be no bigger than a teacup and is quite innocuous), all three books suffer from a lack of human interest. Wirrun is the only major human character. Admittedly his friend Ularra is present in *The Dark Bright Water*—the clashes of personality between these two young men provide much of the interest here, thus making it the most enjoyable book of the trilogy— and Murra, the woman Wirrun creates from the lost water spirit, occupies much of the opening chapters of *Behind the Wind,* but other characters have essentially minor functions; only Merv Bula is given enough attention for the reader to get some impression of what he is like as a person. (Wirrun falls in love with Murra, thus creating the same problems for himself as Llew has to face in the Welsh legend behind Alan Garner's *The Owl Service;* his wife has been created out of flowers and leaves him for another man.) The result of having only one major human character is page after page unrelieved by dialogue; too much cataloging of a solitary man's daily occupations (making fires, eating meals, unrolling a sleeping-bag, etcetera); and lengthy periods when the dramatic tensions wilt.

Wirrun in the first novel defeats the Ninyas, the Ice-Makers, who have escaped from where they belong and are now trying to freeze the whole of Australia; in the second he rescues the lost water-spirit, thus preventing both drought and flood, and by accidentally transforming her into a woman he now has a lover with whom he lives as an Aboriginal would want, free of white city life, roaming the countryside and living off the land. In the final book he loses her—her sisters turn her back into a water spirit (echoes in this of mermaid legends, and the material of Arnold's poem, *The Forsaken Merman*)—and in his task of returning Wulgaru to his rightful place, he confronts his own death. In dying he achieves the status of Immortal, and happiness with Murra, also now Immortal: "Where they went only the land knew." Though the conclusion is convincing, *Behind the Wind* is the weakest book of the trilogy. The prose at times becomes dropsical, a frequent fault with writers who use mythical subjects:

> They did not speak though they knew they might have done, for they were still man and earth-thing; since the barrier of his flesh was put aside they set silence between them. But she lifted her chin with the free, fierce pride of the Yunggamurra and showed him her moonlit eyes full of faith, and he smiled and bent his head and rose up out of the cavern.

It's intended to be solemn and significant, but in fact it's sloppy and faintly ludicrous.

The strength of the trilogy is in its portrayal of the landscapes and peoples of Australia. Here the prose is Patricia Wrightson at her best, even if this particular passage is close to Ursula Le Guin in *The Ones Who Walk Away From Omelas*—

> Along its green margins, clustered in towns here and there, live the Happy Folk with their faces to the sea. They live for happiness; it is their business and their duty. They study it and teach it to their children, debate it, make laws to force it on each other, struggle for it, export and import it. Most of all they buy and sell it. They have no time to look over their shoulders at the old land behind them. Only sometimes, in their search for happiness, they make expensive little explorations into the land with cameras. (*The Ice Is Coming*)

Ularra is described in one brief, telling sentence—"He was tall and loose, not yet having learnt to manage his length"— and Wirrun, striking camp, "set off down the mountain, and it was like leaving some very old person who had been part of his childhood." In deserts there are "hills ground down with age or baring jagged, hacked-out teeth" and

> the ground lies so level that water will not flow, and empty river-courses lead only into clay pans crusted with salt. The sun beats down like a gong on red wind-drifted dunes. (*The Ice Is Coming*)

Wirrun, Ularra, and an acquaintance, Tom Hunter, see Australia from an aeroplane—

> The land lay under them, grey-brown and immense, draped with the purple shadows of clouds. With majestic authority it set forth its cratered hills and looping rivers, its endless plains relentlessly fenced into squares, the patched fur of its forests. The dark eyes watching from little round windows darkened again with awe. Each man travelled alone. (*The Dark Bright Water*)

—and the author, too, seems at times to be observing it from the same viewpoint:

That long coast lay under stars with a pale ruffle of sea
along its edge; wearing scattered brooches of lights
where the towns were clustered, and here and there
pricked with a light from an Inlander's home. But most
of it, lying under the edge of night, was in darkness.
(*Behind the Wind*)

Who owns Australia is a question all three books seem to
be asking. Is it the Happy Folk, the Inlanders, the People (the
name Patricia Wrightson gives to the Aboriginals), or the
Land creatures (the various spirits and monsters)? The answer is: none of them. Each group has its function and place,
and chaos arises when someone, or a whole group, tries to
usurp the function and place of another. Only Wirrun has no
specific place; the entire continent is his, and he is therefore
uniquely qualified to see that place and function are adhered
to. Finally, the matter of ownership that has so preoccupied
Patricia Wrightson's career becomes focussed on people: we
don't own each other. Wirrun says to Murra: "If you want to
stop with me you'll stop. People do what they want when
they come right down to it." Murra says she must "keep old
laws" and leaves him: she was lent, was not his property.

A Little Fear, like the Wirrun trilogy, has only one major
human character, but in this novel, Patricia Wrightson has
solved the problems such a device leads to. It's one of her
shortest books, with a tight, tense plot, and Mrs Tucker, an
eccentric, admirable, "very tall and bony old lady with a
screw of white hair on top" is marvellously well realized—
she does not have to bear the weight of symbolism that
seems to burden Wirrun so often. The other characters are a
delightful dog called Hector, and an Aboriginal spirit, a Njimbin, who is a scavenging, malicious, cuckoo-in-the-nest creature, the most detailed and plausible sketch of a spirit that
Patricia Wrightson has done—he's almost human, a sort of
greedy, spiteful tramp. The story is concerned with the struggle between Mrs Tucker and the Njimbin for the possession
of her hen-house; the Njimbin has moved into it, terrifying
the hens so much that they can't lay any eggs, and he refuses
to leave. Mrs Tucker is no match for the plagues of frogs, ants,
rats and midges he inflicts on her, and deciding anyway that
she is too old to live by herself in an ancient, draughty, re-

mote country house, she moves into town, to "a little place with a yard for Hector" and "a good paling fence between me and the neighbours." The conclusion, as always with Patricia Wrightson, is both unexpected and splendid: there is no question here about ownership; the hen-house belongs to Mrs Tucker, not to the Njimbin, so—

> "Maggoty old fowlhouse," she whispered happily. "John should've put a match to it long ago."

—she burns it down, so the Njimbin, like her, must go elsewhere.

Adults seemed to be banished, in the nineteen thirties and forties, from children's books, but they began to reassume their rightful place in the fifties and sixties. Very old people as major characters, however, are—alas—still rare figures. There are honorable exceptions, of course—Hattie Bartholomew in Philippa Pearce's *Tom's Midnight Garden,* Sammy's grandfather in Betsy Byars' *The House of Wings,* Mrs Oldknow in Lucy Boston's Green Knowe stories, Mrs Shand in Penelope Lively's *A Stitch in Time.* But *A Little Fear* is possibly unique in contemporary children's fiction in having a very old woman as the only human character of any importance. It is full of wise perceptions about ageing and old age—

> When you were old, she knew, you really were a sort of child. When the things you used to do were all done, and your body and mind grew slower, other people took over. They called you dear, or Agnes, just as if you were a child, and kept you in a clean bright nursery, and brought you warm underclothes that you didn't want. They worried and looked after you until, if you weren't careful, you were a prisoner of their care.

Children need to know these things—Grandma doesn't usually live at home with them nowadays. Descriptions of scenery, weather, and animals are also and as usual excellent. "Down at the river swans conversed like ladies at an afternoon tea." The author's sensitivity to sights and sounds, her subtle use of assonance and cadence, is another pleasure—

That night great cream-and-gold scarabs came bumbling at the screens and grumbling under the doors. Little stingless midges swarmed through the wire gauze and danced about the light and tumbled into Mrs Tucker's hair.

A Little Fear is without flaw, a little masterpiece. It may well be that Patricia Wrightson feels that her most important contribution to children's literature is in the Wirrun trilogy, in placing before her audience Aboriginal myth and legend that would not otherwise be widely known, but *The Feather Star, I Own the Racecourse!, The Nargun and the Stars* and *A Little Fear* are her finest books. In these her genius is second to none.

REFERENCES

PATRICIA WRIGHTSON
>*The Crooked Snake,* Angus and Robertson, 1955
>*The Bunyip Hole,* Angus and Robertson, 1958
>*The Rocks of Honey,* Angus and Robertson, 1960
>*The Feather Star,* Hutchinson, 1962; Harcourt Brace, 1963
>*Down to Earth,* Hutchinson, 1965; Harcourt Brace, 1965
>*I Own the Racecourse!,* Hutchinson, 1968; as *A Racecourse for Andy,* Harcourt Brace, 1968
>*An Older Kind of Magic,* Hutchinson, 1972; Harcourt Brace, 1972
>*The Nargun and the Stars,* Hutchinson, 1973; Atheneum, 1974
>*The Ice Is Coming,* Hutchinson, 1977; Atheneum, 1977
>*Night Outside,* not published in Britain; Atheneum, 1985
>*The Dark Bright Water,* Hutchinson, 1979; Atheneum, 1979
>*Behind the Wind,* Hutchinson, 1981; as *Journey Behind the Wind,* Atheneum, 1981
>*A Little Fear,* Hutchinson, 1983; Atheneum, 1983

MATTHEW ARNOLD
>*The Forsaken Merman,* first published 1849

BETSY BYARS
>*The House of Wings,* Viking, 1972; Bodley Head, 1973

ALAN GARNER
>*The Owl Service,* Collins, London, 1967; Walck, 1968

VIRGINIA HAMILTON
  M. C. Higgins, the Great, Macmillan, New York, 1974; Hamish
  Hamilton, 1975

DANIEL KIRKPATRICK, editor
  Twentieth Century Children's Writers, St Martin's Press, 1978

URSULA LE GUIN
  A Wizard of Earthsea, Parnassus, 1968; Gollancz, 1971
  The Tombs of Atuan, Atheneum, 1971; Gollancz, 1972
  The Farthest Shore, Atheneum, 1972; Gollancz, 1973
  The Ones Who Walk Away From Omelas, in *Norton An-
  thology of Short Fiction* compiled by R. V. Cassill, 2nd edi-
  tion, Norton, 1981

PENELOPE LIVELY
  A Stitch in Time, Heinemann, 1976; Dutton, 1976

PHILIPPA PEARCE
  Tom's Midnight Garden, Oxford, 1958; Lippincott, 1959

MACHO MAN, AUSTRALIAN STYLE

Ivan Southall

Ivan Southall's first nine books for children are escapist pulp fiction about a super-hero, Squadron Leader Simon Black of the Royal Australian Air Force, "a form of propaganda," Southall himself says in an essay called "Depth and Direction," "dedicated to the proposition that decorated former officers, particularly of the R.A.A.F., were the hope of the world"—

> Simon possessed in incredible measure virtue, honour, righteous anger, courage and inventiveness. Every incredible difficulty he cheerfully overcame with dignity, grandeur, and a very stiff upper lip . . . these books were limiting the development not only of the reader, but of the writer. Their artificial morality was in fact touching everything else I wrote.

Squadron Leader Black was abandoned, and Southall began to write novels in which assorted groups of children face disasters, both natural and man-made—flood, fire, plane crash, car crash, and so on; with these stories he established himself as a serious and worthwhile writer. *Bread and Honey* (1970) marked a third change in direction: there were no more outside disasters; instead a concentration on one central character and the changes in that character caused by people and events.

Southall is the most popular and most widely discussed Australian author for children; he is also probably the most talented. His greatest strength is his ability to create fear, danger and excitement—the passages in *Ash Road* describing the advance of the bush fire and the children's reactions to it, and the chapter in *To the Wild Sky* in which Gerald takes over the controls of the aeroplane, are possibly the most thrilling, nail-biting episodes in all modern children's fiction. Southall is also very good at creating a large cast of characters, both adult and child, and with a few deft strokes sharply differentiating them one from another; and excellent on small-town life—evoking the ethos of a whole community, its strains and tensions, its pastimes and pleasures. *Hills End, Ash Road* and *Josh* are models of their kind.

But he is too prolific and repetitive. *Bread and Honey* and *Josh* are essentially the same novel about the same character, though the settings and the period are different; and in several of the books one feels there are too many words—particularly in *Bread and Honey, Josh, Matt and Jo,* and *What About Tomorrow,* as the form these stories take is that of an interior monologue, with the central character's thoughts and preoccupations revolving round a few themes that vary little from one book to another. But the main problem is that, impressive and exciting though Southall can be, he is rarely enjoyable. To read his books one after another is an endurance test. There is no stillness, no calm, almost nothing that is ordinary. John Rowe Townsend, in *A Sense of Story,* said "a parody of Southall could be written under the title of *Tether's End*"—though he did not comment if it was the central character's tether or the reader's.

Why is this so? It has a great deal, it seems to me, to do with the nature and morality of Southall's world, the endless hoops through which he puts (indeed, when not at his best he manipulates) his characters; the fact that ultimately, though one may admire the children he creates, one doesn't like them very much. It's a narrow world, and each succeeding book shows little broadening of its vision. It's white, lower middle-class, and essentially Anglo-Saxon. There is not an Aboriginal to be seen in Southall's Australia (though Carol in *To the Wild Sky* had an Aboriginal ancestor) and the only mention of Aboriginal culture is the cave paintings in *Hills End;* nor is there any reference to Australia being a meeting-ground, like the United States, of immigrants of every race, color and creed. It's an old-fashioned world in which most people go to church; if someone swears it's under his breath and considered reprehensible; it's extraordinarily prudish—Colin, in *To the Wild Sky,* is mature enough to rescue a friend from a plane that has crashed into the sea, but then hides in the bush because he can't stand the thought of girls seeing him in his underwear; and it's a world of traditional sex roles and masculine virtues. Strength, dignity, courage and common sense are constantly stressed, but there is no fun, and not a lot of affection. The sex stereotyping becomes tedious—the contrasts between Hugh and Joan, in *The Fox Hole* for example, are characteristic of all the books: "Hugh breaking a window or Hugh falling out of a tree or Hugh putting worms in his sisters' beds," whereas Joan "could make her bed and wash the dishes and use the vacuum cleaner and bake a chocolate cake."

The only one-parent family in Southall is in *King of the Sticks* and its sequel, *The Golden Goose* (two novels in which he belatedly seems to be breaking out of his self-imposed straightjacket). The slang seems old-fashioned—hi-ya, gee, golly, gosh, gee willikins, even fair dinkum. But most tiresome of all is the obsession most of Southall's male children have with becoming a man, a process, it would seem, that is very difficult; only to be achieved through a series of initiation experiences that require physical endurance, a clear head in dangerous situations, and toughness of mind and body. These boys don't seem to enjoy being children or teenagers—Peter, in *Ash Road*, "was running into manhood and leaving childhood behind. He hated childhood"; Gerald, in *To the Wild Sky*, "for six hours, like a giant . . . had burst the bonds of boyhood and become a man." There is little idea of each stage of life being a valid and rewarding experience in itself, that becoming a man isn't something to be striven for like passing an exam but is a natural process, whether one is strong, dignified, brave and sensible—or not. Girls, of course, are a part of this supposed man's world; most Southall males feel that to kiss a girl is a very important milestone to reach, but they never think much beyond that, apart from vague and misty imaginings like running hand in hand over mountains, and "protecting" females. The complexities of boy/girl relationships are rarely discussed, and sexual activity, even in thought, with the exception of Matt in *Matt and Jo,* doesn't exist. Spontaneity and tenderness are lost in the need to preserve the macho male façade—Normie in *Chinaman's Reef*

Is Ours wants to say to his girlfriend when they're stuck on a
roof-top: "'Cherry Cooper; I'd have died if you'd fallen off.'
But he was too shy to say anything as sloppy as that."

One feels sorry for these children, for emotions stunted by
received attitudes, for imprisonment in a rigid set of values
that seems more suited to the pioneering days of nineteenth-
century Australia than to the complex, multi-racial, urban
society of Australia in the second half of the twentieth century. One is intensely irritated by the constant use of words
like "manly" or "unmanly" and phrases like "Be a man"—
does Josh play "manly sports" Aunt Clara asks; "puddles for
splashing in if a fellow weren't supposed to be half a man";
"his teeth were chattering in an unmanly way"; "she hoped
that the man she married some day would have a jaw like this,
clean and square, manly but kind"; "Wallace was a big chap,
burly, almost as rugged as a man; a strong character, Graham
thought"; "Somehow the right words seemed to be there and
Paul said them like a man"; or, an extreme example, this,
"Like Dad says . . . the finer things are for men. Women don't
understand. Shakespeare was a man. Michelangelo was a man.
Mozart was a man. The Beatles are men. Women are slobs."
This world, I suspect, is a world of fantasy in the pejorative
sense; not the real world.

Of the "disaster" novels, *Ash Road* is the most convincing,
Southall's finest book despite the weakness of its conclusion;
in the first, *Hills End,* there is too much manipulation of
events for the plot to be really credible. To achieve a minimum number of unpleasant deaths, Southall empties the remote timber settlement of Hills End of its population when
the storm and the ensuing flood destroy it; most of the inhabitants are miles away on the town's annual outing, and a group
of children and their teacher are in the mountains, discovering, with unbelievable ease, Aboriginal cave paintings. It's too
happy a coincidence. There is also a tendency to pile on the
agony (or the author may be running short of ideas); the
children not only have to fend for themselves, adultless, in
the wrecked buildings, they are forced to cope with a savage
bull and a fire in the store they have chosen to live in. Southall also tends to jump the gun: the opening sentence, though
an arresting invitation to read on—"There was no indication

that Saturday morning that the little town of Hills End was doomed"—tells us too much too quickly. But the characterization is very good, and the children's reactions to events and their behavior in the crisis are entirely believable. The writing is a little hesitant at times, but the descriptions of the storm come off well—

> The heavens split apart and rain and hail fell from the clouds. A mighty wind roared up the valley, and sheets of iron were blasted from rooftops. Chimneys collapsed. Outbuildings vanished. Trees split like sticks, and Frank Tobias couldn't reach shelter. He couldn't stand up. He was beaten into the ground. Again and again he tried to run. Again and again he was stunned and driven back to the earth. He couldn't see in any direction for more than twenty yards. He couldn't draw a breath without pain. Crashing ice and water were as near to solid as they could be.

In *Ash Road* there is no feeling that the author is pulling the strings or lessening the impact of events by referring to them before they happen; only Mr George's heart attack could be said to be an unnecessary piling on of the agony, and the writing is much more confident than in *Hills End.* The sound of the fire siren had "a strange ability to drift about in the air; at one moment close and immediate, a few moments later distant and far away; like a ship on a violent sea heaving into sight then vanishing into troughs." We are constantly aware of the weather and its ability to affect our mood— "that horrid wind roaring in the timber, blustering against him, raising puffs of dust from every area of dry ground, imposing upon the birds extraordinary patterns of flight, flaking leaves from trees, snapping dead twigs."

> And he was frightened of the sky. It was so threatening, so ugly, so unlike anything he had ever seen. It was a hot brown mantle over the earth with pieces breaking off it, little black pieces of ash; an oppressive mantle that did not prevent the penetration of the sun's heat but imprisoned it, added to it, and magnified the hostility of the day.
>
> It was an angry day; not just wild or rough, but savage

in itself, actively angry against every living thing. It
hated plants and trees and birds and animals, and they
wilted from its hatred or withered up and died or pant-
ed in distress in shady places. Above all, it hated Peter.

The relationships between families and within families in a
small community are in this book Southall at his absolute
best—he never again did it so well—and the delaying of the
fire's arrival until the last quarter of the story is a magnificently effective device for screwing up the tension. The only
failure, and it is a serious failure, is the ending: having written
himself into a corner where all his main characters are about
to be burned to death, Southall produces the ultimate cliché
of a deus ex machina to rescue them, a convenient thun-
derstorm that puts the fire out. Why he chose to do this is
very puzzling, for he had given us many hints about where
the characters might find safety—down Grandpa Tanner's
well, under the Fairhalls' house, even wrapped in the Buck-
inghams' soaking wet carpets. Clem Scale's illustrations, by
the way, are perhaps the worst to adorn a modern children's
novel: almost hilariously bad.

  The Fox Hole, a book for younger children, not more than a
long short story, was the successor to *Ash Road;* its main
character, Ken, is a withdrawn, intense, emotional child, almost neurotic, a reworking of Peter Fairhall at a younger age.
Southall was to return again and again to this boy in subsequent books, though he has different names and backgrounds; he is Josh, Michael in *Bread and Honey,* Sam in
What About Tomorrow, and, to a lesser extent, Matt in *Matt
and Jo* and Max in *Finn's Folly.* One feels that he is probably
the boy Southall was himself. The disaster in *The Fox Hole* is
Ken falling down an abandoned mine-shaft, and the excitement and fear—as usual very well done—derive from the
fact that the cushion of humus and debris on which he lands
may give way and plunge him to his death. There are also—as
usual—some well-observed family relationships, and characteristic improbabilities. The behavior of Ken's uncle is not
convincing. It is unlikely that a fond uncle would decide, as
he does, to rescue his nephew without the assistance of the
police and the fire brigade; and his temporary deflection from
his task by the discovery of gold in the mine-shaft is also far-

fetched. But the writing is excellent. This is Ken listening to noises in the night—

> He heard water running, an odd sound, eternal, unending, like glass crinkling or thousands of little diamonds rushing around inside a box; he heard breezes in the leaves as though the pages of books were turning; he heard whispers like distant conversations, like trees talking to each other; he heard insects humming and drumming; he heard splashes, croaking frogs, rustling twigs. He heard the earth stirring and the sky sighing. He heard the world turning round, creaking like an old wheel.

Let the Balloon Go is a companion-piece to *The Fox Hole,* a second brief story for younger children, and the disaster this time is almost its mirror image—instead of being stuck down a hole, the central character is stuck at the top of a tree. For once the macho attitudes of a Southall boy seem right and proper; John is a spastic, and suffers from his unnecessarily over-protective parents. He has to climb the tree in order to prove that he is not a second-class citizen. Interestingly, it's the adults who panic more than he does, and who behave rather badly—for which Southall was unjustifiably attacked by the critics when the book first came out. But *Let the Balloon Go* is not as successful as *The Fox Hole.* It should produce a dizzying sense of vertigo, as does the climbing of the church steeple in Alan Garner's *The Stone Book,* or the descent inside the chimney in Lucy Boston's *The Chimneys of Green Knowe,* but it curiously fails to do this—perhaps the actual climbing of the tree is delayed too long, and John is not worried by it. Much of the book is a monologue, a boy thinking aloud, so it looks forward to *Bread and Honey* and *Josh,* but it's a first experiment with this technique, and Southall doesn't yet know how to handle it successfully.

If one can accept as possible the only adult in an aeroplane, the pilot, dying of a heart attack, leaving a thirteen-year-old boy to fly himself and the other children on board to safety, then nothing in *To the Wild Sky* will divert the reader's attention from the sheer fright and terror of the masterly scenes in which Gerald attempts to stay in the air and eventually land; it's Southall writing from his gut, a recreation, one imagines, of his own experiences as a pilot in the Second World War:

He had never held the controls except in straight and
level flight, and this aircraft was going down, still going
down, yawing from side to side, its altitude constantly
changing, its instrument readings meaningless, and the
pressures relayed from the wheel and the rudder bar
wholly alarming, wholly confusing.

He didn't know where to begin. All he could see was
red earth and a leaning horizon apparently above his
head, a horizon that leaned first one way and then
another . . .

. . . There was a pause, not in movement or in time or
in events, but in the processes of Gerald's thoughts, a
pause when nothing happened, when his only awareness was the dull and approaching certainty of death. It
numbed him as though his body and brain had suffered a
crushing physical blow. It held him motionless, trans-
fixed, hypnotised, stiff-necked, and stiff-backed.

And marvellous, too, is the elation, the sheer joy Gerald experiences when he finds he can, to a limited extent, control the
plane.

His problems are that he has no idea where he is, and he
hasn't the first idea of how to make a landing. He eventually
crashes into the sea, in shallow water off an uninhabited trop-
ical island, which is, maybe, in the Gulf of Carpentaria; it's a
bit hard to believe that the only injury this causes is one
bruised ankle. The book falls into two distinct halves—the
first in the aeroplane, the second on the island with the characters struggling for survival. *To the Wild Sky* ends with the
children discovering they can make fire, and with the possibility (enough hints are given) that they will find food and
water—comparisons with *Lord of the Flies* are inevitable.
Many critics have felt that this conclusion is unsatisfactory
because we are not told whether the children are rescued; do
they die, or—even—do they survive but are not rescued? It
seems fairly clear to me that the children won't die; they have
fire and they'll soon be able to eat and drink. It is quite
reasonable as a conclusion: we don't need to have all the ends
tied up. But Southall was pressed to write a sequel, and,
seventeen years later, *A City Out of Sight* was published. "I
have received many pleas—very many indeed—to go on
with the story," he says in its preface.

It adds little to what was achieved in *To the Wild Sky;* choosing to confine himself (except for the last two pages) entirely to the day following the ending of the previous book, he has no room to develop the characters and their relationships. What is new is interesting—Carol manages to kill a pig (good that for once it's a girl rather than a boy who does this), and Bruce discovers that he fancies Carol, which is obviously going to cause difficulties with Gerald. But the novel ends before this can be gone into. The last two pages, excerpts from a news bulletin eleven years after the events of the story, produce more questions than answers. The lost children, now adults, are still on the island; this is the first time they have been sighted. They were observed from an aircraft, "six adults and three children" living in "a well-established, well-ordered small settlement." Whose children, one asks. There were four boys and two girls in the plane that crashed; what complexities of what relationships led to three offspring? (Particularly when one remembers that Colin and Mark are brothers, and Bruce and Jan are twin brother and sister.) I don't think, however, that Southall is going to write another sequel and answer *those* questions; at least not for children.

The final two books of his "disaster" period are disasters indeed—artistic disasters. Had he continued to write in this vein, there would be no need of John Rowe Townsend's *Tether's End;* Southall would have written it himself. When *Finn's Folly* was published it caused a storm of protest; critics found it terrifying, repulsive and quite unsuitable for children. Catherine Storr, less emotively and more correctly, identified the problem in her essay, "Fear and Evil in Children's Books," as one of credibility—grand guignol had replaced reality; *Finn's Folly* was depressing rather than frightening. The central event of the novel is a crash between a car and a lorry in which the adults are killed—very disturbing, yes, but not, I think, unsuitable for children: it happens every day of the week all over the world, and there are good reasons why fiction for young people should concern itself with such events—they may at least help the reader to come to terms with a similar, real-life catastrophe. When, however, we learn that the crash occurs in dense freezing fog; that the

lorry was carrying barrels of cyanide which is now poisoning
the hillside and covering the children's hands and faces; that
one of the kids is mentally retarded and has run away; that no
one has the sense to fetch the police or an ambulance; that
the eldest boy falls in love with the girl trapped in the cab of
the lorry—then we cease to care or be interested because we
can't believe in anything the author is saying or doing. John
Rowe Townsend says of *Finn's Folly*, in *A Sense of Story*, "in
the absence of belief, the question of moral and emotional
acceptability does not arise." The writing is good—

> The sobs of the boy were different from the strange
> words that had floated for so long in the silence, the
> words that had had little to do with time or place and
> even now seemed like inscriptions read from
> headstones in cemeteries where pioneers were buried

—but the reader is being manipulated all the time, put
through hoops as are the characters. *Finn's Folly* is sheer bad
taste, a major error of judgment.

Chinaman's Reef Is Ours also has a good idea very badly
handled, and the problem is again one of credibility. The
setting is a remote mining community in the desert, once
bustling and active, but now virtually a ghost town in which
only a handful of people live; the company that owns both
the town and the mine want to redevelop the site, which
means the destruction of all the existing property. The end of
a way of life: the remaining inhabitants decide to resist, by
force if necessary. For once in Southall the position of the
women is crucial. They turn out to be stronger than the men
or the children—their lives are limited and full of drudgery;
they have little to lose. At least the men can work and drink,
the children can grow up and move away. The women are
memorable. It could have led to a tense, exciting novel, with
some good atmospheric writing that evokes the town and the
surrounding landscape; but only the odd sentence stands out
in the few moments of scene painting: "Brick piers and arch-
es were there, like parts of ancient temples left behind by
civilizations centuries extinct," or—

> Iron foundations were there set in crazed concrete
> yellow with dust and rust and age. Grass, as dry as splin-
> tered bone, clumped in the cracks. Huge old wheels
> were there, too heavy to roll away, from steam engines
> that had worked the stampers fifty years ago; monstrous
> wheels entangled in scrub and creeping vines . . .

The chief defect is the plot. It's impossible to believe that a
mining company would be allowed to demolish a town
without telling its inhabitants it was going to do so; that it
would send, without prior warning, its bulldozers to do the
job on a Sunday; that its demolition gang wouldn't know that
people still lived there; that the telephone operator, at the
moment of crisis, would refuse to put calls through because
one of the kids insults her; that the chief architect of re-
sistance, the aged Sunday School teacher, Sadie Stevenson,
would absent herself from the action when it occurs . . . and
so on. It is not a failure on the scale of *Finn's Folly,* but, as
with that book, the reader gets bored because he cannot
believe the author is offering any kind of truth. What Southall
has done is to eclipse events that would span months—the
different claims of the mining company and the townspeo-
ple—into one day so he can artificially jack up the tension:
it's a cheat, a trick, and it leads to poor writing, a phoney kind
of tension that isn't real tension at all—

> Cherry's father stepped clear of the prime mover,
> turned from it, and started walking back to town, to-
> wards the women and children whose dark and brood-
> ing stillness was unlike an Australian scene.

"Was unlike an Australian scene"—it doesn't mean anything.
Bread and Honey has a characteristic Southall hero, a
young teenage boy, Michael, who is trying to make sense of
his life and his relationships with other people, in particular
with his father, his grandmother, and the boy next door. He is
in turn both rational and irrational, mature and downright
silly; thoroughly mixed-up. It is a good depiction of the confusion that many kids experience in their teens. He is, as ever
with Southall, preoccupied with the demands of being a man,
but, untypically, he is not prudish about his body—he likes

taking all his clothes off when no one is about and rolling around in the grass. Trouble with the neighbors begins when Mrs Farlow next door observes this and tells his father. Not much happens in *Bread and Honey*—there is no fast-moving story-line, nothing that demands superhuman courage. It is Anzac Day, and Michael intends to see the parade, but he never gets there; he talks instead to a girl he meets on the beach, a strange loner much younger than he is—the best parts of the novel are the weird, circular conversations between these two—and he proves something to himself by fighting one of the local bullies and winning. Michael's inner thoughts, which are concerned with such matters as family, friendship, illusion and reality, violence—his fight with Flackie is in ironic contrast to the solemn ceremony, taking place in the distance, of commemorating the dead of two world wars—are what the book is about. It's a short, almost slight piece, but a welcome change from the two previous novels; it seems entirely unforced, quite unlike the unreal situations of *Finn's Folly* and *Chinaman's Reef Is Ours.* This is one of the key passages; Mike has just come indoors after his naked romp in the garden—

> He dressed over the top of the mud and the wet and the pollen and the grass. He thought about washing it off, but then deliberately dressed; the idea of a shower seemed wrong somehow. It had been terrific out there on the grass; how could he wash *that* off? Like washing something sacred off. It was a fact; a fellow washed half his life down the sink: every game he ever played, nosebleeds, hours of sleep, bread and honey, sweat, inky fingers—washed them all down the sink. Swirled them down the plug hole into the earth and then forgot.

Josh and *What About Tomorrow* are very similar to *Bread and Honey:* they are concerned with teenage boys too thoughtful for their years, emotional and social misfits. Both novels have a strong autobiographical flavor. *Josh* is dedicated to "'Aunt Clara' in fond recall"—Aunt Clara's relationship with Josh, loving, stormy, sensitive and insensitive, is the core of the book—and its central character was born in the same year as Southall; Sam's teenage life in *What About*

Tomorrow is inter-leaved with accounts of his career in his twenties as a fighter pilot in World War Two. Southall, it seems, is using the material of his own early years. As in *Bread and Honey,* nothing much happens; Josh, staying at his great-aunt's house in the country, is bullied by the local kids, and comes to terms with that and himself by leaving before his visit is due to end and walking home to Melbourne, a hundred miles away. The bad feeling and the violence are partly his own fault—Aunt Clara says of him, "Everything so intense. God didn't give us our emotions to turn our lives into a tightrope walk"—and partly her fault, but some of the blame has to be attached to the locals, who wrongly assume Josh is like Clara's other great-nephews, only interested in her money. Josh doesn't learn as much from his experiences as does Michael in *Bread and Honey;* by turning his back on what has happened he is illustrating another of Clara's comments about him—"Heaven preserve me from pig-headed males who want to die for their principles as if in ten minutes it's still going to matter. Too perfect to live with." *Josh* has some very convincing characterization, excellent dialogue, and a deft portrayal of people in a social context; the cross-indexing of relationships in small-town life is done as well as it is in the earlier novels.

In *What About Tomorrow* the social milieu is different; Sam's background is working-class and poverty-stricken. He works as a paper-boy, but, when his inefficient and ancient bicycle—and the newspapers—are wrecked by a tram, he knows he will lose his job: he is so appalled by the prospect of the economic ruin this will bring to his family that he runs away. Nothing very extraordinary occurs as a result—he is befriended by some well-meaning and helpful adults, and in the space of two days he falls in love with three different girls. The third girl, Mary, is the most important. His clumsy experiences with the first two enable him to cope with Mary more maturely; she is the woman in the World War Two passages waiting for the return of Sam, her fighter pilot husband. Stylistically, *What About Tomorrow* is a change from anything Southall had written previously. It is a much more amusing book, and it also seems to show the influence of Leon Garfield. Sam is not unlike the central character of *Smith,* and

there is even a similarity in some of the events, the bath scene
for instance; and Sam stuck under the church and unable to
get out recalls Smith in the chimneys of Newgate gaol. The
writing, too, suggests Garfield—

> Sam—in the ninth grade, five feet eight inches tall (like-
> ly to go five inches taller if he managed to stay alive until
> he grew up—not a certainty, some used to reckon),
> light-boned, light in every way actually, but winner of
> one ferocious fist fight behind the incinerator at school.

Between *Josh* and *What About Tomorrow,* Southall wrote
Matt and Jo, a very short novel about a boy and a girl falling
in love as they observe each other through the glass in a door
that connects two compartments of a crowded train, the train
they catch every day to go to school. The monologue inside
the heads of both characters is fine until they get off the train
and meet—at this point dialogue is needed, but Southall uses
it so sparingly that most of the second half of the book also
takes place inside the heads of each of the characters: the
reader feels frustrated because there seems to be no real
coming together. Also, what happens doesn't convince. Matt
and Jo decide to play truant, catch a train to the end of the
line, find that they don't really have much to say to each
other, and go home; the book ends with Matt telling Mr
McNally, his English teacher, the events of the day. (Or is he
still monologuing in his head? Is the whole book a fantasy
inside his head? It isn't clear.) The style throughout is hyper-
bolic in the extreme; no kid, it seems to this reader, ever felt
or thought like this. Most of it is too much on one note,
screaming fever pitch. At least, however, here is a teenage
boy who's aware of sex; "You could say I've got the ground-
ing, sir, in the mechanics of the art," Matt says to himself.
"There are plenty of books to tell you that. So much they tell
you they almost put you off." It's not something he can discuss with his mother; "She wouldn't know what he was talking about. How could she? Living her protected life . . . And
being a mother. Sort of holy." But—

> It's not like something you can shut away in a drawer
> every time—or forget about every time—or say no to
> every time—or run an extra lap around the oval to

sweat it out of your system every time. You know that, sir, surely. Is that why you looked so sad? I mean, *you* grew up, Mr McNally. Was it all that bad?

King of the Sticks and its sequel, *The Golden Goose,* are set in the Australian bush in the nineteenth century; they are difficult novels—the writing is terse and elliptical, and all the characters are so odd as to be almost crazy—but the perceptive, intelligent teenager may well get something out of both. The central character is Custard (Cuthbert), the son of a widow who owns a small farm in the middle of nowhere; he is a strange child, silent and withdrawn, given to writing poetry in his head. He has the ability to divine water—but, unfortunately for him, his older brother Seth, an alcoholic bully, tells people when he is drunk that Custard can divine gold. He is kidnapped by the sons of a half-mad preacher who think he will make them rich; their father, to save his children from being hanged for this crime, himself kidnaps Custard and forces him to search for gold. Custard's mother, Rebecca, who is also not quite sane (the murder of her husband, the long years of loneliness, and having to look after Bella, her crippled daughter, have taken their toll), sets out to look for him; she eventually finds him and takes him home.

The plot sounds bizarre, but there are many pleasures and rewards in both books. For once Southall takes time to describe the Australian landscape; "Who can comprehend this country?" Rebecca asks. "Who can stand it?"

> Canyons, like great splits in the earth, as if about to split farther, lay below her. Endless, endless were the treetops. Troubled oceans of treetops were there, through which she had to pass. A million gnarled trees were there rooted among a million razor edges, and the softness of the blue distances was an illusion.

Rebecca is a superb piece of characterization; larger than life, ferocious as a tigress in the protection of her children, kowtowing to no one, not even the Governor of the State, who calls at her house. Rebecca offers him tea—

"It's not time for tea," the Governor barked.

"It is, if I say so, in my house."

One of the most interesting aspects of both books is that the characters are not easily divided into goodies and baddies; there is a moral ambiguity about everyone. Preacher Tom's sons are not so much evil as ignorant and easily led astray, and Custard actually enjoys the brief time he is forced to spend with them; though kidnapped, he feels free, ironically—freer than he was at home, subjected to Seth's constant demands and orders: "Time to bring the cow up, kid. Feed the horses. Chop the wood. Hurry. Scurry. Jump to it." He is less happy with Preacher Tom, but weeps when he dies; he explains, later, to Rebecca—"I can't stand the strain of losin' me dads." Rebecca, too, might not have lost Custard in the first place had she attacked the preacher's sons with less viciousness and more forethought. Finally, Custard is partly responsible for his own fate—he could leave Preacher Tom at any time, but he can never plan anything (like his mother). He is a ditherer.

Preacher Tom is pure Garfield: a bogus actor like Dan Coventry in *The Sound of Coaches* and also the kindly quack, Dr Carmody in *Black Jack;* the situation between him and Custard is similar to that between Black Jack and Tolly Dorking, a kidnap that turns into a sort of voluntary stay. Stylistically both books are at times reminiscent of Garfield in his more Dickensian vein, at other times less obviously so—the influence is transmuted into something else, a satisfying richness and density that Southall has not achieved before:

> Stars were out there in the warm silent night, and frogs where the earth was wet and crickets where the earth was dry, and an owl. And many, many things more that Custard saw but couldn't see. Shapes breathing behind trees, stirrings in the air where spirits roamed, creeping feet without legs to lift them from the ground, eyes without heads, hands without arms, and strangely-shaped words looking for voices to give them sound.
>
> "Mum," Bella said, swishing at the jug, "there's not much water here."
>
> "Then leave the tea until we need it more."

> Their voices were whispers. Perhaps the people in the
> night listened at the walls. Perhaps the spirits were
> spies. Perhaps the eyes. Perhaps the words would make
> messages and the hands would write them down and the
> feet would hurry them off to where the enemy
> crouched plotting the next move. And who, thought
> Custard, could say about the owl? Upon whose side was
> he? Seeing all from his bough.

The Long Night Watch is to some extent a return to Southall's earlier preoccupations—a large cast of adults and teenagers, a desert island, an authoritarian father-figure, the
events of the Second World War. The plot revolves round a
strange religious community, the Society for World Order
Under Divine Rule, who leave Australia in the summer of
1941 to live on a remote Pacific island near the Equator; they
are waiting and watching for the Second Coming, or something much like that, but after Pearl Harbor their watch is as
much for invading Japanese as angels descending from the
heavens. There is an interesting parallel with John Rowe
Townsend's *The Islanders,* which is also about a peculiar
community of people on a remote Pacific island. Townsend is
interested in the clash between the island's inhabitants and
outside visitors; Southall is more concerned with the relationships within the community, particularly between its
teenagers—intellectual Hogan and the rather earthier John,
who is in love with Kerry, and whose affections are unre-
quited. (She is in love with a man who is older than her
father, Brigadier Palmer, the leader of the community.) The
island is eventually attacked by the Japanese.

It is an exciting, well-told tale, with some pointed comments en route on racism, mass hysteria, the plight of ordinary people living in a totalitarian state, democracy and dic-
tatorship. Analogies between the Brigadier and Hitler are
suggested:

> There stood the Brigadier at the edge of the stage,
> transported, transformed.
> *"Brigadier! Brigadier!"*
> In Europe they were rising in the great halls and on
> the parade grounds. "Heil Hitler! Heil Hitler!"

But matters are more complex than this: the Brigadier is essentially an honest man, tortured by doubts, trying to do what is best for everybody. It's his followers who see him as some kind of Messiah—he is really quite ordinary. There are some neat comments on people's behavior and attitudes—"Mrs Shuffle liked to be regarded as an Anglophile, though some with a streak of malice called her a cliché." She was also "considered to be a widow woman, though no one remembered the funeral and no one had sent flowers."

> Shufflebottom was the family name, fully spelt out, and pronounced Shaf'll-boe-thum by Mrs Shuffle, when pressed, as at Polling Booths on Voting Days, but differently by Mr Shuffle who said, "What the hell."

Ivan Southall and Patricia Wrightson are the two outstanding authors of contemporary Australian children's fiction, and though they are quite unlike each other in style, content and aims, they are often compared and contrasted. Southall is probably the more gifted writer; but remarkable, indeed brilliant, though some parts of his novels are (*Ash Road, To the Wild Sky, King of the Sticks, The Golden Goose*), I don't think he has achieved the kind of perfection one finds in Patricia Wrightson—in *I Own the Racecourse!, The Nargun and the Stars* or *A Little Fear.*

REFERENCES

IVAN SOUTHALL
> *Hills End,* Angus and Robertson, 1962; St Martin's Press, 1963
> *Ash Road,* Angus and Robertson, 1965; St Martin's Press, 1966
> *The Fox Hole,* Methuen, 1967; St Martin's Press, 1967
> *To the Wild Sky,* Angus and Robertson, 1967; St Martin's Press, 1967
> *Let the Balloon Go,* Methuen, 1968; St Martin's Press, 1968
> "Depth and Direction" in *The Horn Book Magazine,* July 1968
> *Finn's Folly,* Angus and Robertson, 1969; St Martin's Press, 1969
> *Chinaman's Reef Is Ours,* Angus and Robertson, 1970; St Martin's Press, 1970

Bread and Honey, Angus and Robertson, 1970; as *Walk a Mile and Get Nowhere,* Bradbury, 1970

Josh, Angus and Robertson, 1971; Macmillan, New York, 1972

Matt and Jo, Angus and Robertson, 1974; Macmillan, New York, 1973

What About Tomorrow, Angus and Robertson, 1977; Macmillan, New York, 1977

King of the Sticks, Methuen, 1979; Greenwillow, 1979

The Golden Goose, Methuen, 1981; Greenwillow, 1981

The Long Night Watch, Methuen, 1983; Farrar Straus, New York, 1984

A City Out of Sight, Angus and Robertson, 1985; not published in the U.S.A.

L. M. BOSTON

The Chimneys of Green Knowe, Faber, 1958; as *Treasure of Green Knowe,* Harcourt Brace, 1958

LEON GARFIELD

Smith, Constable, 1967; Pantheon, 1967

Black Jack, Longman, 1968; Pantheon, 1969

The Sound of Coaches, Kestrel, 1974; Viking, 1974

ALAN GARNER

The Stone Book, Collins, London, 1976; Collins + World, 1978

WILLIAM GOLDING

Lord of the Flies, Faber, 1954; Putnam, 1959

CATHERINE STORR

"Fear and Evil in Children's Books" in *Children's Literature in Education,* March 1970

JOHN ROWE TOWNSEND

A Sense of Story, Longman, 1971; Lippincott, 1971; revised edition as *A Sounding of Storytellers,* Kestrel, 1979; Lippincott, 1979

The Islanders, Oxford, 1981; Harper, 1981

PATRICIA WRIGHTSON

I Own the Racecourse!, Hutchinson, 1968; as *A Racecourse for Andy,* Harcourt Brace, 1968

The Nargun and the Stars, Hutchinson, 1973; Atheneum, 1974

A Little Fear, Hutchinson, 1983; Atheneum, 1983

BLOOD, THUNDER, MUCK AND BULLETS

Leon Garfield

All Leon Garfield's books are set in the eighteenth or early nineteenth century, but he is not a historical novelist in the conventional sense. There are few signs in his stories of painstaking research or attention to period detail; references to important political events are rare; and there is not much attempt to reproduce the language of the period. Indeed, many of his characters in their speech use modern idioms and slang. Garfield himself says in his cssay, "Writing for Childhood," that "the eighteenth century—or my idea of it—is more a locality than a time. And in this curious locality I find that I can reprcsent quite contemporary characters more vividly than I could otherwise." The comment is interesting, because Garfield does, manage to suggest to the reader that he or she is entering an invented, imaginary locale—which is the technique used by the writers of fantasy, rather than the method of the historical novelist.

Garfield's sources are literary rather than historical. He has often been called the children's Dickens or the children's Stevenson, but only his first book, *Jack Holborn*—a tale of adventure and piracy on the high seas, with, almost inevitably, treasure as an important motif—could truly be labelled Stevensonian. As first novels go, *Jack Holborn* is superior to many, and it shows immediately Garfield's greatest asset—a gift for exciting, action-packed narrative. Few contemporary writers of children's fiction can tell a story as well as Leon Garfield. He subsequently wrote more complex, more subtle books than *Jack Holborn,* which is marred a little by the author being too concerned with what is happening now rather than what is going to happen next; but it certainly keeps the reader turning the pages. The Stevenson influence is there not only in the setting, but in the characterization and in the style. The ambiguous, amoral figure of Solomon Trumpet recalls Long John Silver; Jack Holborn himself is a latter-day Jim Hawkins (though his adolescent emotional changes are entirely his own), and some of the descriptive passages remind one of *Treasure Island:*

> It must have been close on mid-day, for the top of the mist was turning to gold and the great yellow sun came rolling and melting out of it. Out to sea the billowing whiteness began to shiver and be drawn up, like a playhouse curtain, and there lay the great waters again, glittering in the sun. Now was the crew all born again—and we were no more alone by the infformd rail.

The major influence in Garfield's second novel, *Devil-in-the-Fog,* and in much of his later work, is Dickens. Garfield's London with its pickpockets, blackmailers, murderers, thieves and loose women, its teeming working class, its lawyers and judges, the fog, the smells, the exploited innocent child or the engaging street urchin at the center of the action, is Dickensian, even though this London is usually eighteenth rather than nineteenth century. The themes of *Smith, Devil-in-the-Fog, John Diamond,* and *The December Rose,* with their documents and heirlooms promising wealth or property owe a debt to *Bleak House, Great Expectations* and *Our Mutual Friend,* as does that favorite Garfield figure, the foundling child searching for his origins. Garfield often writes like Dickens, imitating him quite closely at times:

> From which I received a distinct notion that heaven was filled with a golden profusion of hoists, that never broke, nor stuck, nor poked young Treets through stained-glass windows.

This is from *Devil-in-the-Fog,* but it could have come out of the first chapter of *Great Expectations:*

> I am indebted for a belief I religiously entertained that they had all been born on their backs with their hands in their trousers-pockets, and had never taken them out in this state of existence.

There are other influences too. Many of the characters in *The Strange Affair of Adelaide Harris* and its sequel, *Bostock and Harris,* with their eccentricities and their grotesque appearances and habits, derive more from Thomas Love Peacock than Dickens; and the anarchists and bomb-throwers, as well as the vignettes of low London life in *The December Rose* are reminiscent of Conrad, particularly the Conrad of *The Secret Agent.* The world of the Red Lion inn in *The Sound of Coaches* is the Farquhar of *The Beaux' Stratagem;* the landlord with his catchphrase "As they say in the north" is very similar to Farquhar's landlord with his repeated "As the saying is." Henrietta Boston in *The Prisoners of September,* with her penchant for Gothic horror novels and her talent for playing the piano frequently and badly, is from Jane Austen— a mixture of Catherine Morland and Mary Bennet. There are echoes of Fielding—the blind justice in *Smith,* Mrs Coker in *The Prisoners of September*—and the coffin on the table at the beginning of *Black Jack,* with the apparently dead man coming to life, is used by Synge in the opening of *The Shadow of the Glen.* Smith's escape from gaol, hidden under his sister's skirts, is from Gunter Grass's *The Tin Drum.* "We lay like a dead ship upon a dead sea"—*Jack Holborn*—is Coleridge (*Kubla Khan*), and from the same novel—

> "What manner of man is he?" I asked uneasily.
> "A wery bad mannered man . . . "

is Shakespeare (*Twelfth Night*).

Other echoes, parallels, and references could be quoted. Some are undoubtedly subconscious—the residue in the mind of one man's study of literature—but many are deliberate: the devices Garfield uses to give his created worlds their authenticity. One is not accusing him of plagiarism, or pallid imitations of the real thing. He has a remarkable ability to transmute these bits of other authors into something that is wholly his own; his style is in fact highly individual, and, at its best, an excellent instrument for his purposes. Parody (even self-parody), irony, a kind of grotesque humor, and a fine eye for the ridiculous are its hallmarks. There are so many genuine "Garfieldisms" that selection is difficult, but these are a few:

All around me chimney-stacks and pots of gigantic size loomed and leaned and scowled and puffed, and balanced themselves uncomfortably on the edges of slate hills, as if they'd decided there was no such thing as gravity and were going to prove it by jumping off. (*John Diamond*)

These gaps in the doctor's talk, popping up between so that he seemed to converse in archipelagos, so to speak, were not of his own making; for he was the most continuous of men. (*Black Jack*)

There are certain individuals, generally of striking presence and volatile nature, who have the ability to become detached from their private calamities, leaving them to stink out other people's houses. They resemble lizards, who, caught by the tail, abandon that limb and rush away to grow another, leaving the severed member, at first wriggling with residual energy, to fester and smell. (*The Prisoners of September*)

"Let us pray," suggested Mr Hudson, the vicar, when the time came; and the congregation knelt—some opening their hearts for relief from private anguish and others endeavouring to close them against the prying eyes of the Almighty. (*The Strange Affair of Adelaide Harris*)

Garfield, however, can write very badly at times. As with William Mayne, the critical adulation he has received has led to over-productiveness and some third-rate work—as well as some near-masterpieces. He has written more than a dozen full-length novels for young people and a wealth of other books—ghost stories, picture books, and two volumes (with Edward Blishen) that re-tell the Greek myths; he has also written for adults, and edited collections of stories. When he is not writing well, his work suffers from cliché—"black as sin" is a favorite, "melancholy as sin," "the sinful smile of crocodiles"—and, when he is not sure of what he is doing, often at the denouement of the story, he can be unconvincing or hysterical. Or he will reach for an improbable coincidence to solve a problem. Even the otherwise excellent *Smith* and *Black Jack* falter at their climaxes. This passage from *Devil-in-the-Fog,* an extremely poor novel from beginning to end, with cardboard characterization and a thin, implausible plot, shows Garfield at his hysterical worst, using vague, emotive, abstract words in an attempt to create feelings he has not experienced, nor can really imagine:

> How he must have sweated with rage and bitterness over the outcome of the duel! Not to've quite killed his brother—and to've quite ruined himself! All of thirteen years' careful cunning—thrown away! He must have tormented himself half to death as he lay in gaol, counting, maybe, the very hours to the uttermost extinction of his hopes . . . He must have cursed himself for that fateful weakness of thirteen years before when he might have dashed out the infant's brains, and did not! His wretched wife, his futile sons—smothering him like sodden curses, sent by Hell as a punishment for evil incompletely done! His black soul screaming: "Is it too late? Even now?"

It sounds more like Mrs Radcliffe's *The Mysteries of Udolpho* than Leon Garfield.

It is perhaps best to comment, briefly, on the weaker books, before concentrating in more detail on the successes. *The Drummer Boy,* like *Devil-in-the-Fog,* is a total failure, almost unbelievably bad. It is an oddity in Garfield's work in that he abandons here his usual straightforward narrative style and realistic characterization for something more symbolic. It has an eighteenth-century setting, and is a war story in which "good," "evil" and "ambiguous" figures play out a kind of literary chess-game of life and death. The style throughout is self-indulgent and pretentiously inflated, peppered with inversions that give a bogus uplift to everything— "Gently Charity wiped her mistress's brow free of sweat," "Palely the drummer boy stared at him," "Savage eyes these children cast upon the dripping survivors." This paragraph is, alas, typical of the whole book's creaking purple upholstery:

> Somewhat tipsily they rolled into the cathedral of trees, like three huge hooded friars creeping to Vespers. Down winding aisles they moved, past chapels of oak and crypts of hawthorn and holly, all stained with the blood of the setting sun.

Long before the end, one ceases to care at all about almost anyone or anything in this story, particularly the surly drummer boy, who is oh! so beautiful and so golden-haired! Mr Shaw, the sycophantic, corrupt surgeon who falls in love with him, seems a rather more interesting person, though he is not intended to be. The homosexual stereotyping irritates: he is "good at sewing."

The Pleasure Garden has a likeable central character, a young clergyman in love; and he is made all the more convincing because he has his share of human weaknesses. Not so the villain, Dr Dormann, who is black throughout, only observed from the outside; and the usual crowd of ragged urchins one finds in most Garfield novels are, in this book, pale caricatures of Smith. The chief problem is that *The Pleasure Garden* is adult fiction trying to squeeze into the conventions of a children's book. Sexual corruption is its theme, and its most interesting ideas—the reasons why Isaac Fisk, the murdered apprentice, liked to dress in women's clothes; the freeing of his killer because the sexual deception is regarded by the authorities as grounds for justifiable homicide; is "the crime against Nature" really a crime against Nature?—are never properly explored. Nor could they be in a children's book. "All is not what it seems" and love as a weakness that invites exploitation and disillusion are common motifs in Garfield's novels, but the cynicism at the heart of this story—love is little more than a desire for the warmth of another body—is too adult a concept. There is, however, a strong narrative (we really do want to discover the murderer's identity) and there are many characteristic felicities:

> Although a widow for seven years, she still wore black, which lent her bulk a certain mystery; sometimes it was hard to see where she ended and the night began. Dr Dormann, standing beside her, looked thinner than ever; really no more than a slice of a man who might have come off Mrs Bray in a carelessly slammed door.

The Confidence Man is one of the few books of Garfield's that is based on a real incident from history. It is the story of a group of German Protestants who decide to emigrate to America to avoid religious persecution; it recounts their sufferings as they walk across Germany to Hamburg, and their subsequent hardships when they find themselves stranded in London, their leader (the con man of the title) having disappeared with all their money. This is a very ambitious, lengthy novel, well-written and interesting throughout, but it is also curiously unattractive; perhaps because the style, the "voice" of the narrator, persistently remains the author's, not that of the central character, Hans, a sharp, intelligent fourteen-year-old, who has an eye for the girls and a genius for getting into trouble. The characters do not seem to live in their own right because they are not sufficiently disengaged from the "voice," which is quirky, jokey, once again "literary"—

> The weather had deteriorated. Between about four and six o'clock, some sudden grief or disaster had turned the sky grey. As yet, this disaster had not been communicated to whomsoever it concerned, so that there was no more than a vague feeling of apprehension throughout Wapping. Sea-captains made fast their vessels, weavers took in their cloth from the bleaching-grounds, and truant apprentices, who had been looking forward to a summer's afternoon on the river, felt that God was in league with their masters, and gave up and went home.

John Diamond and *The December Rose* deserve no more than a passing mention. They are relatively recent books, and they seem to show that Garfield is running out of original ideas, though the bomb-throwing and the setting of *The December Rose*—the Thames with its bargees and river life—are new. But *The December Rose* is really *Smith* in second-hand dress. The central character, Barnacle, is Smith himself, but caricatured and one-dimensional; the opening is that of *Smith*—an illiterate boy steals something important and doesn't know its value—and details like Barnacle being forcibly washed and the chimney climbing are also taken from *Smith*. There is nothing remarkable about the plot, the dialogue, or the atmosphere, and the characters are all stereotypes. *John Diamond* also echoes *Smith* in its London setting, its theme of the good father and the villainous son, and its mysterious document (here a cryptic message left inside a watch); but the central character is a weaker version of Tolly

Dorking from *Black Jack.* Tolly Dorking in the shoes of Smith: it doesn't sound right, psychologically, and leads to excessive emotional straining in the prose style—one ceases, as in *The Drummer Boy,* long before the end, to care very much about the characters or what happens to them.

Garfield's best work is to be found in *Smith* and *Black Jack,* both exciting adventure stories set, for the most part, in eighteenth-century London; in *The Strange Affair of Adelaide Harris* and *Bostock and Harris,* the events of which take place in Brighton and in which we move forward in time to the period of the Regency; and in *The Sound of Coaches* and *The Prisoners of September,* larger, more complex books in theme and scope, set in the rural England of the eighteenth century. (Garfield is often thought to be an almost exclusively "London" novelist, but the facts do not bear this out: the countryside of southern England appears frequently, and he shows considerably more affection for Brighton than he ever does for London.)

Smith is by far and away Garfield's best known and most popular book. It won the Arts Council Award; it was the runner-up for the Carnegie Medal (pipped at the post by Alan Garner's *The Owl Service*); it has been filmed; and most schools in England have several copies of it. It is a rare thing—a favorite with children, parents, teachers, and critics. Beginning with a quite spectacular murder— "Smith was only twelve and, hangings apart, had seen no more than three men murdered in all his life"—its narrative continues at a tremendous pace, doing what *Jack Holborn* does not, making the reader more concerned about what is happening next than what is happening now. *Jack Holborn* had little other than narrative, but *Smith* has much more. There are convincing, vivid characters, particularly Smith himself—rounded, faulty, engaging, and multidimensional. Even such a small part as the highwayman, Lord Tom, seems real: apparently romantic and generous, but actually a squalid crook. There is marvellous atmosphere—the descriptions of London brought to a halt by heavy snow are magnificent—and the chase through the snow-bound countryside not only recalls *Bleak House* but is every bit as good as its original. The scenes of happy family life contrast very effectively with the episodes concerning

villains, thieves and murderers. The combination of realism
and symbol works well—the child, Smith, leading the blind
judge is not just part of the narrative, but it represents justice
tempered by compassion, the way the law should (but
doesn't) work. Smith *is* Mansfield's eyes, guiding him to the
truth. There are nice ironical touches—"a great many peti-
tions had been got up" to save a popular highwayman sen-
tenced to death, but "none had succeeded, and no one in his
heart of hearts was truly sorry, for the death of a hero (even
though he was a murderous ruffian) was a vastly romantic
thing"—and some fine comic moments. Smith at one point
accidentally knocks over a huge pile of books:

> Books in their fluttering and dusty thousands poured
> and thumped down as if the very skies had been loaded
> with them. Histories, Memoirs, Diaries, Lexicons, Gram-
> mars, Atlases, Journals, Biographies, Poems, Plays . . .
> books about heaven, books about hell, huge books about
> pygmies, tiny books about giants—even books about
> books—all, all slid and tumbled into desperate ruin
> overhung by a bitter cloud of dust. And somewhere
> underneath it all, still jerking and twitching, though fee-
> bly now, lay the unlucky bookseller himself!
> Gawd! thought Smith, half-way round the Cathedral
> and going like the wind, 'e must be squashed flatter than
> an old sixpence!

Smith is a rich and colorful novel; the author seems to be
thoroughly enjoying himself, portraying the surface textures
of urban working-class life as well as its undercurrents, in a
narrative and prose style of immense gusto. It certainly deserves its high reputation.

Black Jack occupies much the same world as *Smith*—the
grimy, crowded streets of London—and it has an equally
spectacular opening, in this case a man being hanged at
Tyburn. But the story moves away from London into the
countryside when the central character, Bartholomew
(Tolly) Dorking, meets some itinerant fairground people.
(Traveling entertainers are often found in Garfield's novels:
they are, for instance, important characters in *Devil-in-the-
Fog* and *The Sound of Coaches*.) Tolly is very different from
Smith, not at all ebullient and self-sufficient; he is a quiet,

gentle boy, an innocent adrift in a world of crooks of all sorts, and it is only his inner integrity and his love for the mad girl, Belle, that allow him to survive. Adolescent love is a major theme in *Black Jack*; it is the only novel of Garfield's in which it is seen as a great strength, incapable of being exploited and corrupted. Some of the most attractive parts of the book deal with Tolly's and Belle's feelings for each other. But dominating the entire story is the nightmare figure of Black Jack, the huge and terrifying robber who cheated the gallows; seen at first as an ogre, almost a malevolent giant from a fairy tale, he finally helps Tolly because he comes to respect the boy's love for Belle.

Two themes Garfield explores in almost every book are central to *Black Jack*: the person who is the opposite of what he appears to be, and the unforeseen consequences of a chance meeting. The two brothers in *Devil-in-the-Fog*, for instance, are the complete reverse of what George Treet originally thinks; Captain von Stumpfel in *The Confidence Man* is a petty trickster, not a hero; and there is more to Black Jack than a terrifying footpad. His chance meeting with Tolly alters both their lives, eventually for the better. Garfield accurately pinpoints how and why complete strangers can feel bound to each other:

> The very hugeness, strength and wildness of the giant awed the boy like a phenomenon in Nature. And in due proportion, his contempt was crushing and unendurable. More than anything else in the world, Bartholomew longed to change that contempt into respect. With all his heart and soul he craved for Black Jack's admiration.

Like *Smith, Black Jack* has a powerful narrative that holds the reader's attention; it is only towards the end of the book, when the earthquake occurs, that it becomes a little unstuck—too much happens too quickly here, and some of it is improbable. And also like *Smith* there are a host of well-drawn minor characters, particularly the fairground folk: the blackmailer, Hatch; the astrologer, Mrs Arbuthnot, who, Cassandra-like, can only predict gloom and doom; and the quack doctor, Carmody, who befriends Tolly—a character who is reworked as Dan Coventry, the phoney actor, in *The Sound of Coaches.* (He is himself a reworking of Mr Treet in *Devil-in-the-Fog.*) The same world as *Smith:* but *Black Jack* is no stale repetition. It's a fine novel, which does many new and interesting things, not the least of which is Garfield showing a central character who develops and changes, who moves towards maturity.

The Strange Affair of Adelaide Harris and *Bostock and Harris* stand apart from the rest of Garfield's work, not only because they are set in another period, but their intentions, mood, structure and characterization are very different. These are wholly comic novels, "comedies of humour" in the Ben Jonson sense, in which the characters act out a kind of set-piece dance, with the dancing master (the author) directing and manipulating all the movements. Stylistically, Garfield indulges in frequent—and amusing—parody. He is not only parodying himself; it is reminiscent of Stella Gibbons in *Cold Comfort Farm* poking fun at Thomas Hardy and other novelists of the "agricultural" school:

> On and on went Harris, across the uneven ground and skirting the chalky hollows that glared up abruptly, like the bleached sockets of half-buried giants' skulls.

and

> There is nothing so black as the human heart, came the answer. Under the sea lie poisoned bones and ribs all chipped by knives. Bullets roll inside skulls and ghastly captains lash long-dead cabin boys with whips of trailing weeds, etcetera. Yet the sea's surface is as bland and fair as a baby's cheek. . . .

The plot revolves around the infant Adelaide Harris, who is left on a hillside by her brother and his friend; they are indulging in an experiment—will she be suckled by a passing vixen, just as she-wolves suckled abandoned babies in Ancient Rome? But Adelaide is discovered by a courting couple and promptly taken off to the poorhouse; the rest of the story is concerned with Bostock's and Harris's utterly inept (though eventually successful) attempts to get her out and return her home before her parents discover who is responsible. All this leads to a tremendous commotion: a challenge to a duel, the hiring of an enquiry agent, lovers falling in and out of love, an entire school being turned upside down; betrayal, greed, selfishness, alcoholism. . . . The whole thing is treated as a huge joke, a sort of danse macabre; the manoeuverings of the plot show Garfield at his most skillful and ingenious, and his treatment of the characters displays a gift for pleasing and apt caricature. Bostock and Harris are a delight:

> They suited each other very well, did Bostock and Harris. Each had what the other lacked—and was always ready to part with it: Harris with his powerful mind and Bostock with his powerful limbs. In a way they represented the ancient idea of soul and body, but in a very pure state. Harris was as weak as a kitten and Bostock was as thick as a post.

Harris is, in fact, shifty, selfish, and only marginally more intelligent than Bostock, but Bostock has the redeeming virtues of innocence and honesty. They make a devastating pair, unwittingly causing a whole town to end up in a state of absolute chaos. The minor characters are no less deftly caricatured—Mrs Bunnion, who "slept like a stately ship, rising and falling at anchor"; Mr Raven, the idiotic enquiry agent, with his club foot in a great boot "thumping inquisitively on the ground, as if searching for a weakness or a symptom of dry rot"; the peppery Major Alexander, who "had a fiery and explosive sense of honour which he was inclined to lay like mines under friends and enemies alike." The Peacock influence is strong—there are many similar people in the pages of *Gryll Grange* or *Headlong Hall.* Dr Bunnion is not unlike Dr. Folliott in *Crotchet Castle,* and Mr Brett has something in common with Scythrop, the central character in *Nightmare Abbey.*

Garfield's choice of Brighton during the Regency for the setting means a total departure from his usual "world." There is no squalor, filth, and overcrowding, and there are few working-class people, for the Prince Regent's Brighton is middle-class—hypocrisy, gentility, vanity, keeping up appearances, and a false sense of honor are the vices displayed. Highwaymen, swindlers, thieves and murderers are noticeably absent. The same is true of the book's sequel, *Bostock and Harris,* which is a lesser achievement—*The Strange Affair of Adelaide Harris* would be hard to follow: it is a comic masterpiece, Garfield's finest novel. In the sequel, Dr Harris's household takes center stage, and the emphasis is as much on his daughters as it is on the two boys of the title. Bostock is in love with Mary Harris, who won't even look at him, and much of the comedy revolves round Bostock's attempts to engage her attention—in which he is, as ever, ineptly aided by Harris (who wants Bostock's father's telescope in exchange for his services). In the end, Bostock goes out dancing with Mary, a circumstance Harris plays no part in engineering. Much of the humor is at the expense of the girls, who connive, plan, and deceive their female friends rather more than the boys, a rival of one's own sex being regarded as worse than a boy who has let one down:

> "I would have said, 'Of course, Dolly. I don't mind a bit.' But no! Not you, Dolly Harris! You're just like the rest of them, lying and cheating and being sly . . . like—like weasels and stoats. . . ."
>
> As Miss Hemp's father was a butcher, it was only natural for her to associate the worst failings in character with animals you couldn't eat.

There is a great deal of innocent fun in this book, and the plot, though less convoluted than its predecessor, has an excellent pace, and leads to a satisfying conclusion in which most of the characters achieve what they set out to do at the beginning.

The Sound of Coaches has a more leisurely narrative than is usually found in Garfield's work, and the eighteenth century as observed here has a less grubby, more kindly feel to it than in the other novels, particularly in the opening chapters, which deal with the birth and childhood of Sam Chichester. Looking for a Dickensian parallel, one might say this is the world of *Pickwick Papers,* rosier than the grim battleground of *Our Mutual Friend.* The goodness and generosity of people is emphasized; there *is* room at the inn when the pregnant woman is giving birth. As Sam grows up and wonders about his origins, we are shown many pleasant aspects of country life at this time, and there are some sharp observations of human behavior. Sam's adopted parents, the dour old coachman and his devoted wife, are real, credible people—there is not a hint in this book of caricature. The subtleties of understanding and misunderstanding between parents and children are very well done. As Sam becomes an adult, his world becomes darker; like Lewis Boston in *The Prisoners of September,* he has the unfortunate capacity for doing the wrong thing in a relatively small way that leads to severe, indeed shattering, consequences. Chance events once again cause great calamities: if Sam hadn't shown an interest in the butt of malmsey, his adopted father wouldn't have been shot and paralyzed.

One of the themes is a discussion of honesty, which is seen by some of the characters as a failing; Mr. Chichester's probity, Mr Roggs feels, would drive "a saint to drink":

> Honesty had always been their drawback; the coachman himself was almost fanatical about it, consequently their presence tended to cast a blight on any company more easy-going than themselves.

Elsewhere it is suggested that truth is best hidden if it is likely to cause disaster and ruin—the theme of Ibsen's *The Wild Duck*—and the episodes to do with the actors in the second half of the book add weight to the discussion. This widens into a debate on the inadequacy of words to express emotion, and the way poetry and drama can help in our search for truth. Mrs Jamieson, the actress, says:

> Othello, after all, was a great and glorious hero, dying in a wash of poetry fit to drown the sun. Mr J., I'm sorry to say, was a small, skinny fellow wanting his right eye; and he died with a grunt in a pool of mud. But perhaps . . . the tears I never shed for Mr J. are all mixed in with those for the Moor?

The Sound of Coaches is Garfield's most realistic novel, a straightforward account of a search for origins and identity, growing up, and solving the problem (or at least coming to terms with it) of what have I been put on this earth for? Sam's solution is exchanging a coachman's life for a career on the stage, his relationship with Jenny, and a reconciliation with his adopted father, who finally comes to see that actors do not necessarily inhabit "a world of fraudulent dreams and pretence," that they aren't all "the ever-willing bedfellows of lying, thieving and the crooked way." (Though this is the life of Sam's real father, the hypocritical, drunken actor, Dan Coventry.) This is an impressive book: warm, unhysterical, convincing.

The Prisoners of September is the only major work of Garfield's that has at its center important political events that affect the lives and fates of the characters; it is therefore the only book of his that could be called a historical novel in the conventional sense of the term. The period is the French Revolution, and the events that dominate the plot are the September Massacres of 1792 in Paris. In this story Garfield makes audacious use of two utterly threadbare clichés of the historical novel—Lewis, the dashing young hero, saves a beautiful countess from death in a runaway coach; and the same young man rescues a family of French aristocrats from the Parisian mob and brings them to England. The clichés are brilliantly turned on their heads: the beautiful countess is a thief, and the aristocrats were not put in jail for political reasons, but because they are forgers. Lewis's sister, Henrietta, mocks both clichés, and one senses that Garfield agrees with her:

> You would think my brother had had enough of countesses; but no! He's fetched back a complete *set* from Paris. Picked them up in a prison, it seems, just like we might get hats in the Strand.

But despite its wit, *The Prisoners of September* is a somber, tragic book. Lewis's comfortable background and obvious sex appeal do not help him at all. He is a victim of his own decency and a second-rate mind; drifting against his will into a marriage with the forger's daughter, he realizes he is saddled for ever with his criminal in-laws, and he can do nothing about it. Love, once again, is seen as a weakness, exploited by the selfish and the greedy; "*amor*" doesn't "*vincit omnia*"— it drags people down into a morass of morally unacceptable actions.

This book has a glittering surface—the upper middle-class

world of southern England—but it peels off that surface and reveals sham, nastiness and disillusion. Nothing is ever what it seems: as in *The Pleasure Garden* and *The Strange Affair of Adelaide Harris,* there is little about human nature that Garfield seems to admire. Lewis's friend, Richard, has political ideals—"his soul on fire with destiny"—instead of good looks, but these lead him to commit murder, and he in turn is killed by the British secret service, who are attempting to manipulate political events in France in order to destabilize the country. (A modern theme, this, in period dress; one is reminded of American involvement in Allende's Chile.) Once again, the consequences of a single chance act become more far-reaching than anyone could expect; innocent bystanders and mere acquaintances get caught up in the web of somebody else's life: *all* the characters in this novel are "prisoners of September," affected by the massacres they had no direct, or even indirect, connection with. Illusion and reality are neatly brought together when Mr. Archer, the armchair revolutionary, meets a French soldier who saw the massacres:

> The tutor tended to regard the National Guardsman with awe—as might a mythographer confronted with a unicorn. Here was your actual people—or, rather, your actual person—straight from the volcano of liberty.

"Volcano of liberty" is nice. And even the soldier is a fraud; he faked a stomach illness so he didn't have to storm the Bastille or risk his life fighting. To sum up, the themes and mood of *The Prisoners of September* sound very adult, but they are not above the heads of intelligent teenagers, and the usual cracking pace of the narrative helps a great deal.

Garfield finds it hard not to be an adult novelist. Books like *The Strange Affair of Adelaide Harris, The Sound of Coaches* and *The Prisoners of September* stretch the young reader to his or her limits; though *Smith* and *Black Jack* remain very much within a child's concerns and grasp. At his best, when the wit and the story-line are at their most rumbustious, he is a great writer. His significant contribution to contemporary children's and young adult fiction is that he has given a new lease of life to the historical novel, and created a fresh interest in what was fast becoming an unpopular genre.

REFERENCES

LEON GARFIELD
   Jack Holborn, Constable, 1964; Pantheon, 1965
   Devil-in-the-Fog, Constable, 1966; Pantheon, 1966
   Smith, Constable, 1967; Pantheon, 1967
   Black Jack, Longman, 1968; Pantheon, 1969
   The Drummer Boy, Longman, 1970; Pantheon, 1969
   "Writing for Childhood," *Children's Literature in Education,*
      July 1970
   The Strange Affair of Adelaide Harris, Longman, 1971; Pan-
      theon, 1971
   The Sound of Coaches, Kestrel, 1974; Viking, 1974
   The Prisoners of September, Kestrel, 1975; Viking, 1975
   The Pleasure Garden, Kestrel, 1976; Viking, 1976
   The Confidence Man, Kestrel, 1978; Viking, 1979
   Bostock and Harris, Kestrel, 1979; as *The Night of the Comet,*
      Delacorte, 1979
   John Diamond, Kestrel, 1980; as *Footsteps,* Delacorte, 1980
   The December Rose, Kestrel, 1986; Viking, 1986

S. T. COLERIDGE
   Kubla Khan, first published 1798

JOSEPH CONRAD
   The Secret Agent, first published 1907

CHARLES DICKENS
   Pickwick Papers, first published 1837
   Bleak House, first published 1853
   Great Expectations, first published 1861
   Our Mutual Friend, first published 1865

GEORGE FARQUHAR
   The Beaux' Stratagem, first published 1707

ALAN GARNER
   The Owl Service, Collins, London, 1967; Walck, 1968

STELLA GIBBONS
   Cold Comfort Farm, first published 1932

GUNTER GRASS
   The Tin Drum, Secker & Warburg, 1962; Pantheon, 1961

HENRIK IBSEN
The Wild Duck, first published 1884

THOMAS LOVE PEACOCK
Headlong Hall, first published 1816
Nightmare Abbey, first published 1818
Crotchet Castle, first published 1831
Gryll Grange, first published 1860

ANN RADCLIFFE
The Mysteries of Udolpho, first published 1794

R. L. STEVENSON
Treasure Island, first published 1883

J. M. SYNGE
The Shadow of the Glen, first published 1903

WHAT DO DRACULAS DO?

Margaret Mahy

The simple answer, of course, is that by drinking the blood of young women they recruit their victims to their cause: the young women also become vampires. The world's undiminished fascination, however, with Bram Stoker's *Dracula* is not that it is just a well-told tale of lust and horror, but that its central theme—an evil spirit corrupting people to serve its own wicked purposes—is ages old and universal. It is a metaphor for diabolic possession, for the basic human fear of being (or desire to be) changed into somebody or something else. It questions the very concept of having an identity. It is not surprising, therefore, that it turns up again and again in children's literature. Contemporary fiction for the young abounds with it—Madeleine L'Engle's *A Wrinkle in Time* for example; William Mayne's *It*, the picture books of Maurice Sendak, Penelope Farmer's *Charlotte Sometimes* and *Year King*, Alan Garner's *The Owl Service*, Virginia Hamilton's *Dustland*, and so on. It is a major preoccupation in Margaret Mahy's novels. Cole Scholar in *The Haunting* tries to "possess" his nephew Barney; the ancient and evil spirit in *The Changeover* achieves human shape and power by placing its stamp on the little boy, Jacko Chant, and almost causing him to die; and the spirit manifestations of the dead Teddy Carnival in *The Tricksters* attempt to find permanent human shape and status by corrupting various members of the Hamilton family.

The parallels in Margaret Mahy's work with the Dracula story are quite overt at times; Hadfield Carnival says to Harry Hamilton, "Don't we all become different people once the sun goes down? For instance, I drink blood after dark." Laura, in *The Changeover*, thinks Carmody Braque looks like "an

improbable cross between Dracula and Mr Pickwick," and
Carmody Braque says of himself—

> . . . I've fed on so many by now I'm very very choosy.
> Girls like you, with rather more vitality perhaps, or
> sleeker, or those younger still—eight is an attractive age
> I think, ten is almost too old . . . But one should never
> make hard and fast rules. I enjoy an innocent, sucking
> baby, withering at its mother's breast.

But it is as a metaphor that Margaret Mahy makes her most
striking use of this theme. One recurring idea in her books
from *The Haunting* onwards is that our ancestors have
power over us whether we like it or not; we resemble them
physically, they bequeath us certain characteristics, and there
is little we can do to escape from this inheritance. They are to
some extent spirits molding our lives, though not usually of
the nature of Dracula. Christobel in *The Tricksters* loses her
boyfriend Robert to her best friend Emma, and discovers that
her father, Jack, had an affair with Emma; the baby, Tibby, is
therefore her half-sister. (It sounds like Iris Murdoch on an
off day, but in fact it is a good story):

> "*And* then," Christobel said with new vehemence, "it's
> hard not to feel Emma somehow fixed me with her eye,
> while I was at school, and set herself to invade me, and
> now she's got *my face* for her baby. And I feel I'm the
> one who's been possessed through Jack, and all without
> the chance of saying yes or no."
> "It might have influenced Robert too," Harry said at
> last. "I mean, without realising it. Looking at Tibby he
> saw you again, made all innocent and manageable."

There is little in Margaret Mahy's early writing that suggests she would go on to use such themes. Her career as an
author is rather odd: some thirteen years separate the publication of her first work—the picture books, *The Dragon of
an Ordinary Family* and *A Lion in the Meadow*—and *The
Haunting,* her "first extended novel," as Margery Fisher described it in *Growing Point.* (It's actually very short.) In
between Margaret Mahy showed herself to be immensely
prolific, first with a whole series of picture books and collec-

tions of short stories which are mostly of a fantastic and bizarre nature, then some realistic prose tales—not altogether successful—for younger children, *The Haunting,* and finally, with *The Changeover,* novels for teenagers. Her growth as an author seems to follow the growing up of her own children, which is not an uncommon phenomenon with writers for the young—Penelope Farmer is another instance; in each succeeding book her child hero or heroine is a little older, until with *Year King* she seems to reach the limit of the teenage genre, and after that she writes exclusively for adults. But with Margaret Mahy, the approach to a novel has been remarkably gradual. Thirteen years is a long time to spend being a prolific creator of fiction and *not* write a novel.

Margaret Mahy is a New Zealander, the only contemporary children's author from that country who has received international acclaim and recognition. But if the readers expect New Zealand to be a central issue, as Australia is in the work of Patricia Wrightson and Ivan Southall, they will be disappointed. Wrightson and Southall seem to want to show Australia not only to Australians—Patricia Wrightson said, in *Twentieth Century Children's Writers,* that she was preoccupied with "the use of Aboriginal folk-spirits . . . to enrich Australia's contemporary fantasy"—but also to the outside world: "Who can comprehend this country?" Rebecca asks in Southall's *The Golden Goose.* "Who can stand it?" Many British and American writers for children also make their own particular patch a major theme in their books—Jane Gardam's north-east coast of England, Lucy Boston's house in Huntingdonshire, William Mayne's Yorkshire, Virginia Hamilton's Ohio in *M. C. Higgins, the Great,* Jane Langton's Concord, Massachusetts—but Margaret Mahy does not find this important. Place is certainly there in her work—the countryside in *Clancy's Cabin* and *The Bus Under the Leaves,* the beach and holiday home in *The Tricksters,* the developing suburbs with their carefully noted social gradations in *The Changeover* and *The Catalogue of the Universe;* but with the exception of the differences between the seasons (Christmas, in *The Tricksters,* being at midsummer) we could be almost anywhere in either the northern or the southern hemisphere. This is both a strength and a weakness: one feels that an opportunity to reveal a unique place and culture has been missed; on the other hand, the stories have an immediate universality. The patterns of the relationships within families in Margaret Mahy's novels seem much more generally realistic and up-to-date than, for instance, in the old-fashioned, specifically Australian, pioneer-spirit families in Ivan Southall's books.

With hindsight one can see that some of the gifts Margaret Mahy displays in her novels are present in the earlier picture books—the ability to tell a rattling good tale, a great sense of humor, a constant shifting between fantasy and reality, and a bizarre, vivid imagination. *The Dragon of an Ordinary Family, A Lion in the Meadow,* and *The Witch in the Cherry Tree* are all concerned with a child's fantasy life: in *A Lion in the Meadow* a small boy is convinced that a ferocious lion is skulking in the field outside his house; in *The Witch in the Cherry Tree* a very similar child is sure that a witch is spying on him from a cherry tree in the garden and wants to steal the cakes his mother is baking. The main difference between the two stories is that the mother in *A Lion in the Meadow* refuses to enter into the spirit of the child's imaginings (which leads to a rather unsatisfactory resolution), whereas the mother in *The Witch in the Cherry Tree* behaves quite differently—

> "Look at that!" cried David's mother. "A big black bird just flew up off our lawn."
> "That was the witch," exclaimed David indignantly. "Can't you tell a witch when you see one?"
> "I'm sorry. I just saw her from the corner of my eye," said his mother.

Some of the picture books are pure nonsense, containing wonderfully grotesque characters who are made to seem all the more extraordinary when placed next to humdrum, everyday people who, during the course of the story, achieve a freedom they had previously only dreamed of. The office worker in *The Man Whose Mother Was a Pirate* is liberated from his dull, self-imposed routine by taking his mother (a traditional pirate with eye-patch, ear-rings, cutlass and pistols) to the seaside in a wheelbarrow; the henpecked hus-

band in *Mrs Discombobulous* finds his awful wife stops nag-
ging him after she has fallen into a washing-machine; the
millionaire in *The Great Millionaire Kidnap* gets more pleasure from enriching the lives of his kidnappers than he does
from making money for himself.

Lastly, despite the emphasis on dragons, princesses, pirates,
witches, brigands and other traditional figures of children's
stories, some of the picture books have realistic themes. *The
Wind Between the Stars,* poetic and fantastic though it may
be, deals, unusually for a picture book, with two elderly
women coming to terms with old age—

> "Yet," thought Phoebe, "I don't feel so different. I'm still
> the same. Here I am. Here I am. But who is there to
> remember me? Who is there left to call me by my name,
> 'Phoebe', to know who I really am, and to see the real
> me looking out from behind all these wrinkles?"

Stepmother is concerned with a child's hostile reactions to a
parent's second marriage. *The Changeover* explores this idea
in much greater detail though it isn't marriage itself, in the
latter book, that bothers Laura so much as her mother's relationship with her new boyfriend. The one-parent family, and
its attendant problems, is an important ingredient of *The Catalogue of the Universe,* and a second wife is also a major
character in *The Haunting.* Jenny, in *Stepmother,* sees her
father's girlfriend for the first time as his new wife:

> The stepmother looked to Jenny like a tall golden tree.
> She looked as if beautiful birds might sit on her and sing,
> or butterflies come to visit her for honey. She looked as
> if she might break into wild shining blossoms at the
> sound of a certain magical word.
> But Jenny was not tricked.
> "Being beautiful just makes it worse!" she told her
> small brother, Davey. "There is no excuse."

In *Clancy's Cabin* and *The Bus Under the Leaves,* Margaret
Mahy's first books in which pictures are occasional illustrations rather than being integral to the text, the sure touch is
absent. These realistic long short stories contain too many
clichés—in *Clancy's Cabin* stereotypical middle-class kids

camping out and searching for lost treasure; in *The Bus Under the Leaves,* two boys who make a den during the summer holidays in an old bus they find on a dump. The adults are no more individualized than the children—the old lady in *Clancy's Cabin,* for example, is a very sugary creation—and the dialogue is irritatingly stilted, particularly in *The Bus Under the Leaves:*

> "This boy I have coming to stay with me is called David. He has been sick and the doctor said he must come and stay in the country. He lives in the town and has never been in the country before. I think I might be too old to play with him. Would you like to come down and play with him?"
>
> "Yes!" said Adam. "I would like that. Often I wish I had boys to play with. It is all right when I go to school, but in the holidays I feel a bit lonely."

There are some good images— "The shadows in the creases of the hills grew blurred and soft, as if a giant had smudged them with his thumb"; a dog's tongue "hung joyously out like a pink flag waving at the world"—but both books suffer from being something new that the author is trying. She is ill-at-ease.

Better is *The Pirate Uncle,* a pleasant if unexceptional story about a brother and sister who spend a holiday with an uncle they have never met before; the uncle, aware that the children may find his untidy, bachelor home and his sea-faring way of life difficult to cope with after their regimented, urban existence, successfully entertains them by pretending to be a pirate who needs to be reformed and civilized. The characterization is stronger and the writing more assured than in *Clancy's Cabin* and *The Bus Under the Leaves:* the sea and the atmosphere of childhood holidays are well evoked; Uncle Ludovic walks "around the room next door like a lion in a cage of dreams," and "you could see the studs of the house like the bones of some large creature holding everything else together." Nicholas, observing the house for the first time, thinks it is like a bird's nest—

> for it was overgrown with ivy and other sprawling vines. Through the leaves windows framed in red looked at

them. It all had a nautical air as if built by a ship's carpenter on a desert island. The red door was slightly
open like a surprised mouth.

The nonsense tales that Margaret Mahy wrote next are, in
contrast, brilliantly original creations—endlessly inventive in
the absurdity and humor of their plots and rich in a feeling for
words; her imagination, confined by the limitations of the
realistic story, seems here to be as free and as wild as in the
best of the picture books. *Raging Robots and Unruly Uncles*
is a very amusing story about a pair of contrasting twin brothers, villainous Jasper, whose sons refuse to follow in his
footsteps—

> "What's this?" cried Uncle Jasper in horror as he read
> their school reports.
> "Caligula is at the bottom of the class in Despicable
> Treason, and though Nero is well up in Music he has
> totally failed in Utter Selfishness. Genghis—I hoped
> much from you, but your marks in Persecution are a
> disgrace."

—and virtuous Julian, whose daughter Prudence attends "the
select Academy for Old-Fashioned Heroines, a vegetarian
school for girls." But she is also a disappointment to her
father; she likes brandishing spanners and screw-drivers and
mending old cars, bicycles and television sets, and she hates
being demure and lady-like. How these children outwit their
parents and end up doing what they want to do makes a
delightful story, near to Roald Dahl in his *BFG* vein, but better
than Dahl for it is without nastiness and questionable morality. Margaret Mahy shares with Dahl a love of absurd, invented
language; this could be the BFG talking—

> "Thundering Maledictions! I tell you a laser is a bind-
> lespang device for directing common light in com-
> pletely parallel lines without any grim tucketing diffu-
> sion or snufwinkling dispersion."

—and the book with very small print that Prudence refuses
to read, "One Thousand Improving Little Tales For Pro-

gressive Little Minds" by Nanny Gringe, is a splendid bit of parody.

The Pirates' Mixed-Up Voyage is also extremely amusing, the emphasis, as in *Raging Robots and Unruly Uncles,* being on a fast-moving, ever-changing, complex plot; it is a parody of many genres—pirates' tales, the detective story, the fairy tale, even other contemporary children's books: the Dessert Island is Dahl's chocolate factory without the awful Willie Wonka and the phoney Charlie Bucket, and the pirate ship that operates by pedal power recalls the boat in Russell Hoban's *How Tom Beat Captain Najork and His Hired Sportsmen.* This kind of whimsy is hard to do and even harder to sustain, but the invention in *The Pirates' Mixed-Up Voyage* never flags. The quality can be seen in this extract—

> The manners of pirates are usually very low, but they make up for this by having their hopes very high . . . They had left behind them real life with all its pettifogging rules and complications like library cards, dog licences, parking meters and phone bills, and they were all immensely hopeful . . . They stole kippers from clippers, figs from brigs, lunches from launches . . .

There are some marvellous characters too, such as Mrs Hatchett, who teaches reading from the Silkweed Granulated Readers at Doctor Silkweed's Academy for Literature and Languages (Alive and Dead):

> She wore terrifying black boots and a belt all studded with spikes. At one hip swung a brass chain and at the other, a rather dashing sabre. Over this ensemble she wore the gown and hood of a Doctor of Literature.

She obtains silence in class by firing a pistol at the ceiling (it is "peppered with bullet holes") and threats: "One single, solitary word more and I will shoot your school lunches into smithereens!"

There is a considerable difference in quality between the two books of Margaret Mahy's—*The Haunting* and *The Changeover*—which won Carnegie Medals in 1982 and 1984. *The Changeover* is a rich, powerful, many-layered novel that thoroughly deserved its award, but *The Haunting,* well done though it is, seems a rather slight work to be given such a prestigious accolade as the Carnegie. It has a memorable opening sentence, one of those invitations to plunge immediately into the text—"When, suddenly, on an ordinary Wednesday, it seemed to Barney that the world tilted and ran downhill in all directions, he knew he was about to be haunted again"—and the nature of that haunting, Margaret Mahy's first sinister exploration of the Dracula idea, is conveyed to the reader most successfully—

> He now felt sure he was being haunted by the dead boy who had been his great-uncle. He could feel that fierce owl moving through his mind, touching his memories, his ideas, his fears, his happiness. As this wild spirit moved into him, Barney was himself changed, and perhaps this change was what the Scholar family was recognizing and responding to. Like compass needles turning to the north, they were moving to face that powerful ghost.

The discovery that the dead boy is not dead, but very much alive as Great-uncle Cole, lessens the tension at the wrong moment—Cole is more of a pathetic old fool than a terrifying Dracula figure—and the serious point of the book, that we are all to a certain extent controlled, manipulated and molded by the generations that precede us, gets somewhat lost in the complexities of the denouement. But the main character, Barney, is a convincing creation (though his sisters are tiresome and not totally credible) and there is a nice cast of minor figures, the various aunts, uncles, great-aunts and great-uncles; the spiteful great-grandmother is particularly effective, a sort of latter-day Queen of Spades. Tabitha's comments about her are neat perceptions—a "witch who has lost her magic, but kept her nastiness"; "Her wrinkles are so angry. She's like a wall with furious swear words scribbled all over it." *The Haunting* shows that Margaret Mahy could write a gripping narrative that engenders fear and mystery, but it does not achieve a great deal more than that.

The Changeover is on an altogether different plane. It is another tale of the supernatural—an evil spirit's attempt to remain a human being by destroying little Jacko, an attempt which is thwarted by Jacko's sister's newly-discovered powers when she experiences a "changeover" into a witch. But "changeover" is a double metaphor; this is also a realistic book about an adolescent girl experiencing another kind of shift, that of becoming adult and adjusting to new perceptions about her relationships, particularly with her mother, who is embarking on her first real love-affair since her marriage ended in divorce. On a third level it is a romantic, women's-magazine-type novel about Laura's relationship with her boyfriend, Sorry Carlisle, who, though too sophisticated and knowing at sixteen to be entirely credible, comes over as an attractively sexy young man. The mixing of such different genres could have been a recipe for disaster, but the triumph of *The Changeover* is that the author manages to fuse all three with total success. The chilling and thrilling aspects of the supernatural story sit easily beside Laura's complex and contradictory reactions to her mother's behavior when the new lover, Chris, appears on the scene—

> "You've had your hair done!" Laura cried, outraged. "I thought we were broke this week."
> "I've booked it up again next week," Kate replied. She looked less like a mother in real life, and more like a mother on television, keeping herself nice for husband and family, thrilled to death with her new soap powder.

—and beside the frequent social observations, ironic and amusing, of suburban neighbors:

> "I've been married ten years and I've never let myself go," Laura had once heard her tell a friend, and had thought that, even if Mrs Fangboner did let herself go, she would probably not go far. She defended herself with lipstick, her garden, and cups of tea, and enjoyed her defences too much to leave them behind her.

Margaret Mahy deliberately calls attention to the parallels between Laura's romance with Sorry and the love affairs of romantic fiction—

> He did not look so very different from one of his own pictures, and, once again, just as she had when she saw

him in this room for the first time, he looked more than
himself, a wild man framed in the heavy architraves of
the door . . .
        "If you had read *Wendy's Wayward Heart,*" he said,
    "you would recognize my expression."

Sorry Carlisle would not be out of place in novels like
Daphne du Maurier's *Rebecca.* Margaret Mahy is not afraid to
use the language of romantic fiction, albeit in superior fashion—

> On one side of a kiss was childhood, sunshine, inno-
> cence, toys and, on the other, people embracing,
> darkness, passion and the admittance of a person, who,
> no matter how loved, must always have the quality of
> otherness. . . .

There is one quite splendid moment when all three genres
are experienced almost at the same time—Laura, by means of
a supernatural vision, walking on a beach she once visited
with her father; then feeling romantic as she watches Sorry,
half-naked, tinkering with his motor bike; then being brought
down to earth savagely by realizing that her mother's boyfriend has, for the first time, stayed all night. All three levels
act as metaphors for different layers of adolescent experience.

The characterization throughout is excellent, Jacko, Laura
herself, her mother, Chris: even the minor characters have
time and care spent on them. Julia, Laura's father's second
wife, makes only a fleeting appearance, but her feelings about
Jacko's illness are given attention and ring true; she is
delighted

> at Jacko's recovery, partly because she was naturally
> glad to hear that a sick child was likely to become well
> again, and partly because it would set Stephen free from
> his previous family to belong entirely to her once again.

"Rich variety," a phrase from the book, is the hallmark of *The
Changeover,* and this applies, too, to the quality of the writing, which is strong and impressive throughout, a real pleasure to read—

> She was not thinking of Mr Braque directly but about

Stephen and Julia, Kate and Chris, letting them tumble
over and over in her mind, as if she were watching them
through the round, glass window found in the doors of
certain washing machines. She thought about the tendency the world had to form pairs and then shake every
one up like dice and encourage them to fall into new
arrangements. She thought about love and sex and wondered which one came first . . . Kate believed in true
love which Laura should wait to attain, yet true love had
brought Kate unhappiness, and she herself had turned to
a man she had known for only two days for consolation
and escape. Somewhere, she thought, there must be a
single, unifying principle that would make sense of all
this rich variety, and would explain, too, why suddenly
the sight of Garry standing at the school gate that morning had filled her with a soft electricity, exciting but not
totally amiable.

In *The Catalogue of the Universe* there is no supernatural
element; it is a realistic teenage novel that deals with a further exploration of some of the themes used in *The Changeover*—the one-parent family, the changing nature of relationships between parents and their offspring during
adolescence, the first love affair between boy and girl. The
setting is also similar, the uneasy (and also changing) bound-
ary between suburb and countryside. The chief differences
between the two books are that the boy, Tycho, is not an
idealized male from romantic fiction but a plain, ordinary
eighteen-year-old, intelligent, indeed intellectual, who suffers
from a low opinion of himself particularly in his estimation of
his sexual attractiveness; and the girl, Angela, unlike Laura in
The Changeover, is fascinated by her absent father whom she
has never seen. Much of the plot is concerned with Angela's
search for him and the problems that ensue when she finds
him, confronts him, and is rejected. Tycho helps her to pick
up the pieces, and—unusually even now in a young adult
novel—they end up in bed together. It is a well-written, fast-
moving story, though too much happens in the denouement
(the episode in which Tycho pulls a neighbor from a blazing
wrecked car is unnecessary and unconvincing), with some
insightful comments about the teenage years. The portrayal
of adolescent confusion is good—

> She was offering to let him kiss her and touch her, which
> he did, prepared to give himself up to her, but then he
> accidentally saw himself in the mirror, as much em-
> braced as embracing, and a terrible cupboard in his
> memory burst open, scattering a thousand stored-up
> slights and insults through his head. All that he could
> think was that he looked ridiculous and made love seem
> ridiculous . . .

—but Angela sees Tycho as "more precious than a boyfriend
because he could never be replaced."

Again the minor characters are memorable, Tycho's awful,
garrulous brother and selfish, histrionic sister; Angela's eccentric but loving mother who mows her lawn with a scythe
in the moonlight. These families are real families, with parents who admit they don't know every answer, but who always try to keep open the line of communication with their
children; families that are quarrelsome but caring, capable of
inflicting hurt but also offering love between the generations.
There is, as usual, Margaret Mahy's sense of humor, ironic and
zany in turn; Tycho's comment on the lines from *Kubla
Khan*—

> It was a miracle of rare device
> A sunny pleasure dome with caves of ice

—is "What Coleridge had described was a fridge from a cat's
point of view." *The Catalogue of the Universe* is a fine book,
though perhaps not containing so much "rich variety" as *The
Changeover.*

With *The Tricksters* Margaret Mahy returns to the supernatural, and this aspect of the story is very convincing; the
three young men, triplets, who are in part manifestations of
the dead Teddy Carnival and in part characters from the
slushy romantic novel teenager Harry Hamilton is writing
brought to life, are a sinister, sexy, unpleasant trio who dominate and manipulate the Hamilton family for their own nasty,
selfish reasons. The fact that they are in part people from a
book that is being written—echoes of Pirandello's *Six Characters in Search of an Author*—leads to some interesting
remarks on discoveries that most writers make about work in

progress; that at some point or another in almost any novel the characters take over and tell their creator what to do, and that life can often imitate art. "Everyone would think she was merely copying the outside world," Harry says to herself. "The possibility that the outside world was copying her was unbelievable." Like other writers before her, she finds that the possibility is *not* unbelievable.

But the realistic side of *The Tricksters* shows a falling off in achievement. The setting is the Hamiltons' holiday home, in which a large house-party of family members and their friends is celebrating Christmas; there are too many characters for each to have a proper function in the plot—the English visitor, Anthony, for instance, has no function at all except to pair off with Christobel at the end, so an opportunity to show New Zealand to the outside world (which could have been done via the relationship between this man and his hosts) is lost. The dialogue is immensely wordy and often sounds unreal—

> "It's the national dish," he said lightly. "Our appetite for stewed plums is—oh, it's infinite, isn't it, Hadfield?"
> "Absolutely infinite," Hadfield agreed.
> "Or even more!" concluded Felix.
> Naomi laughed suddenly. "Where are you heading for?" she asked.
> Ovid shrugged. "Wherever we get to," he said. "Anywhere we stop is where we're hoping to get to."
> "But you happen to have stopped here," she said dryly. "Well, you're very welcome."
> "And you're very tolerant," Ovid observed. "It's a virtue I've been spared myself."
> "You'll need massive tolerance to eat the plums," Christobel assured him.
> "Only self-interest," he answered. "I've got plenty of that."

This language is almost parodying itself. As is the plot: when Harry makes love up in the hills with Felix, who is dead Teddy and also one of the creations from her own book, the whole scenario is getting too incredibly bizarre. There are some good comments about life—on the problems parents incur by keeping important secrets from their children, on immaturity and selfishness, on the power of books, on parental example overburdening children—but *The Tricksters* is just too odd to take very seriously; the mix of realistic and supernatural just doesn't work properly here.

Margaret Mahy is a very talented writer who seems equally at home in picture books, nonsense stories for the young, and the teenage novel. One wonders what she will do next: as the age of her central characters has gradually grown older over the years, and her own children are now adults, will she turn to adult fiction? Whatever it will be, it will be a surprise: surprising us is one of her great virtues.

REFERENCES

MARGARET MAHY
> *The Dragon of an Ordinary Family,* Heinemann, 1969; Watts, 1969
>
> *A Lion in the Meadow,* Dent, 1969; Watts, 1969
>
> *Mrs Discombobulous,* Dent, 1969; Watts, 1969
>
> *The Man Whose Mother Was a Pirate,* Dent, 1972; Atheneum, 1973
>
> *The Witch in the Cherry Tree,* Dent, 1974; Parents' Magazine Press, 1974
>
> *Clancy's Cabin,* Dent, 1974
>
> *Stepmother,* Watts, 1974
>
> *The Bus Under the Leaves,* Dent, 1975
>
> *The Great Millionaire Kidnap,* Dent, 1975
>
> *The Wind Between the Stars,* Dent, 1976
>
> *The Pirate Uncle,* Dent, 1977
>
> *Raging Robots and Unruly Uncles,* Dent, 1981
>
> *The Haunting,* Dent, 1982; Atheneum, 1982
>
> *The Pirates' Mixed-Up Voyage,* Dent, 1983
>
> *The Changeover,* Dent, 1984; Macmillan, New York, 1984
>
> *The Catalogue of the Universe,* Dent, 1985; Macmillan, New York, 1986
>
> *The Tricksters,* Dent, 1986; Macmillan, New York, 1987

S. T. COLERIDGE
> *Kubla Khan,* first published 1798

ROALD DAHL
> *The BFG,* Cape, 1982; Farrar Straus, 1982

MADELEINE L'ENGLE
A Wrinkle in Time, Farrar, Straus, 1962; Constable, 1964

PENELOPE FARMER
Charlotte Sometimes, Chatto, 1969; Harcourt, 1969
Year King, Chatto, 1977; Atheneum, 1977

MARGERY FISHER
review in *Growing Point* of *The Haunting,* 1982

ALAN GARNER
The Owl Service, Collins, London, 1967; Walck, 1968

VIRGINIA HAMILTON
M. C. Higgins, the Great, Macmillan, New York, 1974; Hamish Hamilton, 1975
Dustland, Greenwillow, 1980; Julia MacRae, 1980

RUSSELL HOBAN
How Tom Beat Captain Najork and His Hired Sportsmen, Cape, 1974; Atheneum, 1974

DANIEL KIRKPATRICK (editor)
Twentieth Century Children's Writers, St Martin's Press, 1978

DAPHNE DU MAURIER
Rebecca, Gollancz, 1939; Doubleday, 1948

WILLIAM MAYNE
It, Hamish Hamilton, 1977; Greenwillow, 1978

LUIGI PIRANDELLO
Six Characters in Search of an Author, first published 1921

IVAN SOUTHALL
The Golden Goose, Methuen, 1981; Greenwillow, 1981

BRAM STOKER
Dracula, first published 1897

CAVIARE TO THE GENERAL

Jane Gardam

Jane Gardam makes few concessions: for the average or below average reader, all her full-length books are difficult in language and in concept. References to many of the great works of English literature are frequent. She assumes her audience has some knowledge of the geography, customs and speech patterns of Northern England, and—in her first two books—some awareness of the events of the Second World War and the prevailing moods and attitudes of that time. Though their backgrounds are not comfortable or privileged, her protagonists are almost exclusively middle-class and highly intelligent; boys and girls who, like Marigold Green, the heroine of *Bilgewater,* will win open scholarships to Oxbridge. Her novels, therefore, will never be popular in the way, for example, *Charlie and the Chocolate Factory* is popular—but this is not a matter that should concern the critic any more than whether Shakespeare's popularity has any bearing on his merits as a creative artist; it is a question for those who select books, librarians and so· on. But if a story profoundly touches the life of just one child or teenager it is probably worth publishing, and Jane Gardam's young admirers can certainly be counted in more than single figures.

A *Few Fair Days* and *A Long Way from Verona* came out in 1971. The first is a collection of stories ostensibly for young children; *A Long Way from Verona* is for teenagers. Teenagers interest Jane Gardam more than children, for she did not write again for young readers until *Bridget and William* appeared a decade later. The heroines of *A Few Fair Days* and *A Long Way from Verona* have different names, but they seem to be the same person. Both books have an autobiographical air; Margery Fisher said of *A Few Fair Days* that this gives the writing "a positive edge of detail," and indeed it comes over strongly—a feeling that is reinforced when one considers the central characters of *The Summer After the Funeral* and *Bilgewater,* who are really eight-year-old Lucy of *A Few Fair Days* and thirteen-year-old Jessica of *A Long Way from Verona* at sixteen and nearly eighteen. In all four books the setting is the same, or similar—towns on or near the north-east coast of Yorkshire where Jane Gardam was born and grew up—and Dad (always an important figure) is a schoolmaster in *A Few Fair Days* and *Bilgewater,* a schoolmaster who becomes a clergyman in *A Long Way from Verona,* and a clergyman in *The Summer After the Funeral.* The "positive edge of detail"—the minutiae of scenery, houses, gardens, classrooms at school, the physical appearance of people—produce resonances from one story to the next, and are memorable because they seem so personally felt.

The literary interests of Jane Gardam's central characters are evident even in *A Few Fair Days*—

> "'The magus Zoroaster,'" said Lucy, "'my dead child, met his own image walking in the garden.'"
> "I don't know what you're talking about," said Avice Mew.

Nor will the readers who are Avice Mews, and who don't have this kind of childhood—

> —the great shaggy lawn, the sycamore tree and the summerhouse, the houses she made, rounded like nests in the long grass under the apple trees, the cave under the redcurrant bushes with seats made of stones like black sponges from the rockery.

Lucy who

> tired people out, who yearned and squirmed and talked too much and wept and railed and tied her little brother up with ropes and slammed doors and packed suitcases and left home, and came back again five minutes later because she had forgotten a book

is the same iconoclast and misfit as Athene in *The Summer After the Funeral*—"All sunshine she was not, and her sum-

mery face was the very highest achievement, the head behind
it holding dismal and complex troubles"—and prickly, book-
loving Jessica in *A Long Way from Verona*:

> You could tell girls had been putting on pale, pretty
> nicely-made old party dresses in that room for about
> thirty thousand years. An *English* dress, as English as the
> patchwork quilt it was lying on, as English as the rag rug,
> as English as the books on the shelves. A dress whom
> England made, wrought, made aware, for girls at peace
> under an English heaven.

But childhood is easier than adolescence for girls like Lucy;
she has sympathetic parents, a best friend, and spinster and
widowed aunts and great-aunts with time to spare for her.
Even so, like Athene, she is not all sunshine; in the story *One
of Jinnie Love's Fair Days* the destructive and unhappy side
of her personality is revealed when she decides to hurt Mrs
Binge Benson, a friend of her mother's, by contaminating her
sponge cake with seaweed, which has "a smell of dead fish"
and "rather a lot of flies."

In *A Few Fair Days* the chief virtues of Jane Gardam's
writing are already present—a capacity for vivid, visual description, period detail, and a great sense of fun which often
leads to portaits that verge on caricature, people one might
find in a Leon Garfield novel—

> Then a great hustling and creaking and the taxi man and
> his assistant set down a huge wicker chair on wheels
> with a great roll of rugs in it and at the top of the roll,
> nidding and nodding and smiling to herself under a huge
> black straw hat, sat Mrs Hinton. All you could see of her
> face was a big polished old chin with little holes in it and
> an overhanging nose with a long, long water drop on the
> end.

Present, too, are the strong, dominating central character,
and an interest in the theme of illusion and reality, which
comes, almost disastrously, to preoccupy the later heroines;
here Lucy, wanting to dig out "gold and swords and jewels"
from the ship that got buried in the sand, finds only "seagulls' feathers and bed springs and driftwood and sea-coal and

nasty bits of buried newspaper." *A Few Fair Days* also looks forward, as do nearly all its successors; they conclude as if a sequel might follow. Here it is the nineteen thirties coming to an end but aware of the calamities ahead; Lucy's mother's outburst about her children's ignorance as wilful and stupid, with Europe being on the brink of war, looks at something beyond the finish of the book, as does the very last sentence—"Dennis" (the name of a house) "stayed empty till the soldiers came." And *The Tinker at the Door,* the only story in this collection set in Cumberland, is told almost like a private family anecdote, with characters who, one feels, will be resurrected later—in other words, it prefigures *The Hollow Land.*

Growing up during the Second World War was a theme used by several writers of children's books in the late sixties and early seventies; its frequent occurrence was probably due to the fact that the authors were themselves children in the nineteen forties. *The Dolphin Crossing* by Jill Paton Walsh appeared in 1967, and was followed in 1969 by the same author's *Fireweed;* Nina Bawden produced *Carrie's War* in 1973, and Robert Westall's *The Machine-Gunners* and Penelope Lively's *Going Back* were published in 1975. *A Long Way from Verona* is a further example of the genre and is better than most, certainly superior to *The Machine-Gunners,* which shares with it a similar setting, a coastal resort in the north-east of England. There is less emphasis in *A Long Way from Verona* on air-raids than in *Fireweed,* though there is one magnificent, dramatic description of the destruction caused by aerial bombing; no heroic exploits as in *The Dolphin Crossing;* very little about evacuees (*Carrie's War*) or rural life (*Going Back*); and none of the spurious violence and macho posturing of *The Machine-Gunners.* Instead, the humdrum, shabby dreariness of life at this time is at the forefront, the repressive wartime regulations that make school in particular more repressive and regulated than usual; when just having a pot of tea and a piece of cake in a café can seem like a marvellous diversion, and the ultimate joy for a child is if the school gets blasted to bits in the middle of the night. (It is.) It is stressed, too, that adults then were often more censorious and intolerant than they are now—Mrs Baxter, for instance, is shocked when she finds Jessica reading *Jude the Obscure* ("It's a most horrible book. What would your father say?") and has it removed from the library shelves.

But the right teacher at the right time can prove a blessing for the gifted, unhappy child, and it is Miss Philemon, the aged and eccentric Senior English Mistress, who stops Jessica going off the rails by sound advice, kindness, encouragement for her creative writing, and sharing her literary enthusiasms. There are echoes of this theme in *The Summer After the Funeral,* in Athene's relationship with Henry Bell, and in *Bilgewater* with Marigold's teacher, Miss Bex; but the role of these characters is not the same as Miss Philemon's, which is to provide Jessica with what is fundamentally missing in her existence. (Henry Bell, though he takes Athene to see the Brontes' house at Haworth, is essentially a minor figure, and Miss Bex is more interested in Marigold's father than in Marigold—in fact Miss Bex resents her pupil's abilities: a good piece of observation by Jane Gardam of what happens curiously often in real life.)

There are also the bad teachers: Miss Dobbs, who makes her girls read *The Cloister and the Hearth* out loud, and who gives Jessica some appalling advice—if she's pleased with anything she's written she should destroy it. There is, again, some entertaining caricature. Miss Dobbs is "a fine-looking woman,"

> with a noble sort of figure and a great deal of golden hair. Some of it is on her chin. On the hockey field she cries "Up the FIIIIIIELD, Forwards," and she looks just like a Viking.

Much of the book is very amusing: the dotty old woman who claims to have known Henry James—"He was Henry James to all the world," said Mrs Hopkins. "But he was Harry to me"; Jessica describing to her friends the interior of Miss Philemon's living room (pictures of naked women with green bosoms—a Gauguin print, in fact); Jessica's brush at a house-party with upper-class snobbery, people who are

> called things like Auntie Boo and Lady Pap-Fisher (honestly) and they thought I was one of *them* and

> Auntie Boo who was in Red Crawss (you have to call it
> Crawss) uniform with a mouth like a safety pin and
> hardly ever spoke suddenly said, "Good thing these girls
> are away from here, Barby. Raids getting no joke. Tees-
> side," and Lady Pap-Musher said, "But Boo-boo (yes)
> you couldn't send them to a local school *anyway.* I
> mean they're so *crowded* and nobody *does*" . . . . I sud-
> denly said, "How can they be so crowded if nobody
> does?" and there was the most terrible, horrible silence
> all round the room.

A Long Way from Verona is a lengthy, many-layered novel.
Its main achievement is Jessica, an awkward, indiscreet, so-
cially backward but intellectually precocious adolescent —
one of the most complex, in-depth character studies in contemporary teenage fiction. Jane Gardam writes about her
with love and compassion, and these feelings are shared by
the reader. For a first full-length novel *A Long Way from
Verona* is remarkable.

The Summer After the Funeral is a lot shorter, but no less
dense in its texture. A great deal is going on already on page
one; a passage such as this has to be read with care if all the
nuances and ironies are to be picked up—

> Throughout the service and during the stern words in
> the damp graveyard—rowdy rooks above—the Rector's
> family had behaved like heroes. The widow, steady as a
> dwarf oak, had been clearly heard to make the Re-
> sponses, seen to pat a hand upon a pew, at the door to
> kiss a cousin unnoticed earlier, even (surely not) as she
> moved away and through the rectory wicket home,
> even to take a quick glance at her watch, considering
> kettles.
>
> "Dodo has gone home with Boo," people told each
> other with the solemn kindness that obtains at grave-
> sides. They felt proud of her, proud to know her, excited
> by her confident steady face. Unkind people might have
> felt it was a self-satisfied face, but kind ones—and for
> half an hour they were kind—saw only a face grateful to
> its Maker for an opportunity of proclaiming faith.

Yes: Boo. The characters in *The Summer After the Funeral,*
though not rich—in fact somewhat down-at-heel—are more

up-market in origin than in *A Long Way from Verona*, with names and nicknames to match—Primmy (short for Primrose), Posie, Sebastian, Dodo, Beams ("Phoebe at the font") and Athene (nicknamed Ath, Athy, Theeny, Teeny-Weeny, Weeny-Theeny, Assy, At and Mim). Dodo is Athene's mother, loving but unlovable, despite Athene's assertion to the contrary in the last sentence of the book. After her husband's death she cannot immediately cope with her children, so her daughters are sent off to various aunts and friends who don't particularly want them; and her son, Sebastian, goes of his own accord to a monastery in Scotland. Like *A Long Way from Verona, The Summer After the Funeral* is concerned with a precocious adolescent girl who is driven by events and the quirks and contradictions in her prickly character almost to the point of disintegration.

There is a great deal of humor—Dodo's letters are comic masterpieces, "nasty coarse gardens full of dahlias and sunflowers. Church all right but smells damp and the notices on the boards positively *spotted* with age. Low, I should say"— and some wonderfully bizarre eccentrics: pathetic, whining Sybil and her aggressive, tactless friend, Primrose; Aunt Posie who is kind and rich, but obsessed with food and not tiring oneself out; aged, unworldly monks with no understanding of youth. The description of Sybil is again worthy of Leon Garfield—

> Her white riding mac, tightly belted in, made her look thinner than ever, and when she turned sideways she might have been hanging up in a cupboard . . . Her galoshes fluted upwards like bats.

Literary allusions abound. Athene and her father out walking are "tall and lively and talkative, both of them, their hair blown back, the Rector noble as Wordsworth." Hidden here, too, is an allusion to Yeats's description of *his* father in *Beautiful Lofty Things*, "His beautiful mischievous head thrown back," and Maud Gonne in the same poem, "Pallas Athene in that straight back and arrogant head." It is not a book for those with reading difficulties.

Sebastian is Jane Gardam's first successful attempt at portraying an adolescent boy. (Christian in *A Long Way from*

Verona is too much of a caricature to be taken very seriously.) She was to do so again, equally successfully, in *Bilgewater.* Sebastian is a naive, sweet, over-earnest seventeen-year-old, who, one feels, will face a great many problems after the book finishes, when he leaves the monastery for the outside world. The conclusion suggests another story to be told—Athene, who likes to imagine she is the reincarnation of Emily Brontë, at one point glimpses her Heathcliff, a boy who turns out to be a friend of Sebastian's: the novel ends with one of Dodo's innumerable letters that says, among many other things, that Sebastian has invited him home for Christmas.

In *Bilgewater*—the title is another nickname, a roundup down of "Bill's daughter"—the adolescent protagonist is nearly eighteen, and as befits the advance in age, the writing is more adult, sharper in its observation and humor, and more literary in its allusions than its predecessors. Autumn is "the season of UCCA and mellow fruitfulness;" Olivier in the film of *Hamlet* looks "pretty ancient in a gold wig wailing about some battlements in clouds of what looked like steam"; and this long sentence from the opening chapter, with its echoes of Sterne, Dickens and Salinger is characteristic of the book's wit, hyperbole, and complex style:

> I emerged into this cold house in this cold seaside town where you can scarcely even get the telly for the height of the hills behind—I emerged into this great sea of boys and masters at my father's school (St. Wilfrid's) an orange-haired, short-sighted, frog-bodied ancient, a square and solemn baby, a stolid, blinking, slithery-pupilled (it was before they got the glasses which straightened the left eye out) two-year-old, a glooming ten-year-old hanging about the school cloisters ("Hi Bilgie, where's your broomstick?") and a strange, thick-set, hopeless adolescent, friendless and given to taking long idle walks by the sea.

With the heroine nearly eighteen, boys and men, appropriately, have major roles in *Bilgewater.* The men are the teachers at St. Wilfrid's—an all-male boarding school—and the boys are the pupils there. Both are extremely well done; the

teachers a sad, pathetic bunch of losers, the boys eager, ener-
getic and excited about the prospects of adult opportunity
and choice. But nothing is what it seems: Marigold's first
perceptions are for the most part wrong. A few of the masters
are made of sterner stuff than she imagines, and the two boys
who particularly engage her attention, Tom Terrapin and
Jack Rose—a nice use of symbol in the surnames—turn out
to be quite different from how they are at school when observed in their home backgrounds. Intelligent, sexy Tom is in
fact a liar and a fantasist; and handsome, chivalrous Jack is as
selfish and narrowly class-ridden as his parents, who are
bridge bores and alcoholics. One of the main themes of
Bilgewater is the enormous and often fatal consequences of
chance and coincidence—a theme that occupies much of
Leon Garfield's work, particularly *The Sound of Coaches* and
The Prisoners of September. As in *The Sound of Coaches,*
many of the events are inadvertently caused by the central
character. If it hadn't been for Marigold, Tom Terrapin would
not have run off with Grace Gathering and made such a disastrous marriage; Jack Rose would not have eloped with
Grace's mother, and if Marigold could have stopped her
teacher, Miss Bex, from entering her private life, her father
might not have married Paula. (Though in contrast to Tom's
and Jack's actions, Dad's new marriage is likely to be a great
success.)

Bilgewater is the work of someone at full stretch, in total
command of what she is doing. Page after page shows writing
of the highest excellence—the paradoxes of school with its
safeties and securities set against its pettinesses and tedium;
Tom Terrapin's beautiful evocation of the pierrots performing on the beach; the way memory manufactures mood
and atmosphere that never really existed; adolescent naivety
and isolation; how sexual desire can destroy friendship; descriptions of landscape and townscape: there is an almost
Dickensian disgust in this picture of the countryside being
destroyed by suburbia, "the march of the little houses" the
author calls it—

> The hungry, hideous city of Tees-side . . . eating nearer
> bite by bite, the cells of all its little towns floating nearer

to each other, then sticking together in an always denser
and more nondescript mass—like a disease of the blood.
Far away behind the twenty thousand identical streets
were the lights of some unloved tower blocks and beyond these a city of fluorescent light, pencil chimneys
with small orange paint-brush heads of flame, flares,
blazes of fire from furnaces, and wafting smells of gas.

Having brought her heroine up to the age of eighteen—
adulthood—it was obviously important that Jane Gardam
should change direction in her next books. *The Hollow Land*
and *Through the Dolls' House Door* do precisely this. *The
Hollow Land* is a return to the format of *A Few Fair Days*—a
collection of linked short stories—but it is for older readers
than *A Few Fair Days,* being richer and more subtle in its
allusions and images. It is a tale of two families, the rural
working-class Teesdales who have farmed in Cumbria for
centuries, and the Batemans, middle-class Londoners who
rent a cottage on the Teesdales' land for their summer holidays. From uncertain beginnings—the Teesdales resent "in-
comers," and the Batemans do not easily fit in—firm and
lasting friendships develop; the Batemans return year after
year and gradually become accepted as good neighbors, almost as much a part of local life as the people who were born
there. The book has a long timespan; Harry Bateman is five in
the first chapter and twenty-four in the last, and, once again,
the history of the characters after the story has finished is
suggested—Harry may well marry Bell Teesdale's daughter,
thus linking the families in more than friendship, and he will
in any case become the owner of Light Trees rather than the
tenant.

Jane Gardam clearly has a deep affection for this part of
England—its wildness and rugged beauty are evoked in every
story. The unchanging nature and timelessness of the landscape, of the houses built there, are a striking contrast to the
"hungry, hideous city" in *Bilgewater*—

the thick strong walls, the tiny, deep-set windows, the
huge old door that had been made and opened and shut
for the first time by somebody who wore sheepskins and
rags on his feet and spoke a language nobody in the yard

today would understand and who only ever went to the village on special occasions—to sell sheep or see the great Lord of the Marches set off to the coronation in his rubies and pearls.

The humor is gentler but no less ironic than in the previous books; Bell Teesdale, for instance, criticizing Harry for falling into Cumbrian speech patterns—"*Thowt!*" said Bell. "Speak right, can't yer. You'll finish up a savage"—or the amusing tale of Jimmie Metcalf, sitting in a telephone box "like the Buddha in the evening sun, eating a slice of prize apple pie." Jimmie, in the process of keeping an eye on the Teesdales' empty house, is robbed by a gang of thieves of the old kitchen table he had thought was worthless; but it's quickly discovered and is valued at a thousand pounds, which he uses to begin a new life in South America. There are several more eccentric rustics, none of them stock rural types: each is sharply individualized, Bell Teesdale's garrulous old grandfather, Hewitson, being especially memorable.

The Egg Witch is perhaps the most interesting story. Harry and his mother call at a farm on a very hot Sunday afternoon to buy eggs and have tea—but everything about the farm is painted black; the woman who lives there has "steely hair and eyes and mouth and wiry whiskers"; she refuses payment for the eggs because it's Sunday and her tea is a kindness ("I'm a long way from needing to serve *teas.*"). It is a disaster, too—pale heavy cake which "looked rather old" and was "built, like the bristle woman herself, to last." Harry's milk tastes of meat and he cannot drink it: "Waste is a sin," the woman observes. Maddened with frustration, he smashes all the eggs. His mother, later, comments quite truthfully to Mrs Teesdale—

> She was *awful.* She said she'd give us tea and then she wouldn't let us pay. And she said she'd give us eggs but it was a sin if we paid before tomorrow. She just let us make mistakes. She *watched* us making mistakes. She enjoyed us making mistakes.

But the real subtlety is that the person the author makes us feel most sorry for, and most sympathetic to, is neither of the Batemans; it is the old "bristle woman," the egg witch herself.

The successors to *The Hollow Land* were a number of short books for young children—the quality of the writing, the plots and the characterization are just as good as in the longer stories—then, most recently, *Through the Dolls' House Door,* which shows yet another direction. This novel is about toys that talk, the kind of scenario we find in Hans Andersen, or, in the twentieth century, in Russell Hoban's *The Mouse and his Child.* The influence of Hoban is revealed in many ways. Like him, Jane Gardam allows her toys to speak but move only with great difficulty, and much emphasis is given, as in *The Mouse and his Child,* to the inconveniences of such a life. It is reminiscent of Samuel Beckett too: the tragedy and heroism of those who can think, feel and speak, but who are forced to be static, often in uncomfortable places or grotesque positions for long periods of time. Hoban's influence is also present in the dialogue—

> "Earthquake, twaddle," said Miss Bossy. "It's urban disgrace. Case of serious overcrowding. Poverty-line. Authorities. Scandal. Day-and-Age. Bandaid."

—which sounds like the speech of the news-carrying jackdaw in *The Mouse and his Child;* and there is also an echo of the idea of the Last Visible Dog (the label on a tin of dog food that shows a tin of dog food with a label that shows a tin of dog food with a label that . . . etcetera)—

> This was a needle-box that Claire's mother had made into a dolls' house for the dolls' dolls.
> So the needle-box dolls' house stood in the dolls' house.
> And the dolls' house stood in Mary's house.
> One, two, three, like a seed in a pod on a tree in a forest.
> Claire had wanted Mary's mother to make a smaller dolls' house still, to put inside the needle-box for the needle-box dolls to play with. And then an even smaller. . . . And then a smaller. . . .

The whole novel works like this, as if it were a set of Chinese boxes, worlds within worlds, each idea being echoed from one "box" to another. So Claire gets her head stuck in the dolls' house window, and the rag doll, Cry, gets stuck in the dolls' house roof; the Trojan soldiers are stuck in a plastic bag in the chimney, and Bossy, the Dutch doll, once saved Holland from flooding—the famous boy in the poem, Jane Gardam tells us, didn't put his finger in the hole in the dyke, but shoved Bossy's head in instead.

Other books are referred to: the Trojan general passes the time by talking about his role in Homer's *Odyssey,* and the history of the toys—their travels, and their endless waiting to be moved—is also an odyssey, a child's version of Homer. There is also an interesting borrowing from Philippa Pearce; in *Tom's Midnight Garden* Tom, besides being himself, is an invention of Hattie's imagination, in danger of fading away when she no longer needs him. (As she gets older she can see through him.) In *Through the Dolls' House Door,* Sigger is invented by Mary and Claire and only exists because they think about her; as they grow up and need imaginary friends no more, she too is likely to fade away completely.

There is no writing down to children in this book. Though the subject-matter is more traditionally that of a child's world than in most of Jane Gardam's work, she still makes her audience reach in both language and concept—

> "An Abbey-cat is not an alley-cat, you know. It knows its way around the Psalms. I am right, Cat, am I not?"
> "I am not a Mediaevalist," said the Cat, "though I know a thing or two about Christianity that the cats of your abbey never heard of."

The humor, too, is not always likely to be appreciated by the young reader: "Intelligence becomes subdued when someone like Circe is about." *Through the Dolls' House Door,* like its "boxes," works on many levels: it can be read by a child as a straightforward narrative about talking toys, by adults as a saga of something else.

Jane Gardam, in seventeen years, has not been prolific as a writer for children and teenagers. She demands a great deal and her range is not wide, but for the intelligent, bookish child or adolescent she offers many delights. Several of the great modern classics are also for a minority taste—*Tom's Midnight Garden* and *The Mouse and his Child* are obvious examples—so Jane Gardam has nothing to be ashamed of. In my opinion, she is one of the finest and most rewarding of contemporary writers for the young.

REFERENCES

JANE GARDAM

>   *A Few Fair Days,* Hamish Hamilton, 1971; Macmillan, New York, 1972
>
>   *A Long Way from Verona,* Hamish Hamilton, 1971; Macmillan, New York, 1971
>
>   *The Summer After the Funeral,* Hamish Hamilton, 1973; Macmillan, New York, 1973
>
>   *Bilgewater,* Hamish Hamilton, 1976, Greenwillow, 1977
>
>   *The Hollow Land,* Julia MacRae, 1981; Greenwillow, 1982
>
>   *Bridget and William,* Julia MacRae, 1981
>
>   *Through the Dolls' House Door,* Julia MacRae, 1987

NINA BAWDEN

>   *Carrie's War,* Gollancz, 1973; Lippincott, 1973

ROALD DAHL

>   *Charlie and the Chocolate Factory,* Knopf, 1964; Allen and Unwin, 1967

MARGERY FISHER

>   review in *Growing Point* of *A Few Fair Days,* 1971

LEON GARFIELD

>   *The Sound of Coaches,* Kestrel, 1974; Viking, 1974
>
>   *The Prisoners of September,* Kestrel, 1975; Viking, 1975

THOMAS HARDY

>   *Jude the Obscure,* first published 1895

RUSSELL HOBAN

>   *The Mouse and his Child,* Harper, 1967; Faber, 1969

PENELOPE LIVELY

>   *Going Back,* Heinemann, 1975; Dutton, 1975

JILL PATON WALSH

>   *The Dolphin Crossing,* Macmillan, London, 1967; St. Martin's Press, 1967
>
>   *Fireweed,* Macmillan, London, 1969; Farrar Straus, 1970

PHILIPPA PEARCE
   Tom's Midnight Garden, Oxford, 1958; Lippincott, 1959

CHARLES READE
   The Cloister and the Hearth, first published 1861

ROBERT WESTALL
   The Machine-Gunners, Macmillan, London, 1975; Greenwillow, 1976

W. B. YEATS
   Beautiful Lofty Things first published in *Last Poems,* 1939

THE DARK IS RISIBLE

Susan Cooper

> We live in strange times. A character in a story, with his
> mother's help, cuts off his father's genitals, has children
> by his own sister and eats them at birth. This seems to
> be OK for children to read. In a different story, "bastard"
> and "arse" occur, and a teacher sends a letter to chide
> the publisher for printing filth. The crucial difference
> between the stories is that the first is a myth and the
> second is a modern novel.

These are Alan Garner's words in *The Death of Myth* and he
goes on to say that there is an apparent belief that myth is safe
for children to read because it is not "true." He could, perhaps, have added that myth is fashionable, that the use of
complicated Celtic names sounds profound, and that dressing
up any hackneyed cops-and-robbers story in even the most
tawdry mythical costumes is mistaken these days for something "significant" or "cosmic" or "compelling"—adjectives
used by critics at various times to overpraise the work of
Susan Cooper. Not that we get children cutting off their fathers' genitals in the quintet of books called *The Dark Is
Rising,* nothing like that at all: indeed quite the opposite—
the children in her novels are so overprotected from anything really unpleasant that her readers are more likely to be
suffocated with tedium than shocked by horrors.

The quintet—*Over Sea, Under Stone; The Dark Is Rising;
Greenwitch; The Grey King;* and *Silver on the Tree*—was
described by Neil Philip in an essay on Susan Cooper (*Fantasy: Double Cream or Instant Whip?*) as distinctly "instant
whip"—

> The books claim for their events a symbolic value which
> is unjustified because it is neither allied to a fully fledged

metaphysic nor anchored by a believable reality. Above
all, the reader's expectation that myth will be used to
provide, as T. S. Eliot saw it could, "a shape and a significance" to the narratives is continually thwarted.

—an opinion with which I completely agree. Not so the
majority of reviewers and critics. *The Times Literary Supplement* said of *Over Sea, Under Stone* that the story develops
"in the style of the mystical Buchan" (whatever that may
mean); Margery Fisher in *The Sunday Times* found *The Dark
Is Rising* "a totally compelling story"; *The Financial Times*
reviewer proclaimed that "Its mastery of craft and style, its
scholarship and poetry, above all its imaginative force and
power make of it in every sense a major book." *Greenwitch,*
said *The Library Review,* had "magnificence" and a "compelling" narrative; Jill Paton Walsh, in *The Times Literary Supplement,* felt that Susan Cooper "commands, to a rare degree,
the power to thrill the reader, to produce a particular tremor
of excitement and fear," while Natalie Babbitt, in *The New
York Times Book Review* said of the whole quintet that it was
"superbly written and constructed."

The quintet seems to me to have little poetry and no scholarship at all: dull, safe, predictable narratives; cardboard-thin
characterization; immense quantities of cliché; and its prose,
apart from a few felicitous phrases and the ability, in the first
half of *The Dark Is Rising,* to create a believable, wintry,
Christmas atmosphere, is undistinguished, particularly at all
the big climaxes.

To deal with the writing deficiencies first. *Over Sea, Under
Stone* and *Greenwitch* are set in Cornwall, *The Dark Is Rising*
in Buckinghamshire, *The Grey King* and *The Silver on the
Tree* in Wales. All of these very different backgrounds are
made to seem much alike—Cornwall in particular sounds far
from real. It's a picture-postcard, tourists' Cornwall, quite
unlike the bleak, inhospitable landscape of much of the actual
place: stereotyped "hefty, brown-faced" fishermen with
"beaming, wrinkled brown faces," "rosy-cheeked" women, a
"solid, red-faced" police sergeant, and "a sleepy, little shop."
This passage is characteristic:

> Trewissick seemed to be sleeping beneath its grey,
> slate-tiled roofs, along the narrow winding streets down
> the hill. Silent behind their lace-curtained windows, the
> little square houses let the roar of the car bounce back
> from their white-washed walls. Then Great-Uncle Merry
> swung the wheel round, and suddenly they were driving
> along the edge of the harbour, past water rippling and
> flashing golden in the afternoon sun. Sailing dinghies
> bobbed at their moorings along the quay. . . . [*Over Sea,
> Under Stone*]

One notices immediately two disastrous flaws, the reliance on
cliché rather than genuine observation—the town "seemed to
be sleeping," "narrow winding" streets, "swung the wheel
round," the sailing dinghies that "bob"— and the use of far too
many adjectives. This is the Cornwall of travel brochures.

The heavy reliance on adjectives as the words that are
meant to do all the work is an irritating weakness in the early
parts of the quintet, but it becomes worse in the later books,
a substitute for any genuinely felt observation. If she can use
two adjectives instead of one, or none, Susan Cooper will do
so:

> As he was walking through one of the Clwyd fields to-
> wards the river, with a high wild hedge on one side of
> him and the dark ploughed soil on the other, he heard a
> dull muffled thudding somewhere ahead. Then suddenly
> at a curve in the field he saw the figure, moving steadily
> and rhythmically as if in a slow, deliberate dance. [*The
> Grey King*]

At the climaxes in the narrative, there is a complete inability
to make what is happening sound exciting or horrifying.
Nothing is conveyed in any precise detail; empty words are
reached for, "dreadful," "deadly," "terrible," "utter," "des-
perate," "furious," "monstrous" (all adjectives, again, and adjectives that may have once meant something, but through
overuse contain nowadays no real emotion):

> But then a sudden terrible silence like suffocation
> came, blotting out all sound of the storm. In the moment
> of its last desperate chance, breaking across the barrier
> that had been holding it at bay, the Dark came for Will.

> Shutting out the sky and the earth, the deadly spinning
> pillar came at him, dreadful in its furious whirling ener-
> gy and utter quiet. There was no time for fear. Will stood
> alone. And the towering black column rushed to engulf
> him with all the monstrous forces of the Dark arrayed in
> its writhing mist. . . . [*The Dark Is Rising*]

There are also innumerable minor infelicities: few writers
ever began so many sentences with the word "And" as Susan
Cooper; it is meant to add a tone of solemnity to what is
happening, but it is in effect a tiresome mannerism. "There
was no sound anywhere, in all the immensity of space" is a
statement of the obvious; the King of the Lost Land, old and
near death, is described as "frail now" when he walks (as if he
wasn't frail when he was sitting down); "Immensity pressed
in on him, terrifying, threatening" is a characteristic
vagueness masquerading as something profound; but perhaps
the worst piece of English is where the author talks about a
"dark light." The landscape descriptions are downright careless, particularly in their repetitiveness. "Sweep" (again, a
bogus, grand-sounding word) is used dozens of times—"the
sweep of Cardigan Bay," "a sweep of waving green bracken,"
"the downward sweep of the path," "a widening sweep of the
coast" (all these in the same chapter); "exposed sweep of
sand," "a great sweep of brown sand" (on consecutive
pages). This sentence in *Silver on the Tree*—

> And beyond, over the flat stretch of marsh on the other
> side of the river-mouth, the mountain mass of Mid-Wales
> rolled along the skyline, purple and brown and dull
> green, its colours shifting and patching constantly as
> clouds sailed over the summer sky past the sun.

is regurgitated a few pages later as

> And across the valley, beyond its further side patched
> blue with cloud-shadows and dark with close-planted
> fir, there rolled in line after line the massing ancient hills
> of Wales.

The sentence before this one begins with "Far, far below"; a
sentence a few pages previously begins with "Far, far below."

Note, too, the bogus significance given to the prose by such inflated phrases as this, or "the massing ancient hills of Wales." (There is a suggestion here of the cliché "rolling hills," and how can hills roll and mass at the same time?) To sum up, the writing is shoddy throughout, and Natalie Babbitt's judgment that it is "superb" seems to me to be remarkably eccentric.

The narratives of all five books are another major weakness. Each story is concerned with the attempts of the forces of the Dark to overcome the powers of the Light and rule the world; the struggle, we are told, has been going on since the beginning of time, and both sides use human beings in one century or another to help them in their quest. The idea is interesting—Christian, or at least Manichean—and it could be used as an effective symbol for the good and evil that exist in all of us. But the author never relates this central theme to what goes on in the human personality; the Dark and the Light have nothing to do with us (or the human characters in the novels): their struggle is outside our concerns. Though Great-Uncle Merry informs us more than once (again, the repetitiveness is irksome) that the Light is on the side of Man, that the Dark wishes to destroy us, we have no evidence, no proof of this. In fact, the forces of the Dark seem a pretty feeble lot all round. True, they interfere with the weather and cause tremendous snowstorms and so on; they manage to kill a few sheep and a dog in *The Grey King* and kidnap another dog in *Greenwitch,* and in *The Dark Is Rising* they kidnap Will Stanton's sister and injure his mother's leg. But that seems to be the limit of their abilities. The narrative lacks excitement because nobody is ever put in a situation of any real danger at any time. A few magic words are muttered, or a talisman is used, and the Dark is thwarted. Mary is so bewitched, during her kidnap ordeal, that all she remembers is she was taken for a pleasant ride on a horse. Even Mrs Stanton's leg, we discover eventually, isn't broken; it's merely sprained. We are constantly told by Merry that none of the children will come to any harm, will never experience anything dangerous; and when something mildly unpleasant occurs the Light makes the person involved forget what has happened. With the Dark so ineffective as a symbol of power and evil, one wonders what on earth the Light is worried about. Dogs? Sheep? Surely not. The suspicion occurs that maybe it's the Light that is evil; that we're all being deceived by jolly old Uncle Merry and the other Old Ones but in fact it's the *critics* who are deceiving us by telling us how significant and cosmic it all is, when in reality it is nothing of the sort.

The characterization, as I said, is cardboard thin. People are only distinguished by physical appearance, or a few predictable, frequently repeated reactions. Barny's blond hair is always flopping into his eyes; Merry's voice, we are told a score of times, is deeply resonant. Jane, the only girl to play a major role in events, is a stereotypically anxious female, full of warnings to the boys not to do anything rash or dangerous, given to frequent exclamations like "Goodness!" "Oh dear!" and "Good gracious!" There are several comforting middle-aged women—among them Mrs Penhallow, Aunt Jen, Mrs Stanton—busy in the kitchen providing bacon and eggs; and sensible fathers and father-figures to give sound advice at the right moments. It would seem despite the mention of motorways, that the world we are in is the world of children's books of the nineteen thirties—strongly traditional role-playing by the adults, nice middle-class kids who say "super!" and "gosh!" and families renting houses in Cornwall for the holidays complete with housekeeper to wait on them. It's Arthur-Ransome-land, without Arthur Ransome's genius.

The villains are all too obvious. Mr Hastings, in *Over Sea, Under Stone* has "a cold deep voice," smiles "grimly," and has a face "with a frightening coldness behind it"; "Something monstrous blazed behind Mr Hastings's eyes, something not human, that filled her with a horror more vast and dreadful than anything she had felt before." He speaks like any standard crook in a cheap thriller:

> "You may be a stupid little boy," Mr Hastings said, "but not I think as stupid as all that. . . Come along. We know that you have found a map, and that with the help of your esteemed great-uncle, Professor Lyon"—his mouth twisted on the words as if he were tasting something unpleasant—"you have been attempting to trace the place to which it leads."

This is "Ve have vays of making you talk" English. We are, in effect, back to writing faults; the author's inability to visualize Mr Hastings as anything other than a two-dimensional figure leads to the inability to make his voice sound real. Her ear for the music of words is weak. The clashing, repeated "an" sound in these sentences is a good example of verbal deafness:

> He said quietly, his voice eerily echoing, "Bran, if you put your hands out—"
> "I've found them" Bran said. "Like banisters, aren't they?" [*The Grey King*]

The genteel exclamations and reactions in supposedly dangerous or unusual situations lead to bathos:

> "But I know that they wanted only the grail," Great-Uncle Merry said, "to help them on the way to something else. I know what they intend to do, and I know that they must at all costs be stopped. And I am very much afraid that you three, as the finders, will be needed once more to give help—far sooner than I had expected."
> "Shall we?" said Jane slowly.
> "Super," said Simon. [*Greenwitch*]

Great-Uncle Merry is a glaring weakness. He is an "Old One," a chief lord of the Light, immortal, able to appear in various centuries in many different guises, but he is, as Neil Philip says:

> a standard children's-book wise uncle, with his "untidy white hair", his "bleak, craggy face", his "long, wiry fingers", with his improbable scholarship and his mixture of jocose gullibility and reassuring omnipotence.

He has a vague resemblance to Captain Flint in Arthur Ransome's *Swallows and Amazons,* but, again, Ransome's genius is missing—Captain Flint is a properly realized individual; Great-Uncle Merry is not.

The mythological borrowings are another problem. Arthur, Taliesin, the grail, Merlin, Herne the Hunter do not have a genuinely symbolic function in the plot; what goes on does not parallel *their* story: the quest for the grail, for example, lacks the purpose it has in Arthurian legend—Susan Cooper's grail is no more than a stage property, another item among many lost objects needed by the Light for no clearly defined reasons. Much of the narrative in all five books consists of a search for some object or another, but it might as well be a hunt for a lost coin, or any little thing small boys like to collect and hoard; there is no sense that the grail or the golden harp have a specific use of their own and that nothing else will do. Nor is there any excitement, or frustration, or urgency in the search. In *The Dark Is Rising* Will finds all the objects he needs with surprising ease, and in *Greenwitch* there is a particularly bad piece of cheating: the lead case containing the precious manuscript is given to Jane by the Greenwitch in a dream and it is actually there on her pillow in the morning. Thus any real confrontation with the ambiguous figure of the Greenwitch is avoided. Cheating—or at least inexplicable inconsistency—occurs elsewhere. Will, who is both an ordinary eleven-year-old boy in modern times and an "Old One" with tremendous, supernatural powers— he can fly through the air, swim vast distances under the sea—has to borrow Bran's bicycle in *The Grey King* to go and fetch the golden harp. Why does he not just fly to the farmhouse in no time at all? Because if he did so, the danger Bran is in would disappear immediately. But the reader is let down here, too: Bran suddenly discovers new powers in himself, and with a magic trick is free of trouble. Why does the Grey King, who is, we are told, a very potent force on the side of the Dark, choose to exert his influence through such a weak and idiotic man as Caradog Prichard? Why doesn't he appear in a more dangerous human shape? If he did, there might be some suspense; we would not know long before the end that he will inevitably lose the battle. Why does Herne the Hunter in *The Dark Is Rising* repel the assembled armies of the Dark? Is it because he has a real and a symbolic purpose at this point in events? No: it is simply that we happen to be near Windsor Great Park, and Herne the Hunter is an ancient legendary figure associated with this place. So he's dragged in for the author's convenience—no other reason. The mythological borrowings in these books, it seems to me, are cheap short cuts; they are no evidence at all of what *The Financial Times* reviewer chose to label as "scholarship."

Neil Philip talks of "patchy excellence" throughout the quintet, and suggests that the second volume, *The Dark Is Rising,* has "sustained excellence." I can see no excellence anywhere, patchy or sustained. It is true, however, that the five books vary in quality, and I agree with him in thinking that the second volume is the best. Characterization and narrative are weak: the story *should* engage us, telling, as it does, of Will's attempt to save his family who are at the mercy of the Dark; however, the danger the Stantons are in becomes negligible when we see how little the Dark can do. *The Dark Is Rising,* nevertheless, scores in its portrayal of the weather, of a snowbound, freezing landscape that underlines the joys of Christmas. The jollifications indoors seem all the more pleasurable when contrasted with what is happening out of doors, even if those jollifications do not altogether ring true as a faithful rendering of modern Christmas customs. The yule log, the family carol singing at the manor house, the glass of punch given as a reward by the lady of the manor, are not practices common nowadays in the villages of the English home counties, but rituals of times long since dead, or the Christmas "props" of long-ago children's books. The Stantons, we are told, do their shopping in Slough, which is a hideous, modern urban sprawl, synonymous in many jokes with ugliness. John Betjeman was once moved to begin a poem with the lines—

> Come, friendly bombs, and fall on Slough
> It isn't fit for humans now
> There isn't grass to graze a cow

but nothing of this real-life Buckinghamshire is used in *The Dark Is Rising.* The Stantons seem to live in the depths of the countryside, though Buckinghamshire is commuter-land: not genuinely rural England. Atmosphere, however, there certainly is in *The Dark Is Rising:*

> The snow lay thin and apologetic over the world. That
> wide grey sweep was the lawn, with the straggling trees
> of the orchard still dark beyond; the white squares were

the roofs of the garage, the old barn, the rabbit hutches, the chicken coops. Further back there were only the flat fields of Dawsons' Farm, dimly white-striped. All the broad sky was grey, full of more snow that refused to fall. There was no colour anywhere.

"Dimly white-striped" is clumsy, but "the snow lay thin and apologetic" is fine, and the bald simple statement of that last sentence—"There was no colour anywhere"—is effective. Later, when the snow begins to fall in earnest, the same quality of writing is maintained:

All around him the trees stretched to the flat horizon of the valley. The only break in that white world of branches was away over to the south, where the Thames ran; he could see the bend in the river marked like a single stilled wave in this white ocean of forest, and the shape of it looked as though the river were wider than it should have been.

Other, shorter phrases are also striking: chestnut trees inhabited by rooks are "rubbish-roofed with the clutter of their sprawling nests," and James, Will's brother, is described when annoyed as "fuming like a small angry locomotive." Unfortunately, in the second half of the book, when the focus shifts from the background to the battles between the Light and the Dark, the quality of the prose drops into the banal. In contrast, Penelope Lively, in the concluding chapters of *The Whispering Knights,* shows how well this kind of thing can be done.

The other four novels do not have a setting so clearly observed; in consequence the thinness of the plots stands out. *Over Sea, Under Stone* and *The Grey King* have a story that just about works on the kids-outwit-crooks level, but the mythological encumbrances are an embarrassment; and *Greenwitch* doesn't have a narrative that generates any real interest at all. *Silver on the Tree* is the longest book of the five; it is slow, pretentious, and, as Neil Philip says, "the dialogue is suffering from dropsy":

"Go well, Merriman," he said quietly.
"Go well, Will Stanton," Merriman said, his voice tight

with strain. "Into your own place, at this Midsummer
hour, where affairs will take you in the direction you
must go. And we will strive at our separate tasks across
the centuries, through the waves of time, touching and
parting, parting and touching in the pool that whirls
forever. And I shall be with you before long."

In *The Grey King* the season is autumn; in *Greenwitch,* spring;
and in *Silver on the Tree* and *Over Sea, Under Stone,* summer;
but there is no attempt by the author to suggest the influence
of those periods of the year on the characters and the action,
as winter influences events and people in *The Dark Is Rising.*
Maybe it is because the Dark can only create snowstorms?
Causing drought doesn't seem to be one of its abilities. The
festivals of these seasons—Hallowe'en, for instance—are referred to but left curiously unexplored. The spring fertility
rite in *Greenwitch* has no foundation in actuality, and it is the
most unconvincing of all the celebrations mentioned. It is
particularly odd that Susan Cooper should have invented her
own version when one remembers that Cornwall is rich, if
not unique, in the number and variety of pagan spring ceremonies that are still kept up today—the Furry Dance at
Helston, for example, the May Day hobbyhorse at Padstow,
the chasing of the silver ball at St. Columb Major. One sus-
pects, again, that the seasons and their festivals are, like the
mythological elements in the books, mere conveniences—
window-dressing.

"Magnificence," "mastery of craft and style," "imaginative
force and power"? The whole quintet is shallow, relying on a
box of cheap magic tricks to disguise the poverty of the
author's thinking and imagination.

Dawn of Fear and *Seaward* are the only novels for children
that Susan Cooper has written which are not connected with
The Dark Is Rising sequence. *Dawn of Fear* belongs to a
quite different genre, for it is a realistic story set at the beginning of the Second World War. Its faults are, as usual, poor
characterization (it is difficult, as one reads on, to remember
which of the three central characters, Derek, Peter and Geoffrey, did or said what), a prose style that will not often
do what is required of it, and the bathos of genteel reactions:

And then in the second that they still paused on the black asphalt playground, with the grubby concrete boxes that were the air-raid shelters looming ahead of them, they saw the unbelievable happen. Suddenly the rigid, steadily advancing formation of enemy planes broke its pattern, lost its head as plane after plane broke away and dived; and they heard a new higher noise and glimpsed, diving through a broad gap in the clouds out of the sun, a gaggle of other smaller planes scattering the bombers as a dog scatters sheep. It was a furious sky now, full of coughing gunfire.

They heard other guns open up, deeper, closer, on the ground.

"Gosh!" Derek said.

Tom, who is about to be called up to serve in the merchant navy, is an improbable character, quoting at length over the kitchen sink from Winston Churchill's Dunkirk speech at one moment, then, at another, playing mud-balls with a neighborhood gang of young kids. But *Dawn of Fear* has qualities that the quintet lacks; in particular a convincing portrayal of the violence, danger, and excitement that Susan Cooper so scrupulously avoids elsewhere. The sheer nastiness of even young boys is well suggested in a scene in which a rival gang smashes up the secret camp Geoffrey, Derek, and Peter have built; the touch of real horror is provided by the presence of a cat the gang has killed—a cat whose life the three central characters have recently saved. A neat parallel with the mindless violence of fascism that the Allied powers are fighting in the war is implied—real symbolism of Light and Dark. The ending of the story is without any sentimentality: Peter's house is destroyed in an air raid, and he and his parents and their lodger are killed. Derek's stunned grief—an almost physical paralysis—rings true: "He felt tight all over, as if his skin had suddenly become too small." The concluding pages, in which Geoffrey and Derek discover that the only thing which held them together was Peter's friendship for both of them, and that now they will have to find something in each other that was not previously a part of the trio's relationship, is also well done—Peter's death has at least shifted them a step forward on the way to maturity. If Susan Cooper had continued to write realistic fiction, the more rigorous disciplines it demands would perhaps have matured her as a writer: the slapdash short cuts and trivial thinking of the quintet would not have been so easy to get away with. *Dawn of Fear* also differs from the fantasies in that it has a setting (the not-quite-country and not-quite-town of outer London suburbia: the *real* Buckinghamshire?) that is more than adequately described and which has a proper function in the story. It is not a great book, but it is far and away her best.

Seaward is a return to fantasy. Its protagonists are two curiously-named teenagers, Westerly and Cally—Susan Cooper emphasizes that they are children, but coyly suggests an older age by saying of Westerly's chest, "the tentative dark hair that was beginning to thicken there." Cally's parents and Westerly's mother have recently died: the story consists of putting the hero and heroine through a series of meandering, episodic adventures in a mythical country ruled by Lady Taranis (Death). Cally and Westerly fall in love, search for their parents, and, not finding them, opt to return to the real world. Lurgan (Life), Taranis, and their various minions, struggle for possession of the two teenagers, but, as usual, nothing very dramatic happens to them other than being forced to endure a great deal of foul weather and some rather unpleasant landscapes. The writing is worse than in *The Dark Is Rising* quintet; it reads like self-parody. Banal statements of the utterly obvious are intoned with great solemnity: "All things die, so that other things may live"; "The bird cannot fly without the air, the squirrel cannot climb without the tree"; "Like the leaves on the trees each year, you will grow and change." The word "and" is made to work very hard indeed:

> And every tree along the river was flung bending to the ground, and every bloom was ripped from the vines and plants round the house, as suddenly the air all around them roared louder than the waves, and a great wind seized Cally and West and carried them high into the air and away.

Hills, as before, are "rolling"; and everything has "sweep"— "the land rose again in a long bony sweep," "a great sweep of sky," "the long sweep of the plateau." As usual, too, clichéd adjectives are scattered about like pepper: "long rippling hair," "thin cruel line," "dreadful chill menace"; sometimes they are made to work, ungrammatically, as adverbs: "Westerly said, clear and deliberate." Dropsical pace and verbal elephantiasis are the hallmarks of *Seaward*—

> As Cally and Westerly drew level with him he swung round, holding his cloak by its edge, flinging out both arms so that he seemed to enfold them and Taranis in two great golden wings. He drew them forward into the white mist that swirled where there had been a wall, and through the mist into brightness. And they were standing out under the blue sky on a grassy headland high above the sea, with the sweep of that limitless flat horizon before them, and at their backs the rolling green hills and plains inland.

"Fantasy is a difficult literary form, particularly in a critical climate which inclines to overlook inflated and second-hand language in any work whose reliance on magic can be interpreted as psychological or philosophical profundity," says Neil Philip.

Even though critics may talk of literary excellence as the major criterion of assessment, they are often blinded to the second-rate when it is decorated in the safe and familiar fancy clothes, however threadbare, of King Arthur. Other criteria—in particular a longing for a less tangled moral order than that of the second half of the twentieth century—intrude into their thinking. The attraction of the rural present-day in Susan Cooper's books is because it isn't real; her Cornwall is not Cornwall now, nor what it was fifty years ago: it is a hazy, nostalgic memory of childhood middle-class seaside holidays. One would not go so far as to say the current evaluation of her "excellence" is a middle-class conspiracy to give children a sense of supposedly genuine values that have disappeared in modern times, or a plot to provide them with a radical alternative to the problems of getting to grips, in their literature, with the major snags of contemporary living, but I would say that in evaluating the worth of fantasy and myth many critics allow their critical faculties to go to sleep. "Magic," Neil Philip writes, "can replace emotion as the dynamic

of a plot; and fantasy characters and countries are more ame-
nable to lazy depiction than known muscle and earth." It is
small wonder that this is so when critics refuse to see "lazy
depiction" at its most obvious.

REFERENCES

SUSAN COOPER
> *Over Sea, Under Stone,* Harcourt, 1965; Cape, 1965
> *Dawn of Fear,* Harcourt, 1970; Chatto, 1972
> *The Dark Is Rising,* Atheneum, 1973; Chatto, 1973
> *Greenwitch,* Atheneum, 1974; Chatto, 1974
> *The Grey King,* Atheneum, 1975; Chatto, 1975
> *Silver on the Tree,* Atheneum, 1977; Chatto, 1977
> *Seaward,* Atheneum, 1983; Bodley Head, 1983

NATALIE BABBITT
> review of *The Dark Is Rising* quintet in *The New York Times
> Book Review,* 1977

JOHN BETJEMAN
> "Slough" in *Continual Dew,* Murray, 1937

MARGERY FISHER
> review of *The Dark Is Rising* in *The Sunday Times* (London),
> 1973

ALAN GARNER
> "The Death of Myth" in *Children's Literature in Education,*
> November 1970

PENELOPE LIVELY
> *The Whispering Knights,* Heinemann, 1971; Dutton, 1976

JILL PATON WALSH
> review of *The Dark Is Rising* in *The Times Literary Supple-
> ment,* 1973

NEIL PHILIP
> "Fantasy: Double Cream or Instant Whip?" in *Signal,* May 1981

ARTHUR RANSOME
> *Swallows and Amazons,* Cape, 1930; Lippincott, 1931

DAHL'S CHICKENS

Roald Dahl

The sales of *Charlie and the Chocolate Factory* are huge; it was noted number one in a (London) *Sunday Times* survey of the "best" children's books (whatever "best" may mean); it is widely used in schools; it has been filmed. It has also been condemned by critics as racist, sadistic and muddled. "One of the most tasteless books ever written for children," Eleanor Cameron said in *McLuhan, Youth, and Literature*. Her comments, predictably, produced protests from people who seemed to think that because the book is popular it must be good. Popularity equals merit is a not infrequent deduction made by adults about children's fiction, and an unfortunate consequence of this is that the young reader may be led to think the same thing. Roald Dahl has written other stories for children that are more tasteless than *Charlie and the Chocolate Factory,* and some less so—the moral universe he inhabits seems confused and full of contradictions.

The confusions and contradictions are evident in *Boy.* "This is not an autobiography," Dahl writes in its preface; "an autobiography is a book a person writes about his own life and it is usually full of all sorts of boring details." But *Boy is* an autobiography full of details—none of which are, in fact, boring; it is a realistic, but selective, account of Dahl's childhood and adolescence: it omits, for example, because he has a child reader in mind, everything to do with his teenage emotional and sexual development. The comment about autobiography being "usually full of all sorts of boring details" is a sweeping generalization, the purpose of which is, presumably, to suggest to the reader that autobiography is a big word that might deter him/her from buying the book, so it won't be used. Many pages in *Boy* are devoted to unpleasantly detailed accounts of adult men caning children—an obsessive theme in Dahl's work. It also figures in *Lucky Break* (an autobiographical piece in *The Wonderful Story of Henry Sugar and Six More*) and in *Danny the Champion of the World;* and there is a great deal of gratuitous violence in other books: the squashing of the aunts in *James and the Giant Peach,* the poisonous drink given to Grandma in *George's Marvellous Medicine,* "two disgusting people doing disgusting things to each other" in *The Twits,* the fate of the selfish children in *Charlie and the Chocolate Factory,* the bullying of Peter in *The Swan* (a story from the *Henry Sugar* collection), and the attitudes and behavior of many of the characters in *The Witches.* It is difficult to avoid the feeling that Dahl, like Robert Westall, enjoys writing about violence, while at the same time condemning it. In *Boy* the confusion is neatly demonstrated—

> By now I am sure you will be wondering why I lay so much emphasis upon school beatings in these pages. The answer is that I cannot help it. All through my school life I was appalled by the fact that masters and senior boys were allowed literally to wound other boys, and sometimes quite severely. I couldn't get over it. I have never got over it.

In the next paragraph he contradicts this reasonable statement with—

> There is nothing wrong with a few quick sharp tickles on the rump. They probably do a naughty boy a lot of good.

No evidence is produced to substantiate this.

The trouble with Dahl's world is that it is black and white—two-dimensional and unreal—and that he has a habit of elevating personal prejudices, ordinary likes and dislikes, into matters of morality. This is nowhere more evident than in *Charlie and the Chocolate Factory* with "its phony presentation of poverty" as Eleanor Cameron calls it—"a device to make more excruciatingly tantalizing the heavenly vision of being able to live eternally fed upon chocolate. This is Charlie's sole character and being." She added, when Dahl wrote

to *The Horn Book Magazine* to complain about her remarks—

> I find it regrettable . . . that Willy Wonka . . . can tri-
> umphantly convince Charlie that life lived forever inside
> the factory, enclosed as in a prison, is the height of all
> possible bliss, with . . . nothing expressed that would
> question this idea.

an observation with which few discerning readers would dis-
sent. "Bliss" in *Charlie and the Chocolate Factory* is equated
with being perpetually shut up in a sort of Disneyland. Other
parts of the story are just as disturbing. Of the four "bad"
children, one is nasty because she chews gum; another because he eats too much chocolate; a third watches an excessive amount of television; and the fourth is spoiled and over-
indulged by her parents. These faults are displayed as so de-
plorable that the children have to be "cured" by sadistic
punishments. Augustus Gloop, the boy who eats too much
chocolate, is described thus:

> Great flabby folds of fat bulged out from every part of his
> body, and his face was like a monstrous ball of dough
> with two small greedy curranty eyes peering out upon
> the world.

We are being asked to dislike this child because he is fat, and
therefore sanction a prejudice that exists in every school
playground. It is not the only time that Dahl suggests fatness
is a symptom of nastiness; there is Farmer Boggis in *Fantastic
Mr Fox,* the punters at the casino in *The Wonderful Story of
Henry Sugar* and Aunt Sponge in *James and the Giant
Peach*—

> Aunt Sponge was enormously fat and very short. She had
> small piggy eyes, a sunken mouth, and one of those
> white flabby faces that looked exactly as though it had
> been boiled. She was like a great white soggy overboiled
> cabbage.

There is an unnecessary tone of glee and spite in this: and it is
to the gleeful, spiteful aspects of a child's nature that Dahl all
too often appeals.

But *Charlie and the Chocolate Factory* is even more reprehensible for its socio-political attitudes. Willy Wonka is a
dreadful example of the unacceptable face of capitalism—the
owner of an enormous factory that employs slave labor. "The
exclamation mark," Eleanor Cameron says, "is the extent of
his individuality." It would perhaps be all right if Willy
Wonka was portrayed as the villain of the piece, but he's the
hero, the master magician, the fairy godfather who offers
children all the delights of chocolate, the benevolent millionaire who bequeaths his factory to a deserving child. His
employees, the Oompa-Loompas, (the name itself is a racist
putdown) are little people brought from Africa like blacks
who were brought from that continent as slaves in the nineteenth century, they live in the factory and are never allowed
to experience life outside its gates—like slaves on Southern
plantations. We are not asked to feel sorry for them or to see
that their enforced incarceration is monstrous, or to think
that Mr Wonka's use of them in his experiments with new
chocolates is treating humans like laboratory mice; they are
all part of the fun of the factory, entirely happy—so we're
told—singing all day long as they work.

Similar problems of dubious morality plague the subsequent books. *Charlie and the Great Glass Elevator* warns
children not to tamper with medicines they may find in
bathroom cabinets, but it makes no comment on the ethical
questions raised by Mr Wonka's experiments with pills that
can bring eternal youth. Again, the Oompa-Loompas are the
unfortunate laboratory mice; one particular test goes wrong
and causes an Oompa-Loompa to be prematurely aged—
which is seen as comic. Consider also the racism of this
rather infantile joke:

> "It is very difficult to phone people in China, Mr Presi-
> dent," said the Postmaster General. "The country's so
> full of Wings and Wongs, every time you wing you get
> the wong number."

In *Danny the Champion of the World,* poaching pheasants is
not regarded as stealing; it's a great joke, indeed a virtue—
because Mr Hazell, the owner of the pheasants, is snobbish,
drinks too much, and is rude and patronizing to Danny and

his father. Again, phony poverty is contrasted with fake riches. One scene, admittedly very well written, describes nine-year-old Danny driving a car. His motives are made to justify the act—he's attempting to rescue his injured father—but it's shown as exciting rather than dangerous:

> I will not pretend I wasn't petrified. I was. But mixed in with the awful fear was a glorious feeling of excitement. Most of the really exciting things we do in our lives scare us to death. They wouldn't be exciting if they didn't.

Much of the book is concerned with Danny's and his father's plots for cutting Mr Hazell down to size, and one detects the same tone of childish glee and spite as elsewhere. Another fake is the unpleasantness—the only characteristic Dahl mentions—of the farmers in *Fantastic Mr Fox,* which makes the morality of killing foxes simplistically black and white, not the complex issue that it really is. It is much better done in William Mayne's *A Grass Rope.* Dahl does not tell us *why* his farmers are so revolting; they just are, he says, and he seems to think that this is sufficient. He is short-changing the readers, however, by avoiding explanations and leaving an impression that it doesn't really matter if foxes slaughter chickens and geese.

Worse, though, are *The Twits, The Witches,* and *George's Marvellous Medicine.* In *The Twits* facial hair is perceived almost as a moral defect—bearded people are dirty and are trying to hide their real appearance. These remarks do not apply just to Mr Twit (if they did, one would accept them), but to bearded men in general. After three pages on this subject, Dahl homes in on Mr Twit and positively revels in the physically repulsive—

> . . . if you peered deep into the moustachy bristles sticking out over his upper lip, you would probably see . . . things that had been there for months and months, like a piece of maggoty green cheese or a mouldy old cornflake or even the slimy tail of a tinned sardine.

When he turns to Mrs Twit he makes some comparisons between goodness and physical beauty:

> If a person has ugly thoughts, it begins to show on the
> face. And when that person has ugly thoughts every day,
> every week, every year, the face gets uglier and uglier
> until it gets so ugly you can hardly bear to look at it.
>   A person who has good thoughts cannot ever be ugly.

The adult reader, of course, won't take such statements seriously, and maybe the author does not intend that *anyone*
should take them seriously; but this is a book for relatively
young children. Do we want them to think that all ugly
people are evil, that all physically attractive people are virtuous? The first half of *The Twits* consists, as Dahl says, of
"disgusting people doing disgusting things to each other": Mr
Twit puts a frog in his wife's bed; she retaliates by putting
worms in his spaghetti; he ties her up and keeps her a prisoner in the garden, then attempts to get rid of her altogether.
In the second half they both do disgusting things to their pet
monkeys, the birds in the garden, and a group of small boys;
the birds and the monkeys take their revenge and cause the
Twits to die. The net result of all this disgusting behavior is a
disgusting book.

The Witches is sexist and gratuitously frightening. If you
wanted to give children nightmares and thoroughly confuse
them about adult behavior—the behavior of women in particular—then *The Witches* could well do a first-class job:

> I do not wish to speak badly about women. Most women
> are lovely. But the fact remains that all witches are wom-
> en. There is no such thing as a male witch.

Many men, in fact, have been put to death for witchcraft;
several, for instance, after the trials at Salem, Massachusetts,
in 1692. "A real witch," Dahl says, "is easily the most dangerous of all living creatures on earth . . . They all look like
nice ladies." They could, he adds, be the woman next door, a
woman you noticed on a bus, or even your school-teacher
"who is reading these words to you at this very moment"—

> Look carefully at that teacher. Perhaps she is smiling at
> the absurdity of such a suggestion. Don't let that put you
> off. It could be part of her cleverness.

Some readers will see this for the nonsense it's meant to be, but others may well be bewildered and frightened. Frightening children is not always wrong: it would be ridiculously over-protective to banish from books everything that is a possible cause of alarm, for children have to learn how to deal with fear. Indeed, some alarming stories can be therapeutic; Ted Hughes's *The Iron Man* or Maurice Sendak's *Where the Wild Things Are* may well have this function. But a very untherapeutic kind of fear, I think, is likely to result from much of *The Witches,* because what it says is irresponsible, is there for no good reason—

> "Tell me what those English witches do, Grandmamma," I said.
> "Well," she said, sucking away at her stinking cigar, "their favourite ruse is to mix up a powder that will turn a child into some creature or other that all grown-ups hate."
> "What sort of a creature, Grandmamma?"
> "Often it's a slug," she said. "A slug is one of their favourites. Then the grown-ups step on the slug and squish it without knowing it's a child."
> "That's perfectly beastly!" I cried . . .
> . . . "I've known English witches," she went on, "who have turned children into pheasants and then sneaked the pheasants up into the woods the very day before the pheasant-shooting season opened . . . Of course they get shot . . . And then they get plucked and roasted and eaten for supper . . . it gives the English witches great pleasure to stand back and watch the grown-ups doing away with their very own children."

Again, spite, glee, and pleasure. The main character of the book does get turned into something else—a mouse—and has to remain a mouse for the rest of his life: which robs the story of its expected resolution, and leaves a nasty feeling that evil has triumphed. (The suggestion that he likes being a mouse does not convince.)

George's Marvellous Medicine is the most repellent of all Roald Dahl's books for the young. George's grandmother is crotchety, selfish, and a nuisance—as old people sometimes are; so George decides to cure her "or blow off the top of her head" with home-made medicine. He wonders whether to put the contents of the bathroom medicine cabinet in the brew, but decides not to—Dahl, once more, gives the reader a lecture on the follies of experimenting with such things. Fine: but absolute moral confusion follows this, for George throws into the concoction all sorts of household poisons— shampoo, nail varnish, hair remover, deodorant, floor polish, shoe polish, flea powder for dogs, anti-freeze, engine oil, and a quart of paint. This is duly administered to Grandma, and when George's father finds out, he praises and encourages his son! (Dad dislikes his mother-in-law and can also see the possibility of financial gain, for the "medicine" makes things grow to a vast size.) Grandma eventually drinks some more of it, thinking it is tea, but this time it causes her to shrink. Not to her proper dimensions, however (which would be some amends for the cruelty inflicted on her); she dwindles away to nothing and disappears completely. The moral of this is stated by George's father: "That's what happens to you if you're grumpy and bad-tempered," which seems to suggest that Dahl is telling the young reader, "you deserve to be poisoned and killed."

Roald Dahl reminds me of writers in earlier centuries like Mrs Trimmer or Elizabeth Wetherell, who had no qualms about frightening children into being good. A comment of Catherine Storr's in *Fear and Evil in Children's Books* is appropriate—

> And you all, I presume, know about what Mr Fairchild did when he found his children quarrelling about a doll before breakfast? But would any of us think of taking our children to see the body of a condemned murderer now, just as a punishment for quarrelling? Or would we write about it?

Dahl, unlike the Trimmers and Wetherells, parades his own irritations—television addiction (a theme much better handled in the novels of Betsy Byars), over-indulgence in sweets, gum-chewing, shooting foxes, beards, ugly faces, fat bodies, cranky old people, spoiled children—and presents them as moral objections. His black-and-white universe is a sham, its goodness as sham as its evil, the remedies he suggests often more unpalatable than the ills he thinks he sees. I am not at all surprised—human nature being what it is—that he is admired by many adults and eagerly read by large numbers of children.

But he knows how to write, at times most seductively. *Boy* is very readable, a nice mixture of anecdote and incident, laughter and excitement; and when he chooses to comment on inexplicable paradoxes in people, he does it well. Geoffrey Fisher, the headmaster of Repton, who went on to become Archbishop of Canterbury, is seen by the adolescent Roald as "a rather shoddy bandy-legged little fellow with a big bald head and lots of energy but not much charm"—

> He was an ordinary clergyman at this time as well as being Headmaster, and I would sit in the dim light of the school chapel and listen to him preaching about the Lamb of God and about Mercy and Forgiveness and all the rest of it and my young mind would become totally confused. I knew very well that only the night before this preacher had shown neither Forgiveness nor Mercy in flogging some small boy who had broken the rules . . .
> . . . It was all this, I think, that made me begin to have doubts about religion and even about God. If this person, I kept telling myself, was one of God's chosen salesmen on earth, then there must be something very wrong about the whole business.

Other realistic pieces of Dahl's also contain some good writing and sound authentic. One may object to the glorification of stealing in *Danny the Champion of the World,* and it has loose ends—what happened, for instance, to Mr Pratchett's car and his tow-rope?—but it has some very amusing passages, and the father/son relationship is warm, secure, and caring—

> I really loved living in that gipsy caravan. I loved it especially in the evenings when I was tucked up in my bunk and my father was telling me stories. The paraffin lamp was turned low, and I could see lumps of wood glowing red-hot in the old stove and wonderful it was to be lying there snug and warm in my bunk in that little room. Most wonderful of all was the feeling that when I

went to sleep, my father would still be there, very close
to me, sitting in his chair by the fire, or lying in the bunk
above my own.

Some of the realistic tales in *The Wonderful Story of Henry
Sugar and Six More* work well; *The Hitch-hiker* is a humorous, believable character sketch, and *The Swan,* nasty though
it is, is a convincing account of two thugs and their victim, all
drawn to each other like moths to a flame. The best is *The
Mildenhall Treasure:* more "faction" than fiction, it is a recreation of the discovery in 1942 of the biggest hoard of
Roman silverware to be found in Britain. The snowy, winter
atmosphere is excellent, and so is the contrast between the
two men who find the treasure; there is also some neat, ironic
comment—

> . . . he stooped amid the swirling snowflakes, both
> hands embracing, as it were, the treasure, but not actu-
> ally taking it. It was a subtle and canny gesture. It man-
> aged somehow to signify ownership before ownership
> had been discussed. A child plays the same game when
> he reaches out and closes his fingers over the biggest
> chocolate éclair on the plate and then says, "Can I have
> this one, Mummy?" He's already got it.

It is, however, for works of fantasy that Dahl is best known
as a writer for children. *The Magic Finger, James and the
Giant Peach* and *The BFG* are more or less pleasing entertain-
ments, not unduly damaged by the tastelessness and questionable morality of the other books. *The Magic Finger* is the
shortest of the three, and like *Fantastic Mr Fox,* it is about
shooting wild animals—ducks this time. Dahl makes his
points more credibly, though more crudely, than in the fox-
shooting story: perhaps it is easier to take sides when the
species threatened is ducks, not foxes; but, as far as the story
is concerned, he avoids the pitfall of casting his hunters as
totally unsympathetic villains. The Greggs are ordinary
people and their two children are friends of the narrator. The
plot concerns the lessons this family learn when the hunt is
turned on them—having grown wings, they are forced to
build a nest in a tree, as the ducks have moved into their

house. It is all perhaps a bit obvious in what it has to say, but the scenes in which the roles are inverted—the ducks frying fish on the Greggs' kitchen stove, while Mrs Gregg contemplates a supper of wormburgers or slugburgers—are quite amusing. The illustrations, by William Pène du Bois, complement the text very well, and there is one particularly chilling picture of the ducks looking along the barrels of their rifles as they aim them at the unfortunate humans.

Despite echoes of Lewis Carroll and Edward Lear in its characterization and the verses that are scattered throughout, *James and the Giant Peach* is Dahl's most original novel, thoroughly entertaining from beginning to end. He talks in *Lucky Break* of the importance in writing fiction of finding a plot, of the need for stories to build and expand, but almost all his books are episodic. "Good original plots are hard to come by" he says, and he does indeed seem to find it hard, for in some of his work the plots run out of steam. This is particularly obvious in *The Twits* and *Charlie and the Great Glass Elevator,* in which the initial idea abruptly stops half-way through the book, and the second half of both stories seems like an afterthought; in *Charlie and the Great Glass Elevator* a lame, undramatic afterthought that has nothing to do with the plot of the first half. *James and the Giant Peach* is episodic, but the invention is consistently good—bizarre and funny. The most memorable scene is James's response to the attack on the peach by the sharks: The Silkworm and the Spider agree to spin enough thread to lift the peach and its motley crew out of the water—

> "I'm going to take a long silk string," James went on, "and I'm going to loop one end of it round a seagull's neck. And then I'm going to tie the other end to the stem of the peach." He pointed to the peach stem, which was standing up like a short thick mast in the middle of the deck.
> "Then I'm going to get another seagull and do the same thing again, then another and another—"

Five hundred and two seagulls are required. The scenes in New York that conclude the book are also imaginative absurdity of a high order. As the giant peach plummets towards the city, its seagull-power cut off by an aeroplane that inadvertently slices through the silk strings—

> People . . . stood there staring in a sort of stupor at what they thought was the biggest bomb in all the world falling out of the sky and onto their heads. A few women screamed. Others knelt down on the sidewalks and began praying aloud. Strong men turned to one another and said things like, "I guess this is it, Joe."

Small details, too, are excellent; the delays the Centipede causes with his twenty-one pairs of boots, the subsequent careers in America of the Grasshopper—who becomes a musician in the New York Symphony Orchestra —and the Ladybird, worried that her house might be on fire and her children all gone, she marries the Head of the Fire Department. "Each new day demands new ideas," Dahl says in *Boy;* the writer "can never be sure whether he is going to come up with them or not." In *James and the Giant Peach* he came up with them unfailingly.

One idea is the plot that evolves from something quite ordinary growing to a vast and unusual size, in this case the peach; it's a theme Dahl repeats in various guises in many of his books, often accompanied by its opposite, the dwarfing of things or people. Grandma is stretched and shrunk in *George's Marvellous Medicine;* in *The Twits* Mr and Mrs Twit shrink and disappear (like Grandma) altogether; and in *The Witches,* the witches, the hero, and his friend all shrink as part of the process of being turned into mice. The latter may have some resonances with both E. B. White's *Stuart Little* and Kafka's *Metamorphosis,* but the growing/dwarfing theme comes fairly directly from Lewis Carroll, who used it several times in *Alice in Wonderland.* In *The BFG* (short for Big Friendly Giant) nothing actually changes size, but the idea of vastness and smallness is present in the perpetual contrast made between Sophie and the giants; the BFG's ears are "as big as the wheel of a truck" and "each stride he took was as long as a tennis court," which reminds one of the images Ted Hughes invokes to describe the giant in *The Iron Man.* Reminiscent too of *The Iron Man* is the pit that is dug to imprison the flesh-eating giants, "twice the size of a football field and five hundred feet deep," and this sentence is very close to Hughes's story—

> Every earth-digger and mechanical contrivance in the country had been mobilised to dig the colossal hole in which the nine giants were to be imprisoned.

But Dahl's philosophy is the opposite of Hughes's. There is no making friends with these giants, no employment of their energies to serve a useful purpose as in *The Iron Man*; as is normal with Dahl, evil is evil and good is good, and evil is not to be tamed—it is to be punished or destroyed. The resolution of *The BFG*, therefore, with the giants incarcerated for ever in the pit, is much less humane and happy than the ending of *The Iron Man*, with its monster from outer space singing the music of the spheres to make mankind abandon war.

There is too much emphasis in *The BFG* on eating children, but some of the book is pleasant and amusing. The BFG himself—a wimpish, vegetarian giant—is a convincing creation, and the scenes in which he meets the Queen (drawn by Quentin Blake to look exactly like Elizabeth the Second) are excellent. The main achievement is the dialogue; the BFG's difficulties with the English language lead to all sorts of jokes and tongue-twisters, malapropisms and spoonerisms. Charles Dickens, for example, comes out as Dahl's Chickens (though Dahl, obviously pleased with this one, rather spoils the effect by using it twice). "They would be putting me into the zoo or the bunkumhouse with all those squiggling hippodumplings and crocadowndillies," says the giant, and—

> "Here is the repulsant snozzcumber!" cried the BFG, waving it about. "I squoggle it! I dispunge it! But because I is refusing to gobble up human beans like the other giants, I must spend my life guzzling up icky-poo snozzcumbers instead. If I don't, I will be nothing but skin and groans."

It may derive from Lear and Carroll ("human beans" from Mary Norton), but it is done very well.

There are writing faults as well as virtues. Apart from weakness of structure and problems with plots of sufficient length, there is often no real development of his ideas. They tend to be dressed up, second time round, in different clothes, or abandoned half-way through; and he rarely seems to look back at what he has written—no attempts are made when a fresh idea is used to put a hint of it earlier in the story. He can be careless: "The Grand High Witch was starting to talk again," he says when in fact she hasn't stopped. Some things don't mean very much: "We were of a sensible age, between thirteen and eighteen;" and there is a lot of repetition, an emphasis, for example, in almost every book on people spitting when they get angry. His slang is out of date—"by gosh," "by golly," "by gum"—and he resorts to cliché, "for what seemed like hours," "he whizzed past me like a rocket," "as tipsy as a lord," "I oat quiet as a mouse." Minor characters sometimes are stereotypes—

> Sergeant Enoch Samways, as I knew very well, was the village policeman. He was a huge, plump man with a bristly black moustache, and he strode up and down our High Street with the proud and measured tread of a man who knows he is in charge. [*Danny the Champion of the World*]

A veritable Mr Plod. But the same novel has many competent passages—

> Immediately behind the caravan was an old apple tree. It bore lovely apples that ripened in the middle of September and you could go on picking them for the next four or five weeks. Some of the boughs of the tree hung right over the caravan and when the wind blew the apples down in the night they often landed on our roof. I would hear them going *thump . . . thump thump . . .* above my head as I lay in my bunk, but those noises never frightened me because I knew exactly what was making them.

Much of Dahl's appeal to children lies in the way he uses adults. When they have a big role, he manipulates them to fit into a child's world, so that they appear either as supermen (Mr Wonka, Danny's father) or wholly child-like (Grandpa Joe, the BFG) and if they won't fit, they are excluded, made villainous (the witches, Mr Hazell, Mr and Mrs Twit, George's grandmother). Real life is demonstrably not like this; adults enter a child's world in a thousand different moral shapes and sizes. Dahl plays too much to the gallery where the children sit: hence his popularity. He has considerable skills and talents, but they are frequently misused. And there must be quite a number of us—teachers, librarians, parents, critics— who wish that some of the books had never been written.

REFERENCES

ROALD DAHL
>   *James and the Giant Peach,* Knopf, 1961; Allen and Unwin, 1967
>   *Charlie and the Chocolate Factory,* Knopf, 1964; Allen and Unwin, 1967
>   *The Magic Finger,* Harper, 1966; Allen and Unwin, 1968
>   *Fantastic Mr Fox,* Knopf, 1970; Allen and Unwin, 1970
>   *Charlie and the Great Glass Elevator,* Knopf, 1972; Allen and Unwin, 1973
>   *Danny the Champion of the World,* Cape, 1975; Knopf, 1975
>   *The Wonderful Story of Henry Sugar and Six More,* Cape, 1977; in U.S.A. as *The Wonderful World of Henry Sugar,* Knopf, 1977
>   *The Twits,* Cape, 1980; Knopf, 1981
>   *George's Marvellous Medicine,* Cape, 1981; Knopf, 1982
>   *The BFG,* Cape, 1982; Farrar, Straus, 1982
>   *The Witches,* Cape, 1983; Farrar, Straus, 1983
>   *Boy,* Cape, 1984; Farrar, Straus, 1984

ELEANOR CAMERON
>   "McLuhan, Youth and Literature" in *The Horn Book Magazine,* October 1972, December 1972 and February 1973

LEWIS CARROLL
>   *Alice in Wonderland,* first published 1865

TED HUGHES
>   *The Iron Man,* Faber, 1968; in U.S.A. as *The Iron Giant,* Harper, 1968

FRANZ KAFKA
>   *Metamorphosis,* first published in English 1933

WILLIAM MAYNE
   A Grass Rope, Oxford, 1957; Dutton, 1962

MAURICE SENDAK
   Where the Wild Things Are, Harper, 1963; Bodley Head, 1967

CATHERINE STORR
   "Fear and Evil in Children's Books" in *Children's Literature in Education,* March 1970

E. B. WHITE
   Stuart Little, Harper, 1945; Hamish Hamilton, 1946

PERSONS FROM PORLOCK

Helen Cresswell

In a prefatory note to *Kubla Khan* Coleridge attempts to explain why his masterpiece exists only as a fragment; his inspiration, he says, was "interrupted by a person on business from Porlock" who detained him "above an hour," thus causing him to forget what he was going to write next. In an essay called "If It's Someone From Porlock, Don't Answer the Door" Helen Cresswell says that "to children practically all adults are persons from Porlock," interrupting and destroying their creative lives. John Rowe Townsend, she tells us, asked her, "If you don't answer the door how do you know it's someone from Porlock?" which was, she added, "the kind of awful logic that leaves me speechless." It aptly demonstrates, however, the point she was trying to make.

In Helen Cresswell's early work the person from Porlock is nowhere to be seen. "Why I write fantasy," she says in the same essay, ". . . is because I have always had a very strong sense of the miraculous being about to erupt into the everyday." This is an excellent description of such books of hers as *The Piemakers, The Signposters, The Night-Watchmen* and *The Outlanders;* gentle, often comic fantasies in which adult behavior is seen through a child's wondering eyes; a larger-than-life but convincing story given satisfying shape; and, most strikingly, a quality sometimes absent in the novels of many contemporary writers for children—exuberance, joie de vivre. Unfortunately for Helen Cresswell the person from Porlock knocked on *her* door at some time during the mid-nineteen seventies, and he seems to have been detaining her ever since. Her recent books have little of the substance or appeal of *The Piemakers* and the stories that immediately followed it. It is sad to record of any writer's career that her first major work is the best she ever did; but Helen Cresswell has probably not produced a finer novel than *The Piemakers,* which was published more than twenty years ago.

It is difficult to say what went wrong, but it has, I think, something to do with a lack of new ideas, gifted though she is; and she writes far too much. She is one of the most prolific of children's authors; in the seventies alone she had thirty-five books published. Not all of these, of course, are intended to be at full stretch. Many of them are short pieces for very young children, or adaptations of scripts she wrote for television, or brief tales for reluctant older readers; but one cannot help feeling that a talent that should have been allowed to grow and be nurtured has instead exhausted itself

Original though they are, the major books from *The Piemakers* to *The Bongleweed,* but with the exception of *The Night-Watchmen,* owe a considerable debt to Mary Norton's *The Borrowers* and its sequels; indeed one could go so far as to say that without Pod, Homily and Arrietty *The Piemakers* et al. would have been very different stories. As in *The Borrowers* the central character is an imaginative, dreamy, only—and lonely—child; Mum is practical, houseproud, rather snobbish and a bit of a crosspatch; being one up on the relatives or the neighbors is an important theme; and the dialogue is almost identical to the rustic working-class speech patterns of Pod and his family. Pride in a job well done, in one's chosen or inherited craft, is another theme that echoes *The Borrowers,* and the settings of *The Piemakers, The Signposters* and *The Outlanders* occupy a similarly idealized rural past, though Helen Cresswell is less specific about time than Mary Norton—*The Piemakers* and *The Signposters* are vaguely nineteenth century, *The Outlanders* medieval. These books, however, differ sharply from *The Borrowers* in two areas: Dad is never an unimaginative, plodding Pod, nor is he so fearful; he is the adult version of the child central character, ambitious, poetic, sometimes rebellious. Also the child never initiates the action, unlike Arrietty whose unfortunate predilection for talking to the boy causes the whole chain of events that begins in *The Borrowers* and is not resolved until the conclusion of *The Borrowers Avenged.* In Helen Cresswell the child watches. Gravella in *The Pie-*

makers has little to do with her parents' stupendous task of making a pie big enough for two thousand people to eat; in *The Signposters* it is Dyke who organizes the family reunion, not his daughter Barley; the curious lives of the vagrants, Caleb and Josh, in *The Night-Watchmen* would be no different whether Henry were present or not; in *The Outlanders* it is not Piers's decision to journey to the mysterious and terrifying Outlands, but his father's. These books are all about adults, but they are nonetheless quintessentially children's books, because the behavior of the adults is extraordinarily simple, engaging, and child-like; the men floating down the river in the giant pie-dish in *The Piemakers*, Helen Cresswell comments, are "delighted as school-boys."

One of the virtues of these novels is that they are doing something other than they appear to be doing; *The Piemakers*, for example, is ostensibly about making pies, albeit somewhat unusual ones, but it is also a metaphor for every creative attempt and achievement—daring to begin tasks much larger than we have ever dared, but which possibly could, given patience, skill and experience, result in a masterpiece. One critic said it was about the Ark of the Covenant. It is, if we wish it to be; the metaphor is magnificently universal. Dyke's job in *The Signposters* is to measure the distance between signposts in the County of Flockshire, and to repaint them if the miles are more or less than they were last time: it sounds mad, but it stands for any kind of attempt to establish direction, accuracy, purpose. Much of the humor in *The Night-Watchmen* derives from the incongruity of the vagrants (in conventional wisdom, a pretty low form of life) being as obsessively creative and painstaking as Arthy the piemaker, or Tam, the failed poet in *The Outlanders;* Josh is writing a guidebook to England that is already longer than the complete works of Shakespeare, and Caleb is a cordon bleu chef, producing superb dinners on a night-watchman's brazier by a hole in the road. Achievement and happiness, *The Night-Watchmen* seems to be saying, can result from the bleakest of lives and situations.

These books, with the exception of *The Night-Watchmen,* all have a rural setting; each one expresses a child-like delight in the wonders of nature: the summer countryside is almost the main character in *The Signposters,* and the reader shares Barley's naive pleasure in discovering woods, rivers, fields, plants as if for the first time. These examples of Helen Cresswell's writing skills are from *The Piemakers*—

> Then, without warning, he put his hands under Gravella's arms and swung her up, high in the air, so that for a moment she seemed to be flying among the sun-splashed leaves and then whirring down like a bird. She blinked, put out a hand to steady herself, and was looking up at Jarge's delighted face over the rim of the pie-dish.

and:

> In the giant pie, guarded by two snoring Dalesmen, lay on a lake of silver. Moonlight poured through its shattered crust and the moon itself was reflected in the gravy. If Gravella had seen it, tired though she was, she would have realised that this, too, was history. But she was asleep, and past caring, and history had to go on without her.

Not the least of the successes of *The Piemakers* is that from material almost precariously thin the author is able to produce a novel that is absolutely absorbing. (It is entirely devoted to the making of two pies—the first, thanks to the machinations of wicked Uncle Crispin, is a disaster: an overdose of pepper.) Helen Cresswell never brought it off so well again. *The Signposters* is an enjoyable read—her sunniest, most gentle book—but it is too close to *The Piemakers* in ideas and structure: though the names are different, the characters are more or less the same; a similar family quarrel ensues and is resolved; details, such as the fire, and the pigeon post, are repeated. Nothing in *The Piemakers* seems improbable, but here the transformation of bad-tempered Uncle Wick and tearful Aunt Mathilda into genial members of the family strains credulity, as does their unexpected reconciliation with their errant child, Kit.

The Night-Watchmen is based on an interesting idea: men dig holes in the roads, erect braziers and night-watchmen's huts where they drink tea, and we, the general public, assume they are repairing the gas mains or laying pipes for water and sewage; but are they? We never ask; we take it for granted that they are employees of the gas or electricity authorities, or the City Council. It would be perfectly possible, Helen Cresswell suggests, for *anybody* to dig holes in the roads and live undisturbed for months in a night-watchman's hut. Her vagrants, Josh and Caleb, make a profession of this. Much of the comedy comes from the fact that they take themselves very seriously. There is no influence of Mary Norton here— the home life of the central character, the rather colorless child observer of events, Henry—is hardly touched on at all; but there are new sources: Harold Pinter and Samuel Beckett. Both Caleb and Josh have something in common with Davies in *The Caretaker* (Josh's fear of the stove blowing up is an exact parallel), and their quarrelsome but loving relationship of dependence on each other echoes Vladimir and Estragon in *Waiting for Godot. The Night-Watchmen,* however, is not altogether convincing; the plot isn't worked out carefully enough. The sinister Greeneyes who hound the vagrants are merely a device to get Josh and Caleb out of Henry's world and so conclude the story—the author is manipulating the strings. But there is some excellent writing—

> A faint crack of light did in fact splinter the otherwise inky eastern sky, and as Henry watched, a nearby bird let out the first loud jubilant call of the day. By the time he was dressed and had carefully let himself out by the back door the dawn chorus was in full, amazing song. He stole down the dark, deserted streets and from every garden came such ear-splitting whistles and deafening song that he expected at any minute to see windows thrown open and heads peering out to see what the din was.
> "I *sleep* through this every day," he thought with wonder.

The Outlanders is probably Helen Cresswell's finest novel after *The Piemakers.* It has large, serious themes—the need to face frightening, external situations as well as the irrational fears inside oneself; the limited life of the townsfolk of Bray contrasted with the freedom of travelling on the roads; one's duty to fulfill one's potential; who am I, what is my role in life? The scenes in which Tam, Sary and Piers confront their neighbors who want to burn their house down, and in which the child central character, Piers, battles with the wolf and tames it, evoke real terror; and the landscape writing is impressive—the rich, pastoral countryside of the Mid-lands in autumn, the crossing of the Dry Mountains between Bray and the Mid-lands, the sinister rocky beaches of the Outlands where travellers, it is said, disappear and are never seen again. Whole ways of life are created in a few telling sentences—

> "It'll make me cry, sometimes, to think how I had better days and they're all gone. Running and laughing, and a great shiny water called the sea. It was a big world then—further than eye can see. And now I'm shrunk like a nut in a kernel, with walls all about."

This attractive, poetic prose illuminates the whole book—

> Children in Bray who lay awake in the dark at nights saw on their ceilings shadowy, fork-tongued wolves in the light of passing lanterns, and pulled the blankets over their ears when the wind came from the hills howling. And when they grew up, the fears were only half-forgotten, and they spoke of the Outlands in special voices, half-hushed. Or they did not speak of them at all.

There is something of the spirit of Ingmar Bergman's film, *The Seventh Seal,* in *The Outlanders*—the tight-knit, loving family unit persecuted by ignorant people and beset by the superstitions and horrors of medieval life.

The Beachcombers in comparison is a slight book, as if the inspiration for this kind of fantasy was beginning to flag. There is the usual interest in odd trades, crafts and ways of life, but it is hard to see how the beachcombing Dallakers can earn enough to keep themselves from starving; there are villains who are not so much evil as greedy and grubby; the contrasts between the restrictions of town life and the freedom of the open air (the Pickerings' dark basement is set against the shipboard life of the Dallakers); the family unit of father, mother, and only child. But Helen Cresswell has done all this before. There are, admittedly, one or two new ideas—

the manipulation of children by selfish adults is interesting, but unfortunately it isn't central to the plot; and in Mrs Pickering Helen Cresswell creates her most unpleasant female character so far, an uglier version of Meg in Pinter's *The Birthday Party*. She sounds very like Meg; repetitive, unimaginative, silly—

> "There's a Lodger coming," she said, buttering. "Not here yet, but coming. Isn't he, Jack, Arthur? Here in a day or two. Business gentleman—very quiet and respectable. Isn't he, Arthur?"

and:

> "I did a good shop," she said, catching his eye. "Give him a good tea off the train I said, didn't I, Arthur? He'll want a good tea."

But it isn't enough to make one feel that *The Beachcombers* is an advance on the previous novels.

Up the Pier is more worthwhile, but it does not aim very high. It is a nicely atmospheric piece—its chief success is its portrayal of a genteel seaside resort in the fall when all the holiday-makers have gone home—but it is an undemanding tale that shows the author to be so preoccupied with what a child will enjoy that she has omitted what will make a child stretch. (This is characteristic of her later books, in particular the Bagthorpe Saga, which is so encapsulated in an immature world that the adult reader feels there is nothing in it for him.) *Up the Pier* is yet again the story of a lonely, only child who becomes involved with a family who takes pride in an odd sort of job—pier entertainers this time. What is new is that the Pontifexes live in 1921 and have been mysteriously catapulted into 1971; the plot revolves round Carrie's attempts to get them back into their own era. The influence of Mary Norton is once again marked; the Pontifexes' fear of being seen is the same as Pod's and Homily's, their makeshift home in a pier kiosk echoes Pod's and Homily's do-it-yourself houses, and Ellen virtually *is* Homily—

> "And I'll have the house made proper and fit to live in, and curtains up at the windows. Oh oh—I think I shall

> go mad—I can't stand it! We haven't even got our own
> knives and forks! We haven't even got a water closet!
> Half a mile up pier every time we have to go! It's not
> human, and I can't stand it! And we shall be here for ever
> and ever, I know we shall!"

In *The Bongleweed* there is nothing fantastic about the
lives of any of the characters; the unreal is a plant that grows
at an extraordinary rate and threatens to engulf the botanical
gardens in which it first took root—it may even spread over
the whole of the nearby village, the country, the world. The
central child character, Becky, is different from previous heroines—she is nosy and spiteful—and for once she initiates
the action: it is she who sows the seeds of the exotic plant.
Like *The Piemakers*, the material is thin—it is almost entirely
concerned with vegetable growth—but it fails to hold our
attention; perhaps because a rampant bongleweed is intrin-
sically less absorbing than human beings creating a masterpiece, and because the attitude of the main characters to the
plant is unacceptable. They refuse to control it (it's a beautiful living thing) when it is obvious that it must, for reasons
of human survival, be checked—we are being asked to agree
with something we can't agree with. Its ultimate destruction
by a convenient frost shows the author evading the consequences of the problem she has created. The family unit in
The Bongleweed is the same as in the previous books: only
child, dreamy Dad who's tremendously proud of his job
(head gardener), and crosspatch Mum. Elsie Finch is once
again Homily—

> "Two plaice fillets and six bits of finny haddock as tatty
> as ever I saw. I've brought a couple back for you, Becky.
> And I shall have to get the bus into Selling and fetch the
> plaice myself, and if I don't tell that fishy little Welshman
> what I think of him and his finny haddock, my name's
> not Elsie Finch."

The Winter of the Birds is Helen Cresswell's longest, most
ambitious and most serious novel; it is also her last major
work of fantasy. It lacks the humor, caricature and sense of
fun of her previous work—the difference of tone is obvious

from the very first page, which is the monologue of a crazy old man thinking aloud:

> And because I alone in the town am awake at nights, it is
> only I who know of the steel birds. I see the birds who
> do not fly but run on wires. They sweep down in the
> dark straight and hard and cleanly as blades. They are
> terrible and purposeful. They strike. I am afraid of them.

But Mr Rudge manages to convince one of his neighbors, the boy, Edward Flack, of the truth of his visions, and Edward convinces his mother, his Uncle Alfred (who has recently tried to commit suicide because his life is so boring and pointless), and Finn, the Irish taxi-driver who saves Alfred from drowning. The friendships that spring up between this odd and lonely group of people are the core of the book, the relationship between Finn and Alfred being a little like that of Caleb and Josh in *The Night-Watchmen*. Mr Rudge announces that

> On New Year's Day, if those birds have not gone from
> here, if they are still shuttling the night and shining like
> an army of spears over the chimney pots and aerials, on
> New Year's Day I shall give my warning.

but in the early hours of January the first, when a street party is being held in his honor, he dies. The birds do not exist except in the imaginations of the characters; the novel is a persuasive illustration of the ease with which some people can become the victims of auto-suggestion and the delusions of others, but, unexpectedly, the consequences of this are good rather than harmful. Mrs Flack, one of Helen Cresswell's nastiest women, a selfish, narrow-minded nag, discovers a certain amount of neighborly feeling inside herself, and her son Edward, a withdrawn, neurotic boy, obsessed with the role he wishes to play as a hero—

> "I *live* inside my head," he told himself. "So does every-
> one, in a way. So what goes on in there must count. I
> shall always live inside my head, wherever I go or what-
> ever I do for the whole of my life. So why shouldn't I be
> at home in there?"

—begins to find he can live outside his head and form rewarding relationships. The diary he keeps, the style of which is pompous, prim, and unintentionally amusing, is one of the pleasures of the book. Uncle Alfred too (an attempted suicide is extremely rare in a novel for children, but it does not seem out of place here) starts to rebuild his shattered life.

But *The Winter of the Birds* is not as successful as *The Piemakers* or *The Outlanders.* The real hero, the Cuchulain figure Finn, is irritating; a stage Irishman whose speech is the bogus, "top of the morning" blarney that Irish people do *not* use. Some of the points the book is making remain unclear, and all the characters are so odd—grotesques almost—that it is difficult for the reader to identify with or feel sympathy for them. Mr Rudge, in his "glorihi. timeless world" is the most interesting with his speculations on the nature of time and space, but we don't see enough of him. *The Winters of the Birds,* however, *is* Helen Cresswell at full stretch, and the result is a powerful novel that deserves admiration, even though it isn't particularly appealing.

With *Ordinary Jack,* the first book of the Bagthorpe Saga, Helen Cresswell abandoned fantasy for domestic situation comedy; ideal stuff for television, and, as *Twentieth Century Children's Writers* says, "good for sales but not so good for creativity." *Ordinary Jack,* however, and its sequel, *Absolute Zero,* work well enough, though in the latter one can see the signs of the second-rate beginning to emerge; in *Bagthorpes Unlimited, Bagthorpes v. the World, Bagthorpes Abroad* and *Bagthorpes Haunted* the second-rate takes over completely. In these last four books, which have occupied much of Helen Cresswell's writing time for nearly a decade, the reader is sold short—plots based on old, tired formulas; the same slightly larger-than-life characters behaving with total predictability, and in some instances being reduced to hackneyed stereotypes; the same old jokes that weren't even very funny to begin with (how many times is the Bagthorpes' dining room burned or flooded, Uncle Parker almost causing a car crash?); the situations becoming sillier or more incredible. Can one really accept that Mrs Fosdyke, for example, would think passports are needed to visit Wales, that a middle-class stockbroker and his wife would allow their daughter to keep a billygoat as a house-pet, that a five-star hotel would agree to their bringing it onto the premises? This is television sitcom at its unfunny worst. Helen Cresswell has ceased to be child-like and become childish: it is a steep fall from *The Piemakers* to *Bagthorpes Haunted.*

The trouble begins when the author shifts the attention away from Jack, the central character of the first of the series, onto other people. Jack is a very ordinary boy in a family of outstanding talent, and his alliance with his uncle is supposed to lead to his being considered by the others as a genius; the humor in *Ordinary Jack* is the result of their schemes going wrong. Mr Bagthorpe is a successful but bad-tempered and self-regarding writer of TV scripts; his wife is an agony aunt who has a weekly column read by millions. Their eldest son is an electronics whizz-kid and an ace on the tennis court; daughter Tess at thirteen plays the oboe, is a black belt in judo, and she reads Voltaire in French for pleasure; Rosie, aged seven, is a violinist and an excellent portrait painter. Helen Cresswell pokes a great deal of fun at these little super-brats—it is as if she had read the novels of Madeleine L'Engle and had decided to parody *Meet the Austins* or show how ridiculous are the characters in *A Ring of Endless Light.* It works well in *Ordinary Jack* and *Absolute Zero,* which is more than one can say for Madeleine L'Engle's absurd creations, but it palls in succeeding volumes.

Absolute Zero, too, has an original theme: it is a nice piece of satire about people who are addicted to entering competitions advertised on the labels of tins, food packets, and other domestic goods. It begins with Uncle Parker winning a holiday for two in the Caribbean by writing a slogan for a breakfast cereal, Sugar Coated Puffballs. The Bagthorpes, except for Jack and his mother, are green with envy, and they decide to enter for every competition they can lay their hands on. They compete against each other—Helen Cresswell emphasizes that this is not a united, happy family; Jack and Mrs Bagthorpe excepted, they are vain and unpleasantly greedy for success and self-aggrandizement. One of the few really memorable comic episodes in the whole series shows Mr Bagthorpe removing all the labels from the tins in the larder so he can enter the competitions they advertise, and the consequences of this—meals during which nobody knows what will be served up next. The Bagthorpes do win a few things they neither need nor want, a yoghurt maker, a week's holiday at a health farm, and so on, but the real joke of the story is that the most successful member of the family is the dog, Zero, who is unwanted and unloved except by Jack, his constant companion. Zero becomes the smash hit of a TV commercial for a not very popular dog food, Buried Bones, and causes its sales to rise astronomically.

Absolute Zero is a more farcical book than *Ordinary Jack,* and in the scorn it pours on the materialistic greed of an uncaring consumer society it effectively makes a number of serious points. Not so in the third book, *Bagthorpes Unlimited,* and its sequels, though an attempt is made to suggest a serious theme under the comedy. In *Bagthorpes Unlimited* the efforts of people, or groups of people, to do something that will merit an entry in the Guinness Book of Records (the Bagthorpes make the world's longest daisy chain) are seen as vapid and shallow, and in *Bagthorpes Abroad* the dishonesty of people who charge excessively for ill-equipped, sub-standard holiday homes is exposed. But neither of these ideas is allowed sufficient space in the frenetic, ever more improbable situation humor, which, the more frenetic it becomes, the less funny it is. The laughs extracted from Aunt Penelope's vegetarianism, for instance, are cruel and in bad taste. Penelope is also a totally unbelievable stereotype, as is her pious clergyman husband. The writing in these later books is unmemorable and often careless. "He may find this unsatisfactory to his eventual Examining Board" would make more sense as "His eventual Examining Board may find this unsatisfactory"; "The evening was calm and balmy" is unnecessarily ugly, and one use of the word 'all' instead of two would be appropriate in "'My fingers feel all shaky,' Rosie confided in them all." There are many other similar examples of haste, lack of revision, insufficient thought. Whatever happened to the landscape painter of *The Outlanders,* the wordsmith of *The Piemakers*?

The year 1982 saw the publication of two books that are mercifully not part of the Bagthorpe Saga; *Dear Shrink* and *The Secret World of Polly Flint.* The latter, unfortunately,

adds little to Helen Cresswell's reputation, for it is nothing
more than *Up the Pier* retold—the same plot, and the same
characters with different names in a different setting. Here
again is a lonely, imaginative girl being forced by circumstances to stay in the house of an unsympathetic aunt; she
meets a family who belong to another time and who don't
want to be "seen," and as with Carrie in *Up the Pier* she is
instrumental in helping them to return to where they belong.
It's unpretentious but unexceptional. The writing is patchy;
the repetition, for example, of "struck" in this passage is very
careless—"The sun struck fire from dew and leaf and blade.
Dumbstruck, Polly Flint wheeled about for hint or sign, and
saw none"—and "wheeled about" and "dumbstruck" are
clichés. On the other hand, there are some effective moments. Polly's father (he is a coal-miner) explaining why he
keeps pigeons sounds convincing, indeed poetic:

> When you're down there under the ground, hours with-
> out a glimpse of daylight, and working sometimes in
> tunnels that narrow you can hardly stretch—well, the
> thought of them birds, winging and flying and making
> patterns in that great huge sky somewhere up there—
> well, that's a good thought. One you can hold on to
> down there.

His answer to Polly's question about what it is like in a coal
mine is memorable; "Shut off from the world," he says, "and
with a warm wind blowing . . . You'd know you was down
there, even if you was blindfold."

Dear Shrink is a more important book, an unusual venture
for Helen Cresswell into the world of the realistic young
adult novel. Mr and Mrs Saxon, botanists by profession, ar-
range for an old friend to look after their three children when
they decide to spend six months searching for specimens in
the Amazon jungle. This friend, Mrs Bartle, dies very suddenly of a heart attack, so the young Saxons are taken into
care by the Social Services Department, and sent first to ap-
pallingly unsuitable foster parents, then to a children's home.
Oliver, the middle child, writes down his thoughts and feelings about this in his diary, in the form of letters to Carl Jung,
whom he addresses as "Dear Shrink." It's an interesting idea,

thoughtfully worked out, and it has parallels with the experiences of the orphans in Joan Aiken's *The Wolves of Willoughby Chase* and *Midnight Is a Place.* The foster parents, Mr and Mrs Chivers, are horrifying creatures, Mr Chivers in particular giving the reader a sense of revulsion—he seems to be a paedophile, sexually attracted to Oliver's sister, Lucy, aged seven. It's only hinted at—Nina Bawden developed this theme more fully in *Devil by the Sea,* perhaps the only contemporary novel for young people to deal with it.

Dear Shrink is an uneven work. Some of it lacks credibility—it's not likely that the Saxons should have no friends who can look after them when Mrs Bartle dies, and the width of Oliver's reading, the maturity of his comments, and his literary references are highly improbable for a boy of thirteen. "I have measured out my life with roast potatoes!" he says, but would a child really be able to allude so easily to T. S. Eliot's *The Love Song of J. Alfred Prufrock?* (One is reminded of the implausibility of Polly O'Keefe in Madeleine L'Engle's *Dragons in the Waters* regurgitating Yeats's *The Second Coming.*) Oliver seems to suffer no psychological disturbances from his ordeal; he remains unconvincingly cheerful throughout. Also the ending, the nick-of-time rescue by the parents, is contrived, and the style of the book, a teenage first-person confessional narration, is, as is almost inevitable with such novels, another example of the all too pervasive influence on modern young adult fiction of J. D. Salinger's *The Catcher in the Rye.* But *Dear Shrink* has some rounded, believable characters too, good pieces of social observation, nice dialogue, and some well-put perceptions, such as Oliver's explanation of why he likes playing Monopoly—

> It's got a framework . . . and life hasn't. Life spills and spreads all over the place . . . Even Chance and Community Chest are always the same, and they can never truly break anyone, like real-life chances can.

The comments on class distinctions are also effective. It's odd that in such a class-ridden society as Great Britain this subject is usually avoided by today's children's writers. Helen Cresswell tackles here the modern obsession that there's something wrong with being middle-class, that only working-class people are "real" people, and aptly demonstrates what a pernicious nonsense this kind of thinking is.

She could return to the teenage problem novel and produce some worthwhile and original books. I hope it is not much longer that the person from Porlock will detain her, that he'll go away for good; a writer of such talent should definitely *not* have answered the door.

REFERENCES

HELEN CRESSWELL
  The Piemakers, Faber, 1967; Lippincott, 1968
  The Signposters, Faber, 1968
  The Night-Watchmen, Faber, 1969; Macmillan, New York, 1969
  The Outlanders, Faber, 1970
  "If It's Someone From Porlock, Don't Answer the Door," *Children's Literature in Education,* March 1971
  Up the Pier, Faber, 1971; Macmillan, New York, 1972
  The Beachcombers, Faber, 1972; Macmillan, New York, 1972
  The Bongleweed, Faber, 1973; Macmillan, New York, 1974
  The Winter of the Birds, Faber, 1975; Macmillan, New York, 1976
  Ordinary Jack, Faber, 1977; Macmillan, New York, 1977
  Absolute Zero, Faber, 1978; Macmillan, New York, 1978
  Bagthorpes Unlimited, Faber, 1978; Macmillan, New York, 1978
  Bagthorpes v. the World, Faber, 1979; Macmillan, New York, 1979
  Dear Shrink, Faber, 1982; Macmillan, New York, 1982
  The Secret World of Polly Flint, Faber, 1982; Macmillan, New York, 1984
  Bagthorpes Abroad, Faber, 1984; Macmillan, New York, 1984
  Bagthorpes Haunted, Faber, 1985; Macmillan, New York, 1985

JOAN AIKEN
  The Wolves of Willoughby Chase, Cape, 1962; Doubleday, 1963
  Midnight Is a Place, Cape, 1974; Viking, 1974

NINA BAWDEN
  Devil by the Sea, Gollancz, 1976; Lippincott, 1976

SAMUEL BECKETT
Waiting for Godot, Faber, 1956; Grove, 1954

S. T. COLERIDGE
Kubla Khan, first published 1798

T. S. ELIOT
The Love Song of J. Alfred Prufrock, first published 1917

DANIEL KIRKPATRICK (editor)
Twentieth Century Children's Writers, St Martin's Press, 1978

MADELEINE L'ENGLE
Dragons in the Waters, Farrar, Straus, 1976
Meet the Austins, Vanguard, 1960; Collins, London, 1966
A Ring of Endless Light, Farrar, Straus, 1904

MARY NORTON
The Borrowers, Dent, 1952; Harcourt, 1953
The Borrowers Avenged, Kestrel, 1982; Harcourt, 1982

HAROLD PINTER
The Birthday Party, Methuen, 1960; Grove, 1961
The Caretaker, Methuen, 1960; Grove, 1961

J. D. SALINGER
The Catcher in the Rye, Little, 1951; Hamish Hamilton, 1951

W. B. YEATS
The Second Coming, first published 1921

THE WOUND OF PHILOCTETES

David Rees

Katherine Paterson's *Gates of Excellence* is a collection of reviews she wrote for *The Washington Post Book World,* acceptance speeches for her many awards, and transcripts of talks she has given. It is, inevitably, an uneven work, and one may well wonder if it serves any really important purpose. Some of it is on a trivial level (a page is devoted to a description of the interior of her work-room), and there are frequent mentions of her children: the stuff of "chats with the author" at book conferences but hardly worth preserving for posterity. The writing is sometimes inflated—words like "terror," "weep," "ecstasy," "love," and "hate" abound—and there is a flutter of clichéd metaphors: the writing process being compared with a seed that becomes a full-grown plant or the grain of sand which turns into the oyster's pearl. Such statements as "In the beginning of all things was God, and in the beginning of human consciousness was the story" are pretentious, and the prevailing assumption that the members of her audience are, like her, practising Christians irritates: "We Christians have done a lot of preaching about sin," etcetera. There are errors of fact, too: Pooh-Bah in Gilbert and Sullivan's *The Mikado* is misquoted, and Thomas Hardy did not write another novel after *Jude the Obscure* because he was "so appalled, we may guess, by the vision of darkness he had created that he dared not go deeper into it himself," but because he was discouraged by the adverse comment it received in the press: "What has Providence done to Mr Hardy that he should rise up in the arable land of Wessex and shake his fist at his Creator?" asked Edmund Gosse.

There is always an audience for this sort of thing—the people who regard writers as ultra-privileged, larger-than-life geniuses, who feel any little detail about the private existence of authors is gold, not dross. I think it is just as well that we don't know what kind of beer Shakespeare preferred, or the identity of Mr W. H.: it would not help us to understand *Hamlet* or the sonnets any better. *Gates of Excellence,* however, is more interesting than I have suggested; the essay called "A Song of Innocence and Experience," for example, is an absorbing meditation on the power art has and does not have to change our natures, and it is also a spirited defense of the idea that children's authors do not write primarily for the young, but for themselves, for the long-ago children that they once were:

> The reader I want to change is that burdened child within myself. As I begin a book, I am in a way inviting her along to see if there might be some path through this wilderness that we might hack out together, some oasis in this desert where we might find refreshment, some sheltered spot where we might lay our burden down. This is done by means of a story—a story peopled by characters who are me but not simply me.

Many children's novelists have said much the same thing (though their metaphors might be less florid) and, in answering a questioner at a conference, Geraldine Kaye went so far as to suggest that people who write for children do so because they have never grown up totally, that in some way or another they are still immature.

I don't think I would agree with Geraldine Kaye, but my own books for children and young adults, like Katherine Patersons's, are in the first instance for the unhappy child and teenager I once was. There are rearrangements of the patterns of hurt; and my characters, particularly the major characters, are also like Katherine Paterson's, "me but not simply me." Regardless of gender, situation, or historical date, they are a fantasy David Rees who never existed, doesn't exist, and never will exist, but whom I would perhaps like to have existed. I think I give them more of a chance than I had, or let them choose what I was denied or was too frightened to take. So Kim Hooper in *Silence* ceases to wallow in self-pity when his first love-affair turns sour and he goes out with somebody else; Derek Lockwood in *Risks* comes to terms with grief for his murdered friend, Ian, by sharing that grief with Ian's mother. I was nine when the Second World War ended. As a four-year-old my sleep was interrupted night after night by the bombs falling on London, and at the age of seven or eight there were daytime air-raids by buzz-bombs and rockets to contend with. In *The Exeter Blitz* I recreated those childhood terrors, though I first came to Exeter as an adult. The famous Baedeker raid that destroyed the heart of the city in 1942 was something that seemed to demand to be written about anyway, but I was also exorcising the fears and tensions I experienced during the London blitz. For decades I would regularly—four or five times a year—have appalling nightmares about aerial bombing; since writing *The Exeter Blitz* I have had none. In *The Missing German* I recreated the oasis of tranquility that was the period my mother, my brothers, and I spent during 1944 and 1945 in a remote farmhouse on the north coast of Devon, but, though I remember a ship wrecked in a storm, it was not a German submarine. Maybe I wished it was; I certainly played prisoner-of-war games with other children, and doubtless one of us was a missing German. If that time of my life lacked anything, it was excitement, though I was not consciously aware of that; so *The Missing German* gave the long-ago child in myself the thrills and danger he had escaped by leaving London.

Katherine Paterson compares what an author does with what a spider does—both of them spin thread out of their own guts and weave it into a pattern. It's a truthful comment, though it is wise to recall Pope in *Epistle to Dr. Arbuthnot* using the same image:

> Who shames a scribbler? Break one cobweb through,
> He spins the slight, self-pleasing thread anew:
> Destroy his fib or sophistry in vain,
> The creature's at his dirty work again,
> Thron'd in the centre of his thin designs,
> Proud of a vast extent of flimsy lines!

A useful warning to any creative artist's vanity. I think more often of writer and novel as baby and pacifier: I was never allowed a pacifier, or to suck my thumb (in the late nineteen thirties it was thought such habits could lead to worse, quite unmentionable, habits later). My own books are to me a kind of pacifier: the satisfactions of existence are never enough. Why this is so remains a profound mystery to me. My ex-wife once said that if I solved that mystery I would probably stop writing, and I think she may have a point. I don't think real life can ever be totally satisfying to any author—he just wouldn't bother to create imaginary worlds if it was. Wife/husband/lover, 2.4 children, mortgage, car, art, religion, career opportunities and rewards, absorbing hobbies: these are the ways in which most people find the passage of time worthwhile between birth and the grave, but a writer of any sort, including the children's author, for some inexplicable reason does not.

How neurotic all this makes us seem! We aren't neurotic, of course. My fellow-practitioners, those whom I have met, are, with rare exceptions, as cheerful and sane and ordinary as anyone else. Katherine Paterson (whom I have not met) sounds, in *Gates of Excellence* as she does in her novels, to be positively wholesome, yet she says when she examines the events depicted in her books that she is slightly shocked:

> In the first, the hero is a bastard, and the chief female character ends up in a brothel. In the second, the heroine has an illicit love affair, her mother dies in a plague, and most of her companions commit suicide. In the third, which is full of riots in the streets, the hero's best friend is permanently maimed. In the fourth, a central child character dies in an accident.

She adds that she sometimes receives letters of protest from teachers and librarians, but these complaints are invariably about the occasional profanity. "Characters in young people's novels," she says, "should be permitted to do anything, it would seem, except cuss." Which takes us back to Alan Garner's remark in "The Death of Myth" that it's O.K. in a children's book to have someone castrating his father if it's written as a myth, but when a teenager says "arse" it is reprehensible. My own books, though without bastards and brothels, seem to have quite a number of deaths, including a hanging (*The Green Bough of Liberty*). There is disease (cholera) in *The Ferryman;* teenagers making love and living together (*Quintin's Man* and *The Lighthouse*); madness and street riots (*The Ferryman*); and people permanently maimed (*The Exeter Blitz*). No one has ever objected to this; and Jill Paton Walsh is speaking for all of us who are concerned with the young—parents, librarians, publishers, and teachers as well as writers—when she says in "The Lords of Time":

> It is necessary in children's books to mirror death, to show a projected end, to teach that nothing is forever, so that the child may know the nature of the game he is playing and may take a direction, make purposeful moves. It is the plain truth that human life is passing, and that we must find what we will value in the world, and how we will live in the light of that.

I, too, have received complaints about swearing. One headmaster asked his county librarian to remove every copy of *The Missing German* from the shelves of all the libraries in Dorset because on one page—and one page only—I use some four-letter words. *The Missing German* is one of the more innocuous and gentle books I have written; the incident referred to concerns a group of British soldiers stumbling about in thick fog, ordered to search for an escaped enemy sailor they don't even believe exists. They're tired and irritable, and it seems fairly evident to me that they would be swearing, probably rather more than I suggested. Why should we be asked to protect our kids from other people's modes of speech? It's absurd.

Katherine Paterson, however, is wrong in saying that characters in books for young people can do anything these days except curse. There are still many taboo subjects. I know no young adult novel that celebrates the pleasures, as opposed to the trials and tribulations, of an inter-racial love-affair, almost none that suggests teenage sex can be a marvellous experience, and only lip-service is ever paid to feminism. Politics and religion are difficult areas if the author's stance—or the central character's—is biased in favor of one particular organization or philosophy, or is anti-Christian. Homosexuality is still something most people would like to pretend does not exist. As someone who, by birth and upbringing, belongs to at least three minority groups, I tend to view the current consensus of what should or should not be permitted in the children's and young adult novel with a somewhat jaundiced eye.

The children's book establishment attempts to preserve—consciously or subconsciously—a set of values that cannot pertain to every situation in life. These values are of course ostensibly decent and humane, but they are essentially middle-class, family-orientated, Christian (in the sense that Christianity, even if you don't believe in it, has to be respected, not attacked), in favor of preserving the status quo: values, one would not be surprised to find, that Ronald Reagan would think he has. The world of children's books is white Anglo-Saxon Protestant, despite Virginia Hamilton, the Children's Rights Workshop and Leila Berg. I feel myself to be an outsider, walking away from a closed door, even though *The Exeter Blitz* won the Carnegie Medal in 1978. My two novels set in Ireland, in stormy periods of that country's history, have never sold well in Britain. (Winning The Other Award for *The Green Bough of Liberty* in 1980 made little difference.) Irish history from an Irish point of view? Well . . . what can one expect?

In three of my books homosexuality is an important theme. In *Quintin's Man* this, apparently, was all right; the two young men who are gay are minor characters and extremely respectable. But I find it interesting that this novel has not come out in paperback, particularly as Jessica Yates said, in *Signal,* that she had discovered in a survey of London schools in 1978 that it was at the time one of the four novels most widely read by teenagers: perhaps this shows young people are more at ease with the subject-matter than are adults. I should add that *Quintin's Man* was thought to be all right by the *British;* the American edition hacked the text about so much that all references to homosexuality were removed. Jack and Kevin were no longer lovers, just buddies.

In the Tent caused more of a problem. It's the main character this time who is gay, and the book is outspoken in its attack on the Roman Catholic Church, not only for its attitudes toward homosexuality, but its whole teaching that any kind of sexual behavior which is not procreational is

robed in sin. Some county libraries refused to buy it. Others
did so, but keep it under lock and key; in some schools it is
available only for students over the age of 17. *In the Tent,*
however, is a quiet, unobtrusive book in many ways. Tim, the
central character, is an outsider, not only in religion and
sexual orientation, but he's also an intellectual and a somewhat colorless, cerebral person. The reader is not necessarily
asked to identify with him. For much of the story he is agoniz-
ing over his predicament; there's no "glad to be gay" feeling
to it, no political propaganda. A plea for tolerance, yes, but
not much more than that. I was still pussy-footing around
with the subject.

In *The Milkman's On His Way* I was not. Ewan is a much
more ordinary boy than Tim, a sportsman, popular with his
mates and with the girls. He is certainly very uncomfortable
at first with the discovery that it is his own sex he is attracted
to, but by the end of the book, having faced parental disap-
proval—indeed almost total ostracism—and been a witness
to some extremely unpleasant queer-bashing, he is very happy to be what he is. This story, I found, could not be published on a teenage list. It came out as adult fiction, and
proved—irony of ironies—to be the second most successful
novel in terms of sales that I have ever written. Its initial
print-run of eight thousand copies sold out in seven months.
For me, that's good! I realize with some sadness, however,
that its audience is not the one I intended it for. I always have
an ideal reader in mind, someone of about the same age as the
central character, be that five or fifteen (myself?); and in this
case my ideal reader is a muddled kid of perhaps fifteen,
sixteen, or seventeen, struggling with guilt, derision, or despair because he is homosexual. But *The Milkman's On His
Way,* alas, won't be found on the shelves of many school
libraries.

In general, writers of young adult novels are still very shy
of including sex as an important ingredient in their work.
There are, of course, some teenagers who have little interest
in the subject, and no experience. At the other extreme, the
American author Edmund White said in the *San Francisco
Chronicle* that he had had sex with at least five hundred
different people by the age of sixteen, which sounds to me

not so much a pleasure as a gruelling endurance test. On the whole, there is no subject which interests adolescents more, and we are short-changing our readers if we don't show the teenage characters in our books at least *thinking* about sex, experiencing sexual desire, and wondering how to cope with themselves as sexual beings.

I certainly intend to continue exploring, in future books, the themes I find most interesting. I want to write a novel set during the period of the Famine, and one about the subsequent mass emigration of the Irish to North America (*The Hunger,* GMP, 1986); and I don't suppose I shall have many nice things to say about either the British or the American authorities of the time. I want to write a novel in which a child or a young teenager has to come to terms with the fact that his or her parents' marriage broke up because one of the partners was gay (*Out of the Winter Gardens,* Olive Press, 1984). There are several other, as yet less coherent, ideas. But these will be adult novels. Though my own two sons will certainly regret it, I think I've finished with writing for children and young adults. Not because I want to, but because I've come, reluctantly, to the conclusion that I can't at the moment say what I want to say in that kind of book and hope—not for fame and fortune, nice though that would be—but for a little recognition and a minimum amount of money on which to live.

To return to Pope, and to Katherine Paterson. In *Epistle to Dr. Arbuthnot,* Pope asks, part humorously, part seriously:

> Why did I write? What sin to me unknown
> Dipp'd me in ink, my parents', or my own?
> As yet a child, nor yet a fool to fame
> I lisp'd in numbers, for the numbers came.

Katherine Paterson, in *Gates of Excellence,* talks of how miserable she was on returning to her family in the United States after four years in Japan; her relatives failed to recognize how she had changed. "These people," she would say to herself, "don't even know me," and "Language is not simply the instrument by which we communicate thought. The language we speak will shape the thoughts and feelings themselves." Both Pope and Katherine Paterson are only half right. Pope

didn't just "lisp in numbers, for the numbers came." He had
something he wanted to say, and the ordinary method of
communication open to nearly everyone, speech, was not
good enough. Katherine Paterson and I speak the same language, but culturally, ethnically, in our values and the personal experience that has shaped our lives and given us those
values, we are worlds apart.

Written language, William Mayne once remarked, is just
spoken language written down. He's wrong. Writing molds
thoughts and feelings, imposes structures, strikes from us
new thoughts and feelings we would not have if we were not
writing. That is why most of the author's work is done at the
typewriter, not in preparation beforehand. T. S. Eliot in *East
Coker* talks of "the intolerable wrestle with words and mean-
ings." The "intolerable wrestle" is not just the attempt to
impose order on chaos: it is the clash between the thinking
and the feeling that writing produces and the different thinking and feeling going on in our minds and hearts, and in our
speech. What we all have in common as writers is that, for us,
the spoken word is inadequate, not good enough for what we
want to say.

If writers are neurotic at all, they are in this: they're frequently obsessed by the idea that nobody listens to them or
pays them enough attention. A book in which I have largely,
or in part, said what I really wanted to say, gives me a satisfaction no conversation or argument could ever give. If someone reads this book, they are, at last, listening to me! It
doesn't happen often; with only five of my books, *Quintin's
Man, The Ferryman, The Estuary,* and the two Irish novels,
The Green Bough of Liberty and *Miss Duffy Is Still With Us,*
do I have that sense of satisfaction. I sometimes have dreams
in which I'm unable to make myself understood, despite the
fact that my tongue and my lips are moving.

One dream of that nature illustrated, very clearly for me,
the need I have to write. I was swimming in a very rough sea
off the South Devon coast; a gigantic wave flung me against a
rock with such force that one of my feet was almost severed
at the ankle. Somehow I limped ashore, and found myself in
the foyer of a luxurious hotel where a small cocktail party
was being held. There were men in tuxedos and women in

long evening dresses; I was in swimming trunks, wet and bleeding. I knew most of the people, including the host and hostess. I asked the host if he could telephone for a doctor or an ambulance, and he said, yes, but would I first answer the door because some guests had just arrived; I turned to the hostess with the same request and she said, rather crossly, couldn't I see she was busy.

When I was thinking, later, about this dream, I realized it was not only about the need to write, but that it had some resemblance to the story of Philoctetes, the warrior in Greek legend with the incurable wound in his foot, cast away on a desert island. Philoctetes I have always found an interesting and sympathetic figure. After I had finished *The Estuary,* indeed only after reading the galleys, I discovered that I had with all six of the main characters been retelling something of the Philoctetes story. One of them, Aaron (the same Aaron of *Storm Surge* and *In the Tent,* but now an adult, aged 25; all the young people in *The Estuary* are the adults I think some of my children's book characters grow up to be) even suffers a slight stroke, a permanent result of which is that his right leg drags. Most writers are like Philoctetes; wounded, or they imagine they're wounded, and they want others to pay attention, to listen to the tale of that hurt—and also of its healing.

To be a writer means I belong to yet one more minority group, and maybe that is why some of us have a sense of kinship with other minority groups, and some, afraid of the threat posed to the status quo (that is, themselves), attack them. I see from my current reading the flower power hippies of the 1960s taking a few knocks—in Paul Zindel's *I Never Loved Your Mind,* in S. E. Hinton's *That Was Then, This Is Now,* and in Katherine Paterson's *The Great Gilly Hopkins.* Certainly many of the hippies were drug abusers, irresponsible in their relationships and in their sex lives, and there is something sad and depressing about people who turn their backs completely on all the ways society operates. I'm writing this in San Francisco, a city I think without equal in its beauty and as a place in which to live, work, and play. I'm not surprised the flower power people found San Francisco the nearest thing to nirvana. But I'm a little sorry, when I walk through the Haight-Ashbury district, that the sizzling sixties gave way to the somber seventies and the earnest eighties, that not one flower-child is left. For weren't they right, in just a few things? Make love, not war; it's a hackneyed worn-out slogan, of course, but doesn't it contain a truth? If they had been interested in books, and I imagine the vast majority of them were not, they would probably have agreed with Ted Hughes in "Myth and Education" that the great works of imaginative literature are hospitals where we heal; that when they're evil works they are battlegrounds where we get injured. This seems to me to be another way of saying "make love, nor war," and that is what an author should be doing in his or her books.

Katherine Paterson's novels, like any good writer's, are not those battlegrounds. They aren't entirely peopled with bastards, prostitutes, suicides, the incurably crippled, the dead and the dying, any more than mine are filled with executions, swearing soldiers, sex before marriage, disease, faggots and fairies, British stupidity and Irish intransigence. We both have happy, heterosexual children in our stories, discovering with joy the many delights the world has to offer; we have comforting and comfortable mothers and fathers, old people who are wise, the pleasures of friendship, the joys of falling in love, schools that pupils actually like, landscapes and weather that we and our characters are sustained and freshened by. It isn't by any means all hurt. In *Holly, Mud and Whisky* I wrote about cats because I love cats, in *The Lighthouse* about Mykonos and Cambridge because I wanted to convey something I felt of the excitement and beauty of those places. I turn again and again—in *The Exeter Blitz, Quintin's Man, In the Tent, Holly, Mud and Whisky,* and maybe in books not yet written—to the glory of what I consider one of the greatest masterpieces of the European creative imagination—Exeter Cathedral.

Good—though not ideal—parents and loveable, decent kids and teenagers abound in every one of my books from *Storm Surge* to *The Milkman's On His Way.* I advocate no violence, political upheaval, sexual irresponsibility. I do advocate tolerance, particularly of life-styles that are not my own, or of my own if it is not that of the majority of my readers, and granting to children or teenagers time and space to make up their own minds about who they are and what they need to be and to do, a time and a space either denied to me, or which I denied myself, and which I had to fight for in adulthood. My main task as an author is to write those books I still have left to write as well as I possibly can, to please and make happy the eight-year-old or the eighteen-year-old or the twenty-eight-year-old inside me, and hope that in so doing I haven't created a battleground, but that I'm reaching out to those ideal readers of the same age as my characters.

REFERENCES

T. S. ELIOT
East Coker, first published 1940

ALAN GARNER
"The Death of Myth," *Children's Literature in Education,* November 1970

THOMAS HARDY
Jude the Obscure, first published 1895

S. E. HINTON
That Was Then, This Is Now, Viking, 1971; Gollancz, 1971

TED HUGHES
"Myth and Education," *Children's Literature in Education,* March 1970

KATHERINE PATERSON
Gates of Excellence, Elsevier/Nelson, 1981
The Great Gilly Hopkins, Crowell, 1978; Gollancz, 1979

JILL PATON WALSH
"The Lords of Time," *Quarterly Journal of the Library of Congress,* Spring 1979

ALEXANDER POPE
Epistle to Dr. Arbuthnot, first published 1734

DAVID REES
Storm Surge, Lutterworth, 1975
Quintin's Man, Dobson, 1976; Thomas Nelson, 1979

The Missing German, Dobson, 1976
The Ferryman, Dobson, 1977
Risks, Heinemann, 1977; Thomas Nelson, 1978
The Exeter Blitz, Hamish Hamilton, 1978; Elsevier/Nelson,
   1980
In the Tent, Dobson, 1979; Alyson, 1985
Silence, Dobson, 1979; Elsevier/Nelson, 1981
The Green Bough of Liberty, Dobson, 1980
The Lighthouse, Dobson, 1980
Miss Duffy Is Still With Us, Dobson, 1980
Holly, Mud and Whisky, Dobson, 1981
The Milkman's On His Way, GMP, 1982
The Estuary, GMP, 1983
Out of the Winter Gardens, Olive Press, 1984
The Hunger, GMP, 1986

JESSICA YATES
   "Book Post Returns," *Signal,* January 1979

PAUL ZINDEL
   I Never Loved Your Mind, Harper, 1970; Bodley Head, 1971

INDEX